Case Method and Pluralist Economics

Kavous Ardalan

Case Method and Pluralist Economics

Philosophy, Methodology and Practice

Springer

Kavous Ardalan
School of Management
Marist College
Poughkeepsie, NY, USA

ISBN 978-3-319-72070-8 ISBN 978-3-319-72071-5 (eBook)
https://doi.org/10.1007/978-3-319-72071-5

Library of Congress Control Number: 2017960271

Printed on acid-free paper

This Springer imprint is published by Springer Nature
The registered company is Springer International Publishing AG
The registered company address is: Gewerbestrasse 11, 6330 Cham, Switzerland

This work is dedicated to my family.

Preface

This book is the fourth book that reflects the change in the way that I think about the world, and in writing it I hope that it will do the same for others. The writing of my first book[1] began a few years after I received my Ph.D. in Finance from York University in Toronto, Ontario, Canada. But, the origin of it goes back to the time I was a doctoral candidate and took a course in Philosophy and Method with Professor Gareth Morgan. At that time, I was exposed to ideas which were totally new to me. They occupied my mind and every day I found them more helpful than the day before in explaining what I experienced in my daily, practical, and intellectual life.

When in high school, I grew up overseas and I was raised to appreciate mathematics and science at the expense of other fields of study. Then in college, I was exposed only to economics to receive my bachelor of arts. Afterwards, in order to obtain my master's and doctoral degrees in economics, I attended the University of California, Santa Barbara, and I received my specialized training in economics. My further specialized studies in finance at York University ended in another doctoral degree. As is clear, throughout the years of my education, I was trained to see the world in a special narrow way.

Among all courses, which I took during all these years of training, one course stood out as being different and, in the final analysis, as being most influential. It was the Philosophy and Method course which I took with Professor Gareth Morgan at York University. It was most influential because none of the other courses gave me the vision which this one did. Whereas all the other courses trained me to see the world in one special narrow way, this course provided me with the idea that the world can be seen from different vantage points, where each one would be insightful in its own way. Over the years, constant applications of this idea in my daily, practical, and intellectual life were quite an eye-opener for me such that I naturally converted to this new way of thinking about the world. This happened in spite of the fact that my entire education, almost exclusively, trained me to see the world in a narrow and limited way. Since then, I have been writing based on this approach, and

[1] Ardalan (2008).

the current book represents what has been accumulated since the publication of my first three books.[2]

This book crosses two existing lines of literature: philosophy of social science and education. More specifically, its frame of reference is Burrell and Morgan (1979) and Morgan (1983) and applies their ideas and insights to education. Clearly, a thorough treatment of all the relevant issues referred to in this work is well beyond just one book. Within such limits, this book aims at only providing an overview, a review, a taxonomy, or a map of the topics and leaving further discussions of all the relevant issues to the references cited herein. In other words, the aim of this work is not so much to create a new piece of puzzle as it is to fit the existing pieces of puzzle together in order to make sense of it. To implement this aim, and given the specialized and abstract nature of the philosophy of social science, this book discusses the framework of Burrell and Morgan (1979) in the first chapter, and in this context, other chapters bring some of the important dimensions of education into focus. The choice of what to be included in the book and what to be excluded has been a hard one. In numerous occasions, it is decided to refer to some massive topics very briefly. In any case, this book is only an overview but provides a comprehensive set of references to avoid some of its shortcomings.

The main theme of the book is as follows. Social theory can usefully be conceived in terms of four key paradigms: functionalist, interpretive, radical humanist, and radical structuralist. The four paradigms are founded upon different assumptions about the nature of social science and the nature of society. Each generates theories, concepts, and analytical tools, which are different from those of other paradigms.

These four paradigms are not air-tight compartments into which all theories must be squeezed. They are heuristic devices which are created to make sense of the messy reality of education. They are merely useful constructs to aid understanding. They are not claimed to be the only constructs to aid understanding. They are not claimed to be the best constructs to aid understanding. They are only one such construct, among many possible constructs, to aid understanding. They provide an analytically clear and compelling map of the terrain. They help in differentiating the various perspectives that exist with respect to a given phenomenon. Their purpose is to help to understand differences, but not to make invidious comparisons. There is no one paradigm that can capture the essence of reality. Paradigm diversity provides enhanced understanding. In intellectual as well as natural environments, diversity is a *sine qua non* of robust good health. There is no singular approach that in its universality can apprehend the totality of reality. Since academic models are inevitably the product of a partial viewpoint, they will always be biased, and hence a multiplicity of perspectives is required to represent the complexity and diversity of phenomena and activities. The four paradigms provide a full-circle worldview.

The mainstream in most academic fields of study is based upon the functionalist paradigm; and, for the most part, mainstream scholars are not always entirely aware of the traditions to which they belong. Their understanding of different paradigms

[2] Ardalan (2008, 2014, 2016).

leads to a better understanding of the multifaceted nature of their academic field of study. Although a researcher may decide to conduct research from the point of view of a certain paradigm, an understanding of the nature of other paradigms leads to a better understanding of what one is doing.

Knowledge of any phenomenon is ultimately a product of the researcher's paradigmatic approach to that multifaceted phenomenon. Viewed from this angle, the pursuit of knowledge is seen as much an ethical, moral, ideological, and political activity as a technical one. Each paradigm can gain much from the contributions of the other paradigms.

The ancient parable of six blind scholars and their experience with the elephant illustrates the benefits of paradigm diversity. There were six blind scholars who did not know what the elephant looked like and had never even heard its name. They decided to obtain a mental picture—that is, knowledge—by touching the animal. The first blind scholar felt the elephant's trunk and argued that the elephant was like a lively snake. The second blind scholar rubbed along one of the elephant's enormous legs and likened the animal to a rough column of massive proportions. The third blind scholar took hold of the elephant's tail and insisted that the elephant resembled a large, flexible brush. The fourth blind scholar felt the elephant's sharp tusk and declared it to be like a great spear. The fifth blind scholar examined the elephant's waving ear and was convinced that the animal was some sort of a fan. The sixth blind scholar, who occupied the space between the elephant's front and hind legs, could not touch any parts of the elephant and consequently asserted that there were no such beasts as elephant at all and accused his colleagues of making up fantastic stories about nonexistent things. Each of the six blind scholars held firmly to their understanding of an elephant and they argued and fought about which story contained the correct understanding of the elephant. As a result, their entire community was torn apart, and suspicion and distrust became the order of the day.

This parable contains many valuable lessons. First, probably reality is too complex to be fully grasped by imperfect human beings. Second, although each person might correctly identify one aspect of reality, each may incorrectly attempt to reduce the entire phenomenon to their own partial and narrow experience. Third, the maintenance of communal peace and harmony might be worth much more than stubbornly clinging to one's understanding of the world. Fourth, it might be wise for each person to return to reality and exchange positions with others to better appreciate the whole of the reality.[3]

This book, as in my first three books, advocates a multiparadigmatic approach that employs the method of juxtaposing heterogeneous viewpoints in order to illuminate more comprehensively the phenomenon under consideration. The multiparadigmatic approach uses a systematic and structured method to explain the phenomenon from the viewpoint of each paradigm and juxtaposes them in order to transcend the limitations of each of the worldviews.

My first book, entitled *On the Role of Paradigms in Finance*, applied the multiparadigmatic approach to the following phenomena: (1) development of the academic

[3] This parable is taken from Steger (2002).

field of finance, (2) mathematical language of the academic field of finance, (3) mathematical method of the academic field of finance, (4) money, (5) corporate governance, (6) markets, (7) technology, and (8) education.

My second book, entitled *Understanding Globalization: A Multi-Dimensional Approach*, applied, in the context of globalization, the multiparadigmatic approach to the following phenomena: (1) world order, (2) culture, (3) the state, (4) information technology, (5) economics, (6) production, (7) development, and (8) Bretton Woods Institutions.

My third book, entitled *Paradigms in Political Economy*, applied the multiparadigmatic approach to the following phenomena: (1) the state, (2) justice, (3) freedom, (4) democracy, (5) liberal democracy, (6) media, and (7) the great recession. These seven applications of the multiparadigmatic approach continued to show that the multiparadigmatic approach is very versatile in the sense that it can be applied to almost any phenomenon and that the multiparadigmatic approach can be applied not only to categorical concepts such as the state, justice, freedom, and media but also to categorical and subcategorical concepts such as democracy and liberal democracy, as well as practical categories such as the great recession.

The current book applies the multiparadigmatic approach to education. Chapter 1 discusses the four paradigms as the four foundational philosophies. In Chap. 2, the educational philosophies that correspond to the four foundational philosophies are discussed. Chapter 3 discusses the corresponding educational methodologies, i.e., the lecture methodology and the case methodology. Chapters 4 through 9 discuss the corresponding implications of these two methodologies with respect to various practical aspects of teaching, learning, and academic life. In Chap. 10, the difference between the methodology and the method of teaching is discussed. Chapter 11 discusses how the abstract ideas explained in this book can be conveyed to students via the usage of entertaining metaphors. Chapter 12 discusses the major extant schools of economic thought in economics and their correspondence with the four paradigmatic frames of reference.

This book argues that both the case method and pluralist economics emanate from the same foundational philosophy that views the world as being socially constructed and that both of them advocate pluralism. Therefore, the case method seems to be compatible and congruent with pluralist economics. To this end, the book discusses the philosophical, methodological, and practical aspects of the case method through their comparisons with those of the lecture method, which is commonly known by most people. The book also discusses pluralist economics through the exposition of the philosophical foundations of the extant economics schools of thought, which is the focal point of the attention and admiration of pluralist economics.

The book uses a multiparadigmatic approach as its philosophical frame of reference and uses it as its underlying theme throughout the book. The book, therefore, starts with a discussion of the multiparadigmatic approach, which consists of four most diverse paradigms. More specifically, social theory can usefully be conceived in terms of four key paradigms: functionalist, interpretive, radical humanist, and radical structuralist. The four paradigms are founded upon different assumptions about the nature of social science and the nature of society. Each paradigm generates theories, concepts, and analytical tools, which are different from those of other paradigms. An understanding of different paradigms leads to a better understanding of the multifaceted nature of the subject matter.

The book compares the case method with the lecture method through this multiparadigmatic approach. It discusses how foundational philosophies can be located within these four paradigms. Furthermore, it discusses how each foundational philosophy leads to its own educational philosophy. Moreover, it discusses how each educational philosophy leads to its own educational methodology. With this background, the book compares and contrasts the practical applications of the case methodology and the lecture methodology to various aspects of academic life, and shows the pluralism that is advocated by the case method.

The book, then, discusses pluralist economics, in which the contribution of each school of economic thought receives attention and admiration. More specifically, the book discusses the major extant schools of thought in economics—Neo-classical Economics, New Institutional Economics, Behavioral Economics, Austrian Economics, Post-Keynesian Economics, Institutional Economics, Radical Economics, and Marxist Economics. It emphasizes, as pluralist economics does, that these schools of thought in economics are equally scientific and informative; they look at economic phenomena from their certain paradigmatic viewpoint; and together they provide a more balanced understanding of the economic phenomenon under consideration.

In this book, the first chapter reviews the four paradigms and their relation to foundational philosophies. The second chapter discusses the corresponding educational philosophies, namely realism, idealism and pragmatism, reconstructionism, and Marxism. The third chapter discusses the corresponding educational methodologies, namely the lecture methodology and the case methodology. Then, each of the next six chapters provides comparisons of the lecture methodology with the case methodology with respect to various aspects/dimensions of education, namely "course goals, objectives, and contents," "role of teachers and students," "examination," "student-teacher relations," "faculty teaching, research, and service," and "institutional mission and administration." The tenth chapter shows how an educational method (as a tool) is used differently by different educational methodologies. The 11th chapter shows how, in a case-based course, the case methodology can be introduced in comparison with the lecture methodology in a friendly and entertaining manner through the use of entertaining metaphors. The 12th chapter discusses pluralist economics, in which the contribution of each school of economic thought receives attention and praise. The final chapter concludes by emphasizing paradigm diversity, which is the cornerstone of both the case method and pluralist economics.

This book is unique because of its especial characteristics, which are as follows:

1. It is systematic and methodic: It has a multiparadigmatic approach. It starts with foundational philosophies and in a step-by-step fashion arrives at the very

practical applications. It uses a multiparadigmatic approach and in each chapter systematically stays within such multiparadigmatic framework. The learning of this method, by itself, is quite useful. This method of analysis can be applied to any phenomenon as this method is, indeed, quite versatile and resilient.
2. It is foundational and applied: It has a paradigmatic approach. It starts with foundational philosophies and logically arrives at practical applications. It logically connects and relates, in a step-by-step fashion, the philosophical foundations to the very practical applications. It is, therefore, very comprehensive, cohesive, and holistic.
3. It is fair and unbiased: It has a multiparadigmatic approach. In each chapter, it discusses relevant paradigmatic viewpoints with respect to the topic discussed in that chapter. It exposes the reader to various viewpoints and, therefore, provides the reader with a more balanced view of the topic discussed.
4. It is multidimensional: It views phenomena as being multidimensional and emphasizes many different aspects/dimensions of economics and education. It provides a comprehensive approach to the understanding of economics and education, in general, and, in particular, a comprehensive understanding of the lecture methodology in comparison with the case methodology, on the one hand, and various schools of thought in economics, on the other hand.

The writing of the chapters of this book involved extensive work over several years. It required peace of mind and extended uninterrupted research time. My deepest expressions of gratitude go to my wife Haleh, my son Arash, and my daughter Camellia for their prolonged patience, unlimited understanding, sustained support, constant cooperation, and individual independence during all these long years. I hold much respect for my late parents (Javad and Afagholmolouk) who instilled in their children (Ghobad, Golnar, Alireza, and Kavous) the grand Ardalan family's values of tolerance, openness, and love of learning, among others. I sincerely appreciate the heartfelt support of my in-laws (Farideh, Parviz, and Houman) who have always been in close contact with us since the formation of my immediate family.

The ideas expressed in this work are based on the teachings, writings, and insights of Professor Gareth Morgan, to whom the nucleus of this work is owed. Needless to say, I stand responsible for all the errors and omissions. I would like to thank Professor Gareth Morgan who taught me how to diversely view the world and accordingly inspired my work.

I am thankful to the Marist College library staff for their timely provision of the requested literature, which they obtained from various sources. I would also like to thank the publishers, referenced in the endnotes, who allowed me to use their materials. Certainly, I would like to thank the respectable people who work at Springer for their recognition of the significance of my work and for their publication of the book with utmost professionalism.

Poughkeepsie, NY, USA Kavous Ardalan, Ph.D.

References

Ardalan, Kavous. 2008. *On the Role of Paradigms in Finance*. Aldershot, Hampshire, UK: Ashgate Publishing, and Burlington, VT: Ashgate Publishing.

———. 2014. *Understanding Globalization: A Multi-Dimensional Approach*. Piscataway, NJ: Transaction Publishers.

———. 2016. *Paradigms in Political Economy*. Abingdon, Oxon, UK, and New York, NY: Routledge.

Burrell, Gibson, and Gareth Morgan. 1979. *Sociological Paradigms and Organizational Analysis*. Hants, UK: Gower Publishing.

Morgan, Gareth. 1983. *Beyond Method: Strategies for Social Research*. Beverley Hills, CA: Sage.

Steger, Manfred B. 2002. *Globalism: The New Market Ideology*. New York, NY: Rowan & Littlefield Publishers.

Contents

Paradigms and Foundational Philosophies

Social theory can usefully be conceived in terms of four key paradigms: functionalist, interpretive, radical humanist, and radical structuralist. The four paradigms are founded upon different assumptions about the nature of social science and the nature of society. Each generates theories, concepts, and analytical tools which are different from those of other paradigms.

All theories are based on a philosophy of science and a theory of society. Many theorists appear to be unaware of, or ignore, the assumptions underlying these philosophies. They emphasize only some aspects of the phenomenon and ignore others. Unless they bring out the basic philosophical assumptions of the theories, their analysis can be misleading; since by emphasizing differences between theories, they imply diversity in approach. While there appear to be different kinds of theory, they are founded on a certain philosophy, worldview, or paradigm. This becomes evident when these theories are related to the wider background of social theory. The functionalist paradigm has provided the framework for current mainstream academic fields, and accounts for the largest proportion of theory and research in their respective academic fields.

In order to understand a new paradigm, theorists should be fully aware of assumptions upon which their own paradigm is based. Moreover, to understand a new paradigm one has to explore it from within, since the concepts in one paradigm cannot easily be interpreted in terms of those of another. No attempt should be made to criticize or evaluate a paradigm from the outside. This is self-defeating since it is based on a separate paradigm. All four paradigms can be easily criticized and ruined in this way.

These four paradigms are of paramount importance to any scientist, because the process of learning about a favored paradigm is also the process of learning what that paradigm is not. The knowledge of paradigms makes scientists aware of the boundaries within which they approach their subject. Each of the four paradigms implies a different way of social theorizing.

K. Ardalan, *Case Method and Pluralist Economics*,
https://doi.org/10.1007/978-3-319-72071-5_1

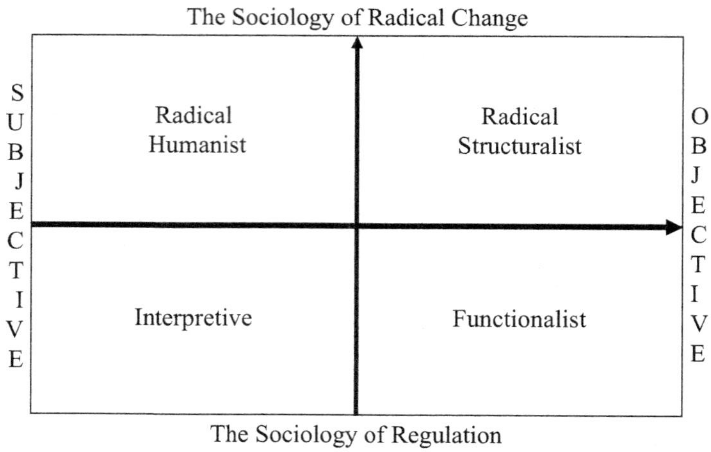

Exhibit 1.1 The four paradigms each paradigm adheres to a set of fundamental assumptions about the nature of science (i.e., the subjective-objective dimension), and the nature of society (i.e., the dimension of regulation-radical change)

Before discussing each paradigm, it is useful to look at the notion of "paradigm." Burrell and Morgan (1979)[1] regard the:

> ... four paradigms as being defined by very basic meta-theoretical assumptions which underwrite the frame of reference, mode of theorizing and modus operandi of the social theorists who operate within them. It is a term which is intended to emphasize the commonality of perspective which binds the work of a group of theorists together in such a way that they can be usefully regarded as approaching social theory within the bounds of the same problematic.
>
> The paradigm does ... have an underlying unity in terms of its basic and often "taken for granted" assumptions, which separate a group of theorists in a very fundamental way from theorists located in other paradigms. The "unity" of the paradigm thus derives from reference to alternative views of reality which lie outside its boundaries and which may not necessarily even be recognized as existing. (pp. 23–24)

Each theory can be related to one of the four broad worldviews. These adhere to different sets of fundamental assumptions about; the nature of science—that is, the subjective-objective dimension—and the nature of society—that is, the dimension of regulation-radical change—as in Exhibit 1.1.[2]

Assumptions related to the nature of science are assumptions with respect to ontology, epistemology, human nature, and methodology.

[1] This work borrows heavily from the ideas and insights of Burrell and Morgan (1979) and Morgan (1983) and applies them to various aspects of the academic life. Burrell and Morgan (1979) state "The scope for applying the analytical scheme to other field of study is enormous … readers interested in applying the scheme in this way should find little difficulty in proceeding from the sociological analyses ... to an analysis of the literature in their own sphere of specialised interest." (page 35)

[2] This can be used as both a classifactory device, or more importantly, as an analytical tool.

The assumptions about ontology are assumptions regarding the very essence of the phenomenon under investigation. That is, to what extent the phenomenon is objective and external to the individual or it is subjective and the product of individual's mind.

The assumptions about epistemology are assumptions about the nature of knowledge. That is, they are assumptions about how one might go about understanding the world, and communicate such knowledge to others. That is, what constitutes knowledge and to what extent it is something which can be acquired or it is something which has to be personally experienced.

The assumptions about human nature are concerned with human nature and, in particular, the relationship between individuals and their environment, which is the object and subject of social sciences. That is, to what extent human beings and their experiences are the products of their environment or human beings are creators of their environment.

The assumptions about methodology are related to the way in which one attempts to investigate and obtain knowledge about the social world. That is, to what extent the methodology treats the social world as being real hard and external to the individual or it is as being of a much softer, personal and more subjective quality. In the former, the focus is on the universal relationship among elements of the phenomenon, whereas in the latter, the focus is on the understanding of the way in which the individual creates, modifies, and interprets the situation which is experienced.

The assumptions related to the nature of society are concerned with the extent of regulation of the society or radical change in the society.

Sociology of regulation provides explanation of society based on the assumption of its unity and cohesiveness. It focuses on the need to understand and explain why society tends to hold together rather than fall apart.

Sociology of radical change provides explanation of society based on the assumption of its deep-seated structural conflict, modes of domination, and structural contradiction. It focuses on the deprivation of human beings, both material and psychic, and it looks towards alternatives rather than the acceptance of *status quo*.

The subjective-objective dimension and the regulation-radical change dimension together define four paradigms, each of which share common fundamental assumptions about the nature of social science and the nature of society. Each paradigm has a fundamentally unique perspective for the analysis of social phenomena.

1 Functionalist Paradigm

The functionalist paradigm assumes that society has a concrete existence and follows certain order. These assumptions lead to the existence of an objective and value-free social science which can produce true explanatory and predictive knowledge of the reality "out there." It assumes scientific theories can be assessed objectively by reference to empirical evidence. Scientists do not see any roles for themselves, within the phenomenon which they analyze, through the rigor and technique of the scientific method. It attributes independence to the observer from the observed. That is, an ability to observe "what is" without affecting it. It assumes there are universal standards of science, which determine what constitutes an adequate explanation of what is observed. It assumes there are external rules and regulations governing the external world. The goal of scientists is to find the orders that prevail within that phenomenon.

The functionalist paradigm seeks to provide rational explanations of social affairs and generate regulative sociology. It assumes a continuing order, pattern, and coherence and tries to explain what is. It emphasizes the importance of understanding order, equilibrium and stability in society and the way in which these can be maintained. It is concerned with the regulation and control of social affairs. It believes in social engineering as a basis for social reform.

The rationality which underlies functionalist science is used to explain the rationality of society. Science provides the basis for structuring and ordering the social world, similar to the structure and order in the natural world. The methods of natural science are used to generate explanations of the social world. The use of mechanical and biological analogies for modeling and understanding the social phenomena are particularly favored.

Functionalists are individualists. That is, the properties of the aggregate are determined by the properties of its units. Their approach to social science is rooted in the tradition of positivism. It assumes that the social world is concrete, meaning it can be identified, studied and measured through approaches derived from the natural sciences.

Functionalists believe that the positivist methods which have triumphed in natural sciences should prevail in social sciences, as well. In addition, the functionalist paradigm has become dominant in academic sociology. The social world is treated as a place of concrete reality, characterized by uniformities and regularities which can be understood and explained in terms of causes and effects. Given these assumptions, the individuals are regarded as taking on a passive role; their behavior is being determined by the environment.

Functionalists are pragmatic in orientation and are concerned to understand society so that the knowledge thus generated can be used in society. It is problem orientated in approach as it is concerned to provide practical solutions to practical problems.

In Exhibit 1.1, the functionalist paradigm occupies the south-east quadrant. Schools of thought within this paradigm can be located on the objective-subjective continuum. From right to left they are: Objectivism, Social System Theory, Integrative Theory, Interactionism, and Social Action Theory.[3]

[3]For classics in this literature see Blau (1955, 1964), Buckley (1967), Comte (1953), Durkheim (1938, 1947), James (1890), Mead (1932a, 1932b, 1934, 1938), Merton (1968), Pareto (1935), Simmel (1936, 1955), Skinner (1953, 1957, 1972), and Spencer (1873).

2 Interpretive Paradigm

The interpretive paradigm assumes that social reality is the result of the subjective interpretations of individuals. It sees the social world as a process which is created by individuals. Social reality, insofar as it exists outside the consciousness of any individual, is regarded as being a network of assumptions and intersubjectively shared meanings. This assumption leads to the belief there are shared multiple realities which are sustained and changed. Researchers recognize their role within the phenomenon under investigation. Their frame of reference is one of participant, as opposed to observer. The goal of the interpretive researchers is to find the orders that prevail within the phenomenon under consideration; however, they are not objective.

The interpretive paradigm is concerned with understanding the world as it is, at the level of subjective experience. It seeks explanations within the realm of individual consciousness and subjectivity. Its analysis of the social world produces sociology of regulation. Its views are underwritten by the assumptions that the social world is cohesive, ordered, and integrated.

Interpretive sociologists seek to understand the source of social reality. They often delve into the depth of human consciousness and subjectivity in their quest for the meanings in social life. They reject the use of mathematics and biological analogies in learning about the society and their approach places emphasis on understanding the social world from the vantage point of the individuals who are actually engaged in social activities.

The interpretive paradigm views the functionalist position as unsatisfactory for two reasons. First, human values affect the process of scientific enquiry. That is, scientific method is not value-free, since the frame of reference of the scientific observer determines the way in which scientific knowledge is obtained. Second, in cultural sciences the subject matter is spiritual in nature. That is, human beings cannot be studied by the methods of the natural sciences, which aim to establish general laws. In the cultural sphere human beings are perceived as free. An understanding of their lives and actions can be obtained by the intuition of the total wholes, which is bound to break down by atomistic analysis of functionalist paradigm.

Cultural phenomena are seen as the external manifestations of inner experience. The cultural sciences, therefore, need to apply analytical methods based on "understanding;" through which the scientist can seek to understand human beings, their minds, and their feelings, and the way these are expressed in their outward actions. The notion of "understanding" is a defining characteristic of all theories located within this paradigm.

The interpretive paradigm believes that science is based on "taken for granted" assumptions; and, like any other social practice, must be understood within a specific context. Therefore, it cannot generate objective and value-free knowledge. Scientific knowledge is socially constructed and socially sustained; its significance and meaning can only be understood within its immediate social context.

The interpretive paradigm regards mainstream economic theorists as belonging to a small and self-sustaining community, who believe that corporations and financial markets exist in a concrete world. They theorize about concepts which have little significance to people outside the community, who practice economic theory, and the limited community whom economic theorists may attempt to serve.

Mainstream academic economic theorists tend to treat their subject of study as a hard, concrete and tangible empirical phenomenon which exists "out there" in the "real world." Interpretive researchers are opposed to such structural absolution. They emphasize that the social world is no more than the subjective construction of individual human beings who create and sustain a social world of intersubjectively shared meaning, which is in a continuous process of reaffirmation or change. Therefore, there are no universally valid rules of behavior. Interpretive economic research enables scientists to examine aggregate behavior together with ethical, cultural, political, and social issues.

In Exhibit 1.1, the interpretive paradigm occupies the south-west quadrant. Schools of thought within this paradigm can be located on the objective-subjective continuum. From left to right they are: Solipsism, Phenomenology, Phenomenological Sociology, and Hermeneutics.[4]

3 Radical Humanist Paradigm

The radical humanist paradigm provides critiques of the status quo and is concerned to articulate, from a subjective standpoint, the sociology of radical change, modes of domination, emancipation, deprivation, and potentiality. Based on its subjectivist approach, it places great emphasis on human consciousness. It tends to view society as anti-human. It views the process of reality creation as feeding back on itself; such that individuals and society are prevented from reaching their highest possible potential. That is, the consciousness of human beings is dominated by the ideological superstructures of the social system, which results in their alienation or false consciousness. This, in turn, prevents true human fulfillment. The social theorist regards the orders that prevail in the society as instruments of ideological domination.

The major concern for theorists is with the way this occurs and finding ways in which human beings can release themselves from constraints which existing social arrangements place upon realization of their full potential. They seek to change the social world through a change in consciousness.

Radical humanists believe that everything must be grasped as a whole, because the whole dominates the parts in an all-embracing sense. Moreover, truth is

[4]For classics in this literature see Berkeley (1962), Dilthey (1976), Gadamer (1965), Garfinkel (1967), Hegel (1931), Husserl (1929), Schutz (1964, 1966, 1967), Winch (1958), and Wittgenstein (1963).

historically specific, relative to a given set of circumstances, so that one should not search for generalizations for the laws of motion of societies.

The radical humanists believe the functionalist paradigm accepts purposive rationality, logic of science, positive functions of technology, and neutrality of language, and uses them in the construction of "value-free" social theories. The radical humanist theorists intend to demolish this structure, emphasizing the political and repressive nature of it. They aim to show the role that science, ideology, technology, language, and other aspects of the superstructure play in sustaining and developing the system of power and domination, within the totality of the social formation. Their function is to influence the consciousness of human beings for eventual emancipation and formation of alternative social formations.

The radical humanists note that functionalist sociologists create and sustain a view of social reality which maintains the *status quo* and which forms one aspect of the network of ideological domination of the society.

The focus of the radical humanists upon the "superstructural" aspects of society reflects their attempt to move away from the economism of orthodox Marxism and emphasize the Hegelian dialectics. It is through the dialectic that the objective and subjective aspects of social life interact. The superstructure of society is believed to be the medium through which the consciousness of human beings is controlled and molded to fit the requirements of the social formation as a whole. The concepts of structural conflict, contradiction, and crisis do not play a major role in this paradigm, because these are more objectivist view of social reality, that is, the ones which fall in the radical structuralist paradigm. In the radical humanist paradigm, the concepts of consciousness, alienation, and critique form their concerns.

In Exhibit 1.1, the radical humanist paradigm occupies the north-west quadrant. Schools of thought within this paradigm can be located on the objective-subjective continuum. From left to right they are: Solipsism, French Existentialism, Anarchistic Individualism, and Critical Theory.[5]

4 Radical Structuralist Paradigm

The radical structuralist paradigm assumes that reality is objective and concrete, as it is rooted in the materialist view of natural and social world. The social world, similar to the natural world, has an independent existence, that is, it exists outside the minds of human beings. Sociologists aim at discovering and understanding the patterns and regularities which characterize the social world. Scientists do not see any roles for themselves in the phenomenon under investigation. They use scientific methods to find the order that prevails in the phenomenon. This paradigm views

[5]For classics in this literature see Bookchin (1974), Fichte (1970), Goldmann (1969), Gouldner (1954a, 1954b, 1970, 1973, 1976), Gramsci (1971), Habermas (1970a, 1970b, 1971, 1972, 1974, 1976), Horkheimer (1972), Lukacs (1971), Marcuse (1954, 1964, 1966, 1968), Marx (1975), Meszaros (1970, 1971), Sartre (1966, 1974, 1976), and Stirner (1907).

society as a potentially dominating force. Sociologists working within this paradigm have an objectivist standpoint and are committed to radical change, emancipation, and potentiality. In their analysis they emphasize structural conflict, modes of domination, contradiction, and deprivation. They analyze the basic interrelationships within the total social formation and emphasize the fact that radical change is inherent in the structure of society and the radical change takes place though political and economic crises. This radical change necessarily disrupts the *status quo* and replaces it by a radically different social formation. It is through this radical change that the emancipation of human beings from the social structure is materialized.

For radical structuralists, an understanding of classes in society is essential for understanding the nature of knowledge. They argue that all knowledge is class specific. That is, it is determined by the place one occupies in the productive process. Knowledge is more than a reflection of the material world in thought. It is determined by one's relation to that reality. Since different classes occupy different positions in the process of material transformation, there are different kinds of knowledge. Hence class knowledge is produced by and for classes, and exists in a struggle for domination. Knowledge is thus ideological. That is, it formulates views of reality and solves problems from class points of view.

Radical structuralists reject the idea that it is possible to verify knowledge in an absolute sense through comparison with socially neutral theories or data. But, emphasize that there is the possibility of producing a "correct" knowledge from a class standpoint. They argue that the dominated class is uniquely positioned to obtain an objectively "correct" knowledge of social reality and its contradictions. It is the class with the most direct and widest access to the process of material transformation that ultimately produces and reproduces that reality. Radical structuralists' analysis indicates that the social scientist, as a producer of class-based knowledge, is a part of the class struggle.

Radical structuralists believe truth is the whole, and emphasize the need to understand the social order as a totality rather than as a collection of small truths about various parts and aspects of society. The economic empiricists are seen as relying almost exclusively upon a number of seemingly disparate, data-packed, problem-centered studies. Such studies, therefore, are irrelevant exercises in mathematical methods.

This paradigm is based on four central notions. First, there is the notion of totality. All theories address the total social formation. This notion emphasizes that the parts reflect the totality, not the totality the parts.

Second, there is the notion of structure. The focus is upon the configurations of social relationships, called structures, which are treated as persistent and enduring concrete facilities.

The third notion is that of contradiction. Structures, or social formations, contain contradictory and antagonistic relationships within them which act as seeds of their own decay.

The fourth notion is that of crisis. Contradictions within a given totality reach a point at which they can no longer be contained. The resulting political, economic crises indicate the point of transformation from one totality to another, in which one set of structures is replaced by another of a fundamentally different kind.

In Exhibit 1.1, the radical structuralist paradigm occupies the north-east quadrant. Schools of thought within this paradigm can be located on the objective-subjective continuum. From right to left they are: Russian Social Theory, Conflict Theory, and Contemporary Mediterranean Marxism.[6]

5 Conclusion

This chapter briefly discussed social theory, its complexity, and diversity. It indicated that theorists are not always entirely aware of the traditions to which they belong. The diversity of theories presented in this section is vast. While each paradigm advocates a research strategy that is logically coherent, in terms of underlying assumptions, these vary from paradigm to paradigm. The phenomenon to be researched is conceptualized and studied in many different ways, each generating distinctive kinds of insight and understanding. There are many different ways of studying the same social phenomenon, and given that the insights generated by any one approach are at best partial and incomplete, the social researcher can gain much by reflecting on the nature and merits of different approaches before engaging in a particular mode of research practice.

Knowledge is ultimately a product of the researcher's paradigmatic approach to this multifaceted phenomenon. Viewed from this angle, the pursuit of knowledge is seen as much an ethical, moral, ideological, and political activity, as a technical one. Researchers can gain much by exploiting the new insights coming from other paradigms.

References

Althusser, L. 1969. *For Marx*. Harmondsworth, England: Penguin.

———. 1971. *Lenin and Philosophy and Other Essays*. London, England: New Left Books.

Althusser, L., and E. Balibar. 1970. *Reading Capital*. London, England: New Left Books.

Berkeley, G. 1962. *The Principles of Human Knowledge and Three Dialogues between Hylas and Philonous*. London, England: Collins.

Blau, P.M. 1955. *The Dynamics of Bureaucracy*. Chicago, IL: University of Chicago Press.

———. 1964. *Exchange and Power in Social Life*. New York, NY: Wiley.

Bookchin, Murray. 1974. *Post-Scarcity Anarchism*. London, England: Wildwood House.

Buckley, William. 1967. *Sociology and Modern Systems Theory*. Englewood Cliffs, NJ: Prentice-Hall.

[6]For classics in this literature see Althusser (1969, 1971), Althusser and Balibar (1970), Bukharin (1965), Colletti (1972, 1974, 1975), Dahrendorf (1959), Marx (1973, 1976), Marx and Engels (1965, 1968), Plekhanov (1974), and Rex (1961, 1974).

Bukharin, N. 1965. *Historical Materialism: A System of Sociology*. New York, NY: Russell and Russell.
Burrell, Gibson, and Gareth Morgan. 1979. *Sociological Paradigms and Organizational Analysis*. Hants, England: Gower Publishing.
Colletti, L. 1972. *From Rousseau to Lenin*. London, England: New Left Books.
———. 1974. A Political and Philosophical Interview. *New Left Review* 86: 3–28.
———. 1975. Marxism and the Dialectics. *New Left Review* 93: 3–29.
Comte, Auguste. 1953. *The Positivist Philosophy*. Vol. I. London, England: Chapman.
Dahrendorf, R. 1959. *Class and Class Conflict in Industrial Society*. London, England: Routledge and Kegan Paul.
Dilthey, Wilhelm. 1976. In *Selected Writings*, ed. H.P. Rickman. London, England: Cambridge University Press.
Durkheim, Emile. 1938. *The Rules of Sociological Method*. Glencoe, IL: Free Press.
———. 1947. *The Division of Labor in Society*. Glencoe, IL: Free Press.
Fichte, J.F. 1970. In *Science of Knowledge*, ed. P. Heath and J. Lachs. New York, NY: Century Philosophy Sourcebooks.
Gadamer, H.G. 1965. *Wahrheit und Method*. Tubingen, Germany: J.C.B. Mohr.
Garfinkel, Harold. 1967. *Studies in Ethnomethodology*. Englewood Cliffs, NJ: Prentice-Hall.
Goldmann, Lucien. 1969. *The Human Sciences and Philosophy*. London, England: Cape.
Gouldner, Alvin W. 1954a. *Patterns of Industrial Bureaucracy*. Glencoe, IL: Free Press.
———. 1954b. *Wildcat Strike*. New York, NY: Antioch Press.
———. 1970. *The Coming Crisis of Western Sociology*. London, England: Heinemann.
———. 1973. *For Sociology*. Harmondsworth, England: Allen Lane.
———. 1976. *The Dialectic of Ideology and Technology*. New York, NY: Macmillan.
Gramsci, Antonio. 1971. In *Selections from the Prison Notebooks of Antonio Gramsci*, ed. Quinton Hoare and Geoffrey Nowell-Smith. London, England: Lawrence and Wishart.
Habermas, Jurgen. 1970a. On Systematically Distorted Communications. *Inquiry* 13: 205–218.
———. 1970b. Towards a Theory of Communicative Competence. *Inquiry* 13: 360–375.
———. 1971. *Toward a Rational Society*. London, England: Heinemann.
———. 1972. *Knowledge and Human Interests*. London, England: Heinemann.
———. 1974. *Theory and Practice*. London, England: Heinemann.
———. 1976. *Legitimation Crisis*. London, England: Heinemann.
Hegel, G. 1931. *The Phenomenology of Mind*. London, England: George Allen and Unwin.
Horkheimer, M. 1972. *Critical Theory: Selected Essays*. New York, NY: Herder.
Husserl, Edmund. 1929. Entry on 'Phenomenology'. In *Encyclopedia Britannica*, 14th ed.
James, William. 1890. *Principles of Psychology*. London, England: Macmillan.
Lukacs, Georg. 1971. *History and Class Consciousness*. London, England: Merlin.
Marcuse, H. 1954. *Reason and Revolution*. New York, NY: Humanities Press.
———. 1964. *One-Dimensional Man*. London, England: Routledge and Kegan Paul.
———. 1966. *Eros and Civilisation*. Boston, MA: Beason.
———. 1968. *Negations: Essays in Critical Theory*. London, England: Heinemann.
Marx, Karl. 1973. *Grundrisse: Foundations of the Critique of Political Economy*. Harmondsworth, England: Penguin.
———. 1975. *Early Writings*. Harmondsworth, England: Penguin.
———. 1976. *Capital: A Critique of Political Economy*. Vol. I–III. Harmondsworth, England: Penguin.
Marx, Karl, and Fredrick Engels. 1965. *The German Ideology*. London, England: Lawrence and Wishart.
———. 1968. *Selected Works*. London, England: Lawrence and Wishart.
Mead, George Herbert. 1932a. In *Movements of Thought in the Nineteenth Century*, ed. M.N. Moore. Chicago, IL: University of Chicago Press.
———. 1932b. In *The Philosophy of the Present*, ed. A.E. Murphy. Chicago, IL: Open Court Publishing.

———. 1934. In *Mind, Self and Society*, ed. Charles Morris. Chicago, IL: University of Chicago Press.
———. 1938. In *The Philosophy of the Act*, ed. Charles Morris. Chicago, IL: University of Chicago Press.
Merton, Robert K. 1968. *Social Theory and Social Structure*. New York, NY: Free Press.
Meszaros, I. 1970. *Marx's Theory of Alienation*. London, England: Merlin.
———. 1971. *Aspects of History and Class Consciousness*. London, England: Routledge and Kegan Paul.
Morgan, Gareth, ed. 1983. *Beyond Method: Strategies for Social Research*. Beverly Hills, CA: Sage.
Pareto, Vilfredo. 1935. *The Mind and Society, 4 Volumes*. New York, NY: Harcourt, Brace, Jovanovich.
Plekhanov, G. 1974. *Selected Philosophical Works*. Vol. I. Moscow, Russia: Progress.
Rex, J. 1961. *Key Problems in Sociological Theory*. London, England: Routledge and Kegan Paul.
———. 1974. *Approaches to Sociology*. London, England: Routledge and Kegan Paul.
Sartre, Jean-Paul. 1966. *Being and Nothingness*. New York, NY: Washington Square Press.
———. 1974. *Between Existentialism and Marxism*. London, England: Pantheon.
———. 1976. *Critique of Dialectical Reason*. Vol. I. London, England: New Left Books.
Schutz, Alfred. 1964. *Collected Papers II: Studies in Social Theory*. The Hague, The Netherlands: Martinus Nijhoff.
———. 1966. *Collected Papers III: Studies in Phenomenological Philosophy*. The Hague, The Netherlands: Martinus Nijhoff.
———. 1967. *Collected Papers I: The Problem of Social Reality*. 2nd ed. The Hague, The Netherlands: Martinus Nijhoff.
Simmel, Georg. 1936. *The Metropolis and Mental Life*. Chicago, IL: University of Chicago Press.
———. 1955. *Conflict and the Web of Group Affiliations*. Glencoe, IL: Free Press.
Skinner, B.F. 1953. *Science and Human Behaviour*. New York, NY: Macmillan.
———. 1957. *Verbal Behavior*. New York, NY: Appleton-Century-Crofts.
———. 1972. *Beyond Freedom and Dignity*. New York, NY: Alfred Knopf.
Spencer, Herbert. 1873. *The Study of Sociology*. London, England: Kegan Paul and Tench.
Stirner, Max. 1907. *The Ego and His Own*. New York, NY: Libertarian Book Club.
Winch, P. 1958. *The Idea of a Social Science*. London, England: Routledge and Kegan Paul.
Wittgenstein, L. 1963. *Philosophical Investigations*. Oxford, England: Blackwell.

Educational Philosophies

Any adequate comparison between the lecture and the case educational methodologies necessarily requires a comparison of their underlying philosophies. This is based on the premise that foundational philosophies underlie educational philosophies, and each educational philosophy favors a certain educational methodology. This chapter, therefore, builds on the previous chapter that discussed how any foundational philosophy can be positioned on a continuum formed by four basic paradigms: functionalist, interpretive, radical humanist, and radical structuralist. This chapter discusses the major educational philosophies, namely: realism; idealism and pragmatism; reconstructionism; and Marxism. It also notes the correspondence between these educational philosophies and the four paradigms. It, furthermore, notes that each educational philosophy favors a certain instructional methodology and when any educational method is utilized, it is used within the bounds of that educational methodology which is based on its educational philosophy and foundational philosophy. That is, different educational methodologies use a given educational method differently.

Each educational philosophy, through its underlying foundational philosophy, can be related to one of the four paradigms. Any philosophy of education is the application of a foundational philosophy to educational problems. The practice of education, in turn, leads to the refinement of philosophical ideas. The philosophy of education becomes important when educators recognize the need for thinking clearly about what they are doing and to see what they are doing in the larger context of society. Educational philosophy is not only a basis for generating educational ideas, but also a basis for how to provide education, i.e., educational methodology. In turn, the educational methodology determines how an educational method should be used.

This chapter discusses the major extant educational philosophies.[1] It notes that the major educational philosophies, namely: realism; idealism and pragmatism;

[1] For this literature see Barrow and Woods (1989), Blake et al. (2002), Cahn (1996, 2009), Carr (2003), Chambliss (1996), Christensen and Garvin (1991), Cromer (1997), Curren (2003, 2007),

K. Ardalan, *Case Method and Pluralist Economics*,
https://doi.org/10.1007/978-3-319-72071-5_2

reconstructionism; and Marxism; respectively correspond to the four basic paradigms, namely: functionalist; interpretive; radical humanist; and radical structuralist. These major educational philosophies occupy an area in Exhibit 1.1, as shown in Exhibit 2.1. More specifically, realism lies in the functionalist quadrant in Exhibit 1.1 and is located on the right-hand side on the objective-subjective continuum, as shown in Exhibit 2.1. Idealism is located in the interpretive quadrant in Exhibit 1.1 and is located on the left-hand side on the objective-subjective continuum, as shown in Exhibit 2.1. Pragmatism lies in the interpretive quadrant, but to the right of idealism, as shown in Exhibit 2.1. Reconstructionism lies in the radical humanist quadrant in Exhibit 1.1 and belongs to the same position on the objective-subjective continuum as pragmatism, as shown in Exhibit 2.1. Marxism lies in the radical structuralist quadrant in Exhibit 1.1 and belongs to the right-hand side on the objective-subjective continuum, as shown in Exhibit 2.1. In the same vein, other non-major educational philosophies which are not discussed here, fall in between the major extant educational philosophies in Exhibit 2.1. This is in the same spirit as the foundational philosophies covering an area in Exhibit 1.1.[2] In combination, they show that each foundational philosophy is located within a paradigm and underlies an educational philosophy, as shown in Exhibit 2.2.

This chapter, further, notes that each educational philosophy favors a certain educational methodology, which in turn favors a certain way of applying educational methods, as shown in Exhibit 2.3. The former point will be discussed in Chaps. 3 through 9, and the latter point will be discussed in Chap. 10. As will be made clear, there is a difference between "educational method" and "educational methodology." The former refers to a tool, whereas the latter signifies an approach, an orientation, and a way of thinking about how to generate and apply educational methods. It is worth noting that Exhibit 2.3 is, indeed, the continuation of Exhibit 2.2.

1 Realism and Education

Realists strongly promote the study of science and the scientific method.[3] They believe that knowledge of the world is needed for humankind's proper use of it for his or her survival. The idea of survival has important implications for education. It places self-preservation as the primary aim of education.

Ellis et al. (1991), Freedman (1996), Gutek (2000a, 2000b, 2003), Hare and Portelli (2001), Hickman and Alexander (1998), Larochelle et al. (1998), Marples (1999), McLaren (1998), Noddings (2016), Ozmon (2011), Philosophy of Education Society (2003), Popkewitz and Fendler (1999), Power (1995), Rocha (2014), Rorty (1998), Sadovnik et al. (2000), Schrag (1995), Siegel (2012), Talisse and Hester (2002), and Winch and Gingell (1999). This chapter is based on Ardalan (2003).

[2] See Burrell and Morgan's (1979) exhibit on page 29.

[3] See, for example, Cromer (1997) and Schrag (1995).

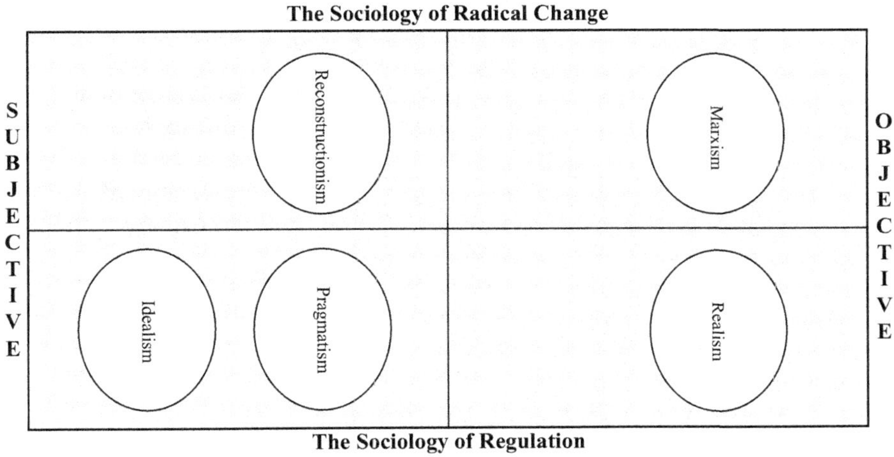

Exhibit 2.1 Major extant schools of thought in education located within the four paradigms

Realists maintain that knowing the world requires an understanding of facts and classifying the knowledge obtained about them. Schools should teach essential facts about the universe and the method of arriving at facts. Realists place enormous emphasis upon critical reason based on observation and experimentation.

Realists emphasize the practical side of education. Their concept of "practical" includes education for moral and character development, where moral education is founded on knowledge itself. Realists' essentials and the practicalities of education lead themselves further. They proceed from matter to idea, from imperfection to perfection, and all to the good life.

Realists promote the education which is primarily technical and leads to specialization. The idea of specialization is the natural outcome of the efforts to refine and establish definitive scientific knowledge. The expansion of our knowledge can be accomplished by many people, each one working on a small component of knowledge.

Realists support the lecture methodology and other formalized methodologies of teaching. They maintain that such objectives as self-realization can best occur when the learner is knowledgeable about the external world. Consequently, the learner must be exposed to the facts, and the lecture method can be an efficient, organized, and orderly way to accomplish this. Realists insist that any method used should be characterized by the integrity which comes from systematic, organized, and dependable knowledge.

Realists consider the role of the teacher in the educational process to be of primary importance. The teacher presents material in a way which is systematic and

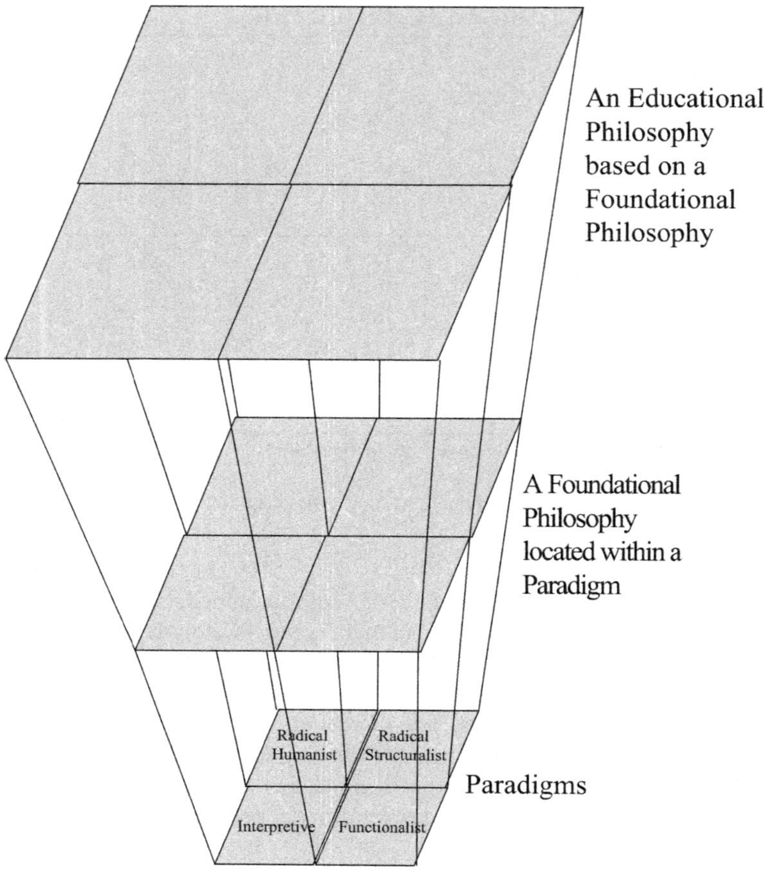

Exhibit 2.2 The structure within a paradigm

organized. He or she promotes the idea that there are clearly defined criteria making judgement about art, economics, politics, and education. For example, in education there are certain objective criteria to judge whether particular educational activities are worthwhile, such as type of material presented, how it is organized, whether or not it suits the psychological make-up of the learner, whether the delivery system is suitable, and whether it achieves the desired results.

Realists expect that institutions of higher education turn out teaching specialists who are knowledgeable, and who can serve as role models for their students. Realists place a lower priority on the personality and character of the teacher than they do on the effectiveness of the teacher to impart knowledge about the world that the learner can use.

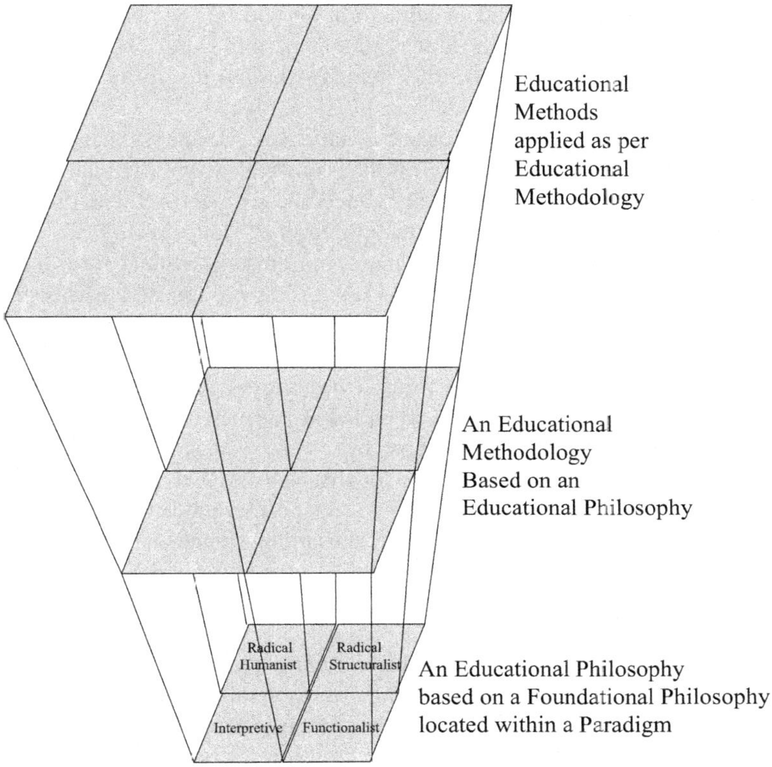

Exhibit 2.3 The structure within a paradigm

Realism results in practices with five formal steps of learning: preparation, presentation, association, systematization-generalization, and application. This is due to the realists' desire for precision and order. These desires are found in such school practices as ringing bells, set time periods for study, departmentalization, daily lesson plans, course scheduling, increasing specialization in curriculum, pre-packaged curriculum materials, and line-staff forms of administrative organization.

2 Idealism and Education

Idealists believe that truth cannot be found in the world of matter because it is an ever-changing world. Truth can be attained in the world of ideas, which are of substantial value and endurance, if not perfect and eternal.

Idealists believe that the aim of education should be the search for wisdom and true ideas. This leads to the development of mind and requires character development, as the search for truth demands personal discipline and steadfast character.

The concept of "self" lies at the center of idealistic metaphysics and, therefore, at the center of idealistic education. Self is the prime reality of individual experience and, hence, education becomes primarily concerned with self-realization. Idealists view self in the context of society and the totality of existence.

Idealists believe that human development and education stand in a dialectical relationship with respect to each other. Education is the process of a learner growing into the likeness of a universe of mind, i.e., an infinite ideal. Idealists view the student as one who has enormous potential for both moral and cognitive growth. The teacher guides the immature learner toward the infinite. To guide the student, the teacher should possess the necessary knowledge and personal qualities. Idealists favor a more philosophically-oriented teacher.

Idealists favor holistic curriculums. Idealists stress that a proper education includes study of classical writings, art, and science. The aim is to teach students to think and to demonstrate creative and critical thinking. Idealists believe that much of the great literature of the past is relevant to contemporary problems since many of these problems have been debated extensively by great philosophers and thinkers.

Idealists believe that the best method of learning is dialectic. The dialectic is a process in which ideas are put into battle against each other with the more substantial ideas enduring in the discussion. Essentially, it is a matter of disputation and only if ideas emerge victorious there is some reason for believing in them. It is a way of looking at both sides of the question and allowing the truth to emerge. Through this critical method of thinking, individuals can develop their ideas in ways that achieve syntheses and develop universal concepts. Idealists have a high regard for the inner powers of human beings, such as intuition. They believe that dialectic is the proper tool for stimulating intuition.

Idealists favor discussion-oriented learning methodologies. They might use the lecture method, but it is viewed more as a means of stimulating thought than merely passing on information. Idealists also utilize other methods like projects, supplemental activities, library research, and artwork.

Self-realization is an important aim of education and, therefore, idealists stress the importance of self-activity in education. Idealists believe that true learning occurs only within the individual self. The teacher cannot get inside a learner's mind, but he or she can provide materials and activities which influence learning. It is the response of the learners to these materials and activities that constitutes real education. This action is personal and private, therefore, all education is self-education. The teacher cannot always be present when learning occurs. Therefore, he or she stimulates the student such that the student continues to learn even when the teacher is absent.

Pragmatism and Education

Pragmatism seeks out the processes which work best to achieve desirable ends. Pragmatism examines traditional ways of thinking and doing to reconstruct approaches to life more in line with contemporary conditions.

Pragmatists stress that educational aims grow out of existing conditions. They are tentative and flexible, at least in the beginning. People—parents, students, and citizens—are the ones who have educational aims, and not the process of education.

Pragmatists point out that the philosophy of education is the formation of proper mental and moral attitudes to be used in tackling contemporary problems. When social life changes, the educational program must be reconstructed to meet the change.

For pragmatists, the process of education is fulfilled only when the student really understands why he or she does things. School fosters habits of thought, invention, and initiative which assist the individual in growing in the desired direction. School is a place where the other environments which the student encounters—the family environment, the religious environment, the work environment, and others—are combined into a meaningful whole.

Pragmatists do not view education as preparation for life, but as life itself. The lives of learners are important to them. Thus, educators should be aware of the background, interests, and motivations of the learners. Pragmatists believe that educators should also look at learners in terms of their cognitive, physical, emotional, and all their other factors. Pragmatists maintain that individuals should be educated as social beings, capable of participating in and directing their social affairs.

Pragmatists champion a diversified and integrated curriculum. It is composed of both process and content, but it is not fixed or an end in itself. Pragmatists recommend developing a "core" approach to curriculum. Learners can select an area of concentration or "core" for a period of study such that all other subject areas revolve around it. Learners are capable of knowing the general operating principles of nature and social conditions, which serve as general guides for participation.

Pragmatists believe that life is ever-changing and there is a constant need for improvement. Therefore, pragmatic education is based on experimental method which realizes that there are no fixed or absolute conclusions. The students learn the process of discovery and self-sufficiency as much as the facts which are uncovered. One of the approaches suggested by pragmatic educators is the project approach to learning. Students cooperate in pursuing the goals of the project. Projects are decided by group discussion with the teacher as moderator. Pragmatists favor the use of case methodology in class.

Pragmatists adhere to action-oriented education. They suggest an activity-oriented core approach. School can arrange for students to reconstruct past events and life situations in order to better appreciate the difficulties involved in a given actual situation. Learners become involved with the fundamentals of knowledge in a practical and applied way so that the usefulness of knowledge becomes more apparent to them. This approach demonstrates the relationship of various disciplines, shows the wholeness of knowledge, and helps learners to utilize such a knowledge in novel and creative ways when tackling problems.

Pragmatism is closely linked with reconstructionism in education in some aspects.[4] However, pragmatists are often critical of the excesses of reconstructionism.

3 Reconstructionism and Education

Reconstructionists believe that society is in need of constant reconstruction or change in order to adequately deal with social problems to make life better than it is.[5]

Reconstructionists stress that education and schools should be viewed in the much wider societal context. Radical changes in education cannot occur without radical changes in the structure of society itself. Educational reform follows social reforms and rarely, if ever, precedes or causes it. Therefore, an educator must be both an educator and a social activist.

Reconstructionists believe in the ideals of world community, brotherhood, and democracy. Schools should promote these ideals through curricular, administrative, and instructional practices. Schools cannot be expected to reconstruct society by themselves, but by the adoption of these ideals, they can serve as models for the rest of society.

Reconstructionists are critical of the teaching methods presently used at all levels of education. These methods promote traditional values and attitudes underlying the status quo and reinforce resistance to change. For instance, where teachers are viewed as dispensers of knowledge and students as passive recipients of knowledge, students uncritically accept whatever is presented. This results in producing students who think in the same way and who are uncritical of society, the economy, and the political structure.

Reconstructionists hold that teachers should begin by focusing on critical social issues not usually found in textbooks or discussed in schools. Teachers must become critical, analytical, and discriminating in judgement. They should encourage similar development in students. Reconstructionists believe that such a development in class can be brought about by the discussion methodology, including the case methodology. In this way, teachers help develop democratic approaches to social problems by enabling students to deal with social life intelligently. In fact, democratic procedures should be utilized on every level of schooling. This implies that students play an active part in the formulation of all objectives, methods, and curricula used in the educational process.

---

[4] They both certainly agree with the philosophy of John Dewey.

[5] See, for example, Larochelle et al. (1998) and Popkewitz and Fendler (1999).

Reconstructionists' favored curriculum is a modification of the core plan advocated by pragmatists. The core may be viewed as the central theme of the school. The core is complemented by related activities such as discussion groups, field experience, content and skill studies, and vocational studies. Finally, there is the synthesizing and unifying capacity. The reconstructionists' curriculum draws the people of the community together in common studies and it extends from the school into the wider community. Thus, it has the capacity to help bring about cultural transformation because of the dynamic relationship between school and society.

Reconstructionists believe that curriculum should be action-oriented by engaging students in projects such as collecting funds for worthy causes, informing the citizenry about social problems, and engaging in petition and protests. Reconstructionists favor students' participation in society, where they can both learn and apply what they learn. A curriculum which engages students in some social activity can produce far more learning than any sterile lecture in a classroom.

Reconstructionists favor a world curriculum which is future-oriented. They encourage reading the literature of other nations that deals with issues on a worldwide basis. They recommend teachers to be internationally oriented and humanitarian in their outlook.

4 Marxism and Education

Marxists find the definition of education which limits the term to the school system as too narrow since it leaves out the learning which Marxists regard as fundamental.[6] They see the world as it is in order to change it. Therefore, they regard education as those processes which contribute to the formation and changing of a person's consciousness and character. Consciousness is based on the worldview, and character involves how a person behaves in relation to that worldview and society. In this, Marxists not only combine education and socialization, but also impart to them the necessary critical perspective in the light of Marxist goals. By imparting such perspectives in class, Marxists favor the lecture methodology.

Marxists agree that the most obvious agent of education is the school. However, they doubt whether the really important learning takes place there. Other agents include the family, youth organizations, peer groups, work, the mass media, religious institutions, trade unions, political parties, and armed forces. These educative agents are classified as socializing agents. Work is the most important socializing agent for those who perform it.

Marxists' vision of communism as a period when man becomes increasingly self-conscious and self-determining has important implications for education. This performs both as a criterion for judging current efforts and as a guide for setting aims and methods. Communism is the movement that abolishes the present state of affairs, including the activities of both teacher and students throughout the process.

[6] See, for example, Brosio (1998) and McLaren (1998).

In fact, the relationship is dialectical: a change of social circumstances is required to establish a proper system of education, and a proper system of education is required to bring about a change of social circumstances. This implies that the major concern of education should be moral-political; the development of the socialist consciousness.

Marxists are careful about the ideology an individual adopts. School is the crucial agency within which the conflict of class values is worked out. The ruling class ideology consciously or unconsciously permeates the school system. It is a reflection of the interests of the dominant class, but is also accepted by wide sections of other classes.

Marxists define education in conjunction with productive labor: mental education, bodily education, and technological training. The combination of paid productive labor, mental education, bodily exercise, and polytechnic training will raise the working class far above the level of the higher and middle classes. Polytechnic training is a cognitive activity centered on an interaction of human and non-human nature. The combination of productive labor and mental education is primarily social, an interaction of one human with another human. Marxists see working together on a meaningful task as potentially humanizing. The young, brought up to take their place in the great work of social production, learn to play their part. Moreover, it is obvious that the fact of the collective working group being composed of individuals of both sexes and all ages, must necessarily, under suitable conditions, become a source of humane development.

Marxists' concepts of the relationship of the proletariat and permanent revolution have profound implications for education. Democracy can only be learned through the practice of democracy, and this must apply to schools as well as to all other sectors of society. The rotation of positions of responsibility and control is essential if people are to learn to exercise power. The spread of information in open government and the discussion of matters before policies are formulated are considered as constituting both education and execution. The performance of ordinary, manual labor by government and industrial leaders is an essential educational process, but the converse, government and management by the masses, is also essential if society is to become really classless.

5 Conclusion

This chapter built on the previous chapter and discussed how any foundational philosophy or worldview can be positioned within the four paradigms, namely: functionalist, interpretive, radical humanist, and radical structuralist. That is, the chapter discussed that the major educational philosophies, namely: realism; idealism and pragmatism; reconstructionism; and Marxism; respectively correspond to the four paradigms: functionalist; interpretive; radical humanist; and radical structuralist. It further noted that each educational philosophy underlies its instructional methodology, which in turn underlies the way it uses instruction methods.

References

Ardalan, Kavous. 2003. The Lecture-versus-Case Controversy: Its Philosophical Foundation. *Southwestern Economic Review* 30 (1): 99–118.

Barrow, Robin, and Ronald Woods. 1989. *An Introduction to Philosophy of Education*. New York, NY: Routledge.

Blake, Nigel, Paul Smeyers, Richard Smith, and Paul Standish, eds. 2002. *The Blackwell Guide to the Philosophy of Education*. New York, NY: Blackwell.

Brosio, Richard A. 1998. *The Continuing Correspondence Between Political Economy and Schooling: Telling the News, Journal of Thought*, Fall 33 (3): 85–105.

Burrell, Gibson, and Gareth Morgan. 1979. *Sociological Paradigms and Organizational Analysis*. Hants, England: Gower Publishing.

Cahn, Steven M., ed. 1996. *Classic and Contemporary Readings in the Philosophy of Education*. New York, NY: McGraw-Hill, College Division.

———., ed. 2009. *Philosophy of Education: The Essential Texts*. New York, NY: Routledge.

Carr, David. 2003. *Making Sense of Education: An Introduction to the Philosophy and Theory of Education*. New York, NY: Routledge.

Chambliss, J.J., ed. 1996. *Philosophy of Education: An Encyclopedia*. New York, NY: Garland Publishers.

Christensen, C. Roland, and David A. Garvin, eds. 1991. *Education for Judgment*. Cambridge, MA: Harvard Business School Press.

Cromer, Alan H. 1997. *Connected Knowledge: Science, Philosophy, and Education*. Oxford, England: Oxford University Press.

Curren, Randall R., ed. 2003. *Companion to the Philosophy of Education*. New York, NY: Blackwell.

———., ed. 2007. *Philosophy of Education: An Anthology*. Malden, MA: Blackwell.

Ellis, Arthur K., John J. Cogan, and Kenneth R. Howey. 1991. *Introduction to the Foundations of Education*. Upper Saddle River, NJ: Prentice Hall.

Freedman, James O. 1996. *Idealism and Liberal Education*. Ann Harbor, MI: University of Michigan Press.

Gutek, Gerald Lee. 2000a. *Philosophical and Ideological Perspectives on Education*. 3rd ed. New York, NY: Allyn & Bacon.

———. 2000b. *Historical and Philosophical Foundations of Education: Selected Readings*. Upper Saddle River, NJ: Prentice Hall, College Division.

———. 2003. *Philosophical and Ideological Voices in Education*. 1st ed. New York, NY: Allyn & Bacon.

Hare, William, and John P. Portelli, eds. 2001. *Philosophy of Education: Introductory Readings*. 3rd ed. New York, NY: Detseling Enterprises.

Hickman, Larry, and Thomas M. Alexander, eds. 1998. *The Essential Dewey: Pragmatism, Education, Democracy*. Bloomington, IN: Indiana University Press.

Larochelle, Marie, Nadine Bednarz, and Jim Garrison, eds. 1998. *Constructivism and Education*. Cambridge, England: Cambridge University Press.

Marples, Roger, ed. 1999. *The Aims of Education*. New York, NY: Routledge.

McLaren, Peter. 1998. Revolutionary Pedagogy in Post-Revolutionary Times: Rethinking the Political Economy of Critical Education. *Educational Theory* 48 (4): 431–462.

Noddings, Nel. 2016. *Philosophy of Education*. Boulder, CO: Westview Press.

Ozmon, Howard A. 2011. *Philosophical Foundations of Education*. 7th ed. New York, NY: Pearson.

Philosophy of Education Society. 2003. *Philosophy of Education 2002*. New York, NY: Philosophy of Education Society Press.

Popkewitz, Thomas S., and Lynn Fendler, eds. 1999. *Critical Theories in Education: Changing Terrains of Knowledge and Politics*. New York, NY: Routledge.

Power, Edward J. 1995. *Educational Philosophy: A History from the Ancient World to Modern America*. New York, NY: Garland Publishers.
Rocha, Samuel D. 2014. *A Primer for Philosophy and Education*. Eugene, OR: Cascade Books.
Rorty, Amelie Oksenberg, ed. 1998. *Philosophers on Education: Historical Perspectives*. New York, NY: Routledge.
Sadovnik, Alan R., Susan Semel, and Peter Cookson. 2000. *Exploring Education: An Introduction to the Foundations of Education*. 2nd ed. New York, NY: Allyn & Bacon.
Schrag, Francis. 1995. *Back to Basics: Fundamental Educational Questions Reexamined*. San Francisco, CA: Jossey-Bass Education Series.
Siegel, Harvey. 2012. *The Oxford Handbook of Philosophy of Education*. Oxford, England: Oxford University Press.
Talisse, Robert B., and D. Micah Hester. 2002. *On the Philosophy of Education*. New York, NY: Wadsworth Publishing.
Winch, Christopher, and John Gingell. 1999. *Key Concepts in the Philosophy of Education*. New York, NY: Routledge.

Educational Methodologies

This chapter discusses the implications of the previous two chapters with respect to educational methodologies. For this purpose, this chapter brings major aspects of the previous two chapters to the forefront, and elaborates on their connections and implications for the way educational methodologies are formed.[1]

The previous two chapters, in essence, discussed that foundational philosophies underlie educational philosophies, and each educational philosophy favors a certain educational methodology. It was also noted that there is a difference between "educational method" and "educational methodology." The former refers to a tool, whereas the latter signifies an approach, an orientation, and a way of thinking about how to generate and apply educational methods. That is, educational methodologies determine the way such educational methodologies are applied to determine various aspects of the way education is performed.

As one moves from the objective to the subjective end of the spectrum in Exhibit 1.1 of Chap. 1, the in-class instructional methodology favored changes from totally having a lecture-oriented educational methodology to completely having a discussion-oriented educational methodology, e.g., a case-oriented educational methodology.

In fact, for the realist, whose position on the objective-subjective continuum in Exhibit 1.1 of Chap. 1 is to the far right, the teacher is a guide. The real world exists,

[1]For this literature see Ardalan (2003a, 2003b, 2006, 2008, 2013, 2015), Barnes et al. (1994), Barrow and White (1993), Barrow and Woods (1989), Blake et al. (2002), Brosio (1998), Burrell and Morgan (1979), Cahn (1996, 2009), Carr (2003), Chambliss (1996), Christensen and Garvin (1991), Cromer (1997), Curren (2003, 2007), Dooley and Skinner (1977), Ellis et al. (1991), Erskine et al. (2003), Freedman (1996), Gragg (1954), Gutek (2000a, 2000b, 2003), Hancock (1999), Hare and Portelli (2001), Hickman and Alexander (1998), Kimball and Orrill (1995), Larochelle et al. (1998), Marples (1999), Mauffette-Leenders et al. (2007), McLaren (1998), Morgan (1983, 1985), Noddings (2016), Orrill (1999), Ozmon (2011), Philosophy of Education Society (2003), Popkewitz and Fendler (1999), Power (1995), Reynolds (1978), Rocha (2014), Rorty (1998), Sadovnik et al. (2000), Schrag (1995), Siegel (2012), Talisse and Hester (2002), and Winch and Gingell (1999). This chapter is based on Ardalan (2003a).

K. Ardalan, *Case Method and Pluralist Economics*,
https://doi.org/10.1007/978-3-319-72071-5_3

and the teacher is responsible for introducing the student to it. To do this, the teacher uses lectures, demonstrations, and sensory experiences. The teacher does not do it in a random or haphazard way; he/she must not only introduce the students to nature, but also show them its regularities.

At the other (subjective) extreme on the objective-subjective continuum in Exhibit 1.1:

> Where truth is relative, where reality is probabilistic, and where structural relationships are contingent, teaching and learning are most effectively accomplished through discussion rather than exploration. With intrinsically complex phenomena and the limited usefulness of simple theoretical relationships, little of value can be communicated directly from teacher to student. The learning process must emphasize the development of understanding, judgement, and even intuition.
>
> Discussion teaching requires a major change in an instructor's role and classroom responsibilities. Traditional teaching, and the lecture mode with which it is so often associated, gives primacy to the instructor. Classroom activity derives from the teacher's presentation of subject matter and follows his or her class plan. The student's role is clearly subordinate. (Christensen et al. 1989, p. 20)

In short, as one moves from the objective to the subjective end of the continuum in Exhibit 1.1 the nature of reality viewed changes and along with it changes the foundational philosophy, its corresponding educational philosophy, and its educational methodology.[2] That is, a move from lecture methodology to discussion methodology, e.g., case methodology.

In the lecture methodology teaching is telling, knowledge is facts, and learning is recall. Teachers deliver content, in the form of factual information, and students receive it. Learning is satisfactorily completed when the student transfers the material back to the teacher at the specified time.

The lecture methodology is efficient with respect to the use of time, energy, and the patience of instructor and student. A student trained under the lecture method possesses a certainty, a precision, and a firming of grasp which is remarkable for the relatively short time he/she spends on acquiring his/her knowledge.

The lecture methodology is of great power when the transfer of knowledge is the primary academic objective. But when the objective is critical thinking (in the liberal arts setting, for example) or problem-solving (in the professional school milieu), and the development of qualities such as sensitivity, cooperation, and zest for discovery, then discussion pedagogy offers substantial advantages. To achieve these goals, both teachers and students must modify their traditional roles and responsibilities.

The case methodology has an entirely different purpose and provides an entirely different result. Businesspeople must be able to solve problems arising in new situations in the real life. Accordingly, education would consist of acquiring skills to act in a changing environment. It is not that how a student may be trained to know, but how a student is to be trained to act. The case methodology is most effective

---

[2] Similarly, Morgan (1983) elaborately and extensively shows how different worldviews along the objective-subjective continuum in Exhibit 1.1 underlie different research methodologies.

wherever decisions are to be made and problems are to be solved. There is no one best way of teaching with cases.

The case methodology is a learning process which consists of the interaction of the case situation, individual student, overall class section, and the teacher. It blends cognitive and affective learning modes.

There are other methods of teaching such as lectures, movies, field trips, readings. Any way students can learn is a good way. There are situations where the case methodology is not a good match. But, in business environment it is one of the best fit.

Next, Chaps. 4 through 9 show that the sequence of foundational philosophy, educational philosophy, and educational methodology affects the way that education is performed in practice. In order to show this, each one of those chapters focuses on certain aspects of the applications of the lecture methodology and the case methodology and compares them. Since most readers are familiar with the lecture methodology, the discussions in these chapters elaborate more on the case methodology. Chapter 10 shows how different educational methodologies use a given educational method differently.

1 Conclusion

This chapter discussed how foundational philosophies or worldviews underlie educational philosophies, and each educational philosophy favors a certain educational methodology, which in turn implies a certain way or method of education.

References

Ardalan, Kavous. 2003a. The Lecture-versus-Case Controversy: Its Philosophical Foundation. *Southwestern Economic Review* 30 (1): 99–118.

———. 2003b. Alternative Approaches Utilized in the Case Method: Their Philosophical Foundations. *Academy of Educational Leadership Journal* 30 (3): 103–120.

———. 2006. The Philosophical Foundation of the Lecture-versus-Case Controversy: Its Implications for Faculty Teaching, Research, and Service. *International Journal of Social Economics* 33 (3): 261–281.

———. 2008. The Philosophical Foundation of the Lecture-versus-Case Controversy: Its Implications for Course Goals, Objectives, and Contents. *International Journal of Social Economics* 35 (1/2): 15–34.

———. 2013. The Philosophical Foundation of the Lecture Method of Instruction and the Case Method of Instruction: Implications for Examinations. *Contemporary Issues in Education Research* 6 (1): 1–7.

———. 2015. Chapter 3: Using Entertaining Metaphors in the Introduction of the Case Method in a Case-Based Course. In *Exploring Learning and Teaching In Higher Education*, ed. Mang Li and Yong Zhao, 69–96. New York, NY: Springer.

Barnes, Louis B., Abby J. Hansen, and C. Roland Christensen. 1994. *Teaching and the Case Method: Text, Cases, and Readings*. Boston, MA: Harvard Business School.

Barrow, Robin, and Patricia White, eds. 1993. *Beyond Liberal Education: Essays in Honor of Paul H. Hirst*. New York, NY: Routledge.
Barrow, Robin, and Ronald Woods. 1989. *An Introduction to Philosophy of Education*. New York, NY: Routledge.
Blake, Nigel, Paul Smeyers, Richard Smith, and Paul Standish, eds. 2002. *The Blackwell Guide to the Philosophy of Education*. New York, NY: Blackwell.
Brosio, Richard A. 1998. The Continuing Correspondence between Political Economy and Schooling: Telling the News. *Journal of Thought* 33 (3): 85–105.
Burrell, Gibson, and Gareth Morgan. 1979. *Sociological Paradigms and Organizational Analysis*. Hants, England: Gower Publishing.
Cahn, Steven M., ed. 1996. *Classic and Contemporary Readings in the Philosophy of Education*. New York, NY: McGraw-Hill College Division.
———., ed. 2009. *Philosophy of Education: The Essential Texts*. New York, NY: Routledge.
Carr, David. 2003. *Making Sense of Education: An Introduction to the Philosophy and Theory of Education*. New York, NY: Routledge.
Chambliss, J.J., ed. 1996. *Philosophy of Education: An Encyclopedia*. New York, NY: Garland Publishers.
Christensen, C. Roland, and Abby J. Hansen. 1989. *Teaching and the Case Method: Text, Cases, and Readings*, Harvard Business School, Boston, Massachusetts.
———., eds. 1991. *Education for Judgment*. Cambridge, MA: Harvard Business School Press.
Cromer, Alan H. 1997. *Connected Knowledge: Science, Philosophy, and Education*. Oxford, England: Oxford University Press.
Curren, Randall R., ed. 2003. *Companion to the Philosophy of Education*. New York, NY: Blackwell.
———., ed. 2007. *Philosophy of Education: An Anthology*. Malden, MA: Blackwell.
Dooley, Arch R., and Wickham Skinner. 1977. Casing Casemethod Methods. *Academy of Management Review* 2 (2): 277–289.
Ellis, Arthur K., John J. Cogan, and Kenneth R. Howey. 1991. *Introduction to the Foundations of Education*. Upper Saddle River, NJ: Prentice Hall.
Erskine, James A., Michiel R. Leenders, and Louise A. Mauffette-Leenders. 2003. *Teaching with Cases*. 3rd ed. London, ON, Canada: Ivey Business School, University of Western Ontario, Erskine Associate Inc., and Leenders and Associates Inc..
Freedman, James O. 1996. *Idealism and Liberal Education*. Ann Harbor, MI: University of Michigan Press.
Gragg, Charles I. 1954. Because Wisdom Can't Be Told. In *The Case Method at the Harvard Business School*, ed. Malcolm P. McNair. New York, NY: McGraw-Hill Book Company, Inc.
Gutek, Gerald Lee. 2000a. *Philosophical and Ideological Perspectives on Education*. 3rd ed. New York, NY: Allyn & Bacon.
———. 2000b. *Historical and Philosophical Foundations of Education: Selected Readings*. Upper Saddle River, NJ: Prentice Hall College Division.
———. 2003. *Philosophical and Ideological Voices in Education*. 1st ed. New York, NY: Allyn & Bacon.
Hancock, Ralph C., ed. 1999. *America, the West, and Liberal Education*. New York, NY: Rowman & Littlefield.
Hare, William, and John P. Portelli, eds. 2001. *Philosophy of Education: Introductory Readings*. 3rd ed. New York, NY: Detseling Enterprises.
Hickman, Larry, and Thomas M. Alexander, eds. 1998. *The Essential Dewey: Pragmatism, Education, Democracy*. Bloomington, IN: Indiana University Press.
Kimball, Bruce A., and Robert Orrill, eds. 1995. *The Condition of American Liberal Education: Pragmatism and a Changing Tradition*. New York, NY: College Entrance Examination Board.
Larochelle, Marie, Nadine Bednarz, and Jim Garrison, eds. 1998. *Constructivism and Education*. Cambridge, England: Cambridge University Press.
Marples, Roger, ed. 1999. *The Aims of Education*. New York, NY: Routledge.

Mauffette-Leenders, Louise A., James A. Erskine, and Michiel R. Leenders. 2007. *Learning with Cases*. 4th ed. London, ON, Canada: Ivey Publishing, Ivey Business School, University of Western Ontario.

McLaren, Peter. 1998. Revolutionary Pedagogy in Post-Revolutionary Times: Rethinking the Political Economy of Critical Education. *Educational Theory* 48 (4): 431–462.

Morgan, Gareth. 1983. *Beyond Method: Strategies for Social Research*. Beverley Hills, CA: Sage.

———. 1985. Qualitative and Action Based Research. In *Actes du Colloque, Perspective de Recherche Pour lo Praticien*, ed. Y. Allaire, M. Landry, H. Mintzberg, and G. Morgan, 81–187. Rouyn-Noranda, QC, Canada: University of Quebec at Abitibi-Temiscaminque.

Noddings, Nel. 2016. *Philosophy of Education*. Boulder, CO: Westview Press.

Orrill, Robert, ed. 1999. *Education and Democracy: Re-Imaging Liberal Learning in America*. New York, NY: College Entrance Examination Board.

Ozmon, Howard A. 2011. *Philosophical Foundations of Education*. 7th ed. New York, NY: Pearson.

Philosophy of Education Society. 2003. *Philosophy of Education 2002*. New York, NY: Philosophy of Education Society Press.

Popkewitz, Thomas S., and Lynn Fendler, eds. 1999. *Critical Theories in Education: Changing Terrains of Knowledge and Politics*. New York, NY: Routledge.

Power, Edward J. 1995. *Educational Philosophy: A History from the Ancient World to Modern America*. New York, NY: Garland Publishers.

Reynolds, John I. 1978. There's Method in Cases. *Academy of Management Review* 3 (1): 129–133.

Rocha, Samuel D. 2014. *A Primer for Philosophy and Education*. Eugene, OR: Cascade Books.

Rorty, Amelie Oksenberg, ed. 1998. *Philosophers on Education: Historical Perspectives*. New York, NY: Routledge.

Sadovnik, Alan R., Susan Semel, and Peter Cookson. 2000. *Exploring Education: An Introduction to the Foundations of Education*. 2nd ed. New York, NY: Allyn & Bacon.

Schrag, Francis. 1995. *Back to Basics: Fundamental Educational Questions Reexamined*. San Francisco, CA: Jossey-Bass Education Series.

Siegel, Harvey. 2012. *The Oxford Handbook of Philosophy of Education*. Oxford, England: Oxford University Press.

Talisse, Robert B., and D. Micah Hester. 2002. *On the Philosophy of Education*. New York, NY: Wadsworth Publishing.

Winch, Christopher, and John Gingell. 1999. *Key Concepts in the Philosophy of Education*. New York, NY: Routledge.

Educational Methodologies: Implications for Course Goals, Objectives, and Contents

This chapter discusses the implications of the first three chapters with respect to the course goals, objectives, and contents. For this purpose, this chapter brings major aspects of the first three chapters to the forefront, and elaborates on their connections and implications for the way educational methodologies are applied.[1]

The first three chapters, in essence, discussed that, within the framework of the four paradigms, foundational philosophies underlie educational philosophies, and each educational philosophy favors a certain educational methodology.[2] In other words, as one moves from the objective to the subjective end of the spectrum in Exhibit 1.1 of Chap. 1, the in-class instructional methodology favored changes from totally having a lecture-oriented educational methodology to completely having a discussion-oriented educational methodology, e.g., a case-oriented educational methodology. This chapter discusses how these educational methodologies, in turn, determine the way such educational methodologies are applied to determine the type of course goals, objectives, and contents. In order to show this, this chapter focuses on certain aspects of the applications of the lecture methodology and the case methodology and compares them. Since most readers are familiar

---

[1] For this literature see Ardalan (2003a, 2003b, 2006, 2008, 2013, 2015), Barnes et al. (1994), Barrow and White (1993), Barrow and Woods (1989), Blake et al. (2002), Brosio (1998), Burrell and Morgan (1979), Cahn (1996), Cahn (2009), Carr (2003), Chambliss (1996), Christensen and Garvin (1991), Cromer (1997), Curren (2003, 2007), Dooley and Skinner (1977), Ellis et al. (1991), Erskine et al. (2003), Freedman (1996), Gragg (1954), Gutek (2000a, 2000b, 2003), Hancock (1999), Hare and Portelli (2001), Hickman and Alexander (1998), Kimball and Orrill (1995), Larochelle et al. (1998), Marples (1999), Mauffette-Leenders et al. (2007), McLaren (1998), Morgan (1983, 1985), Noddings (2016), Orrill (1999), Ozmon (2011), Philosophy of Education Society (2003), Popkewitz and Fendler (1999), Power (1995), Reynolds (1978), Rocha (2014), Rorty (1998), Sadovnik et al. (2000), Schrag (1995), Siegel (2012), Talisse and Hester (2002), and Winch and Gingell (1999). This chapter is based on Ardalan (2008), Erskine et al. (2003), and Mauffette-Leenders et al. (2007).

[2] The difference between "educational method" and "educational methodology" should be kept in mind. The former refers to a tool, whereas the latter signifies an approach, an orientation, and a way of thinking about how to generate and apply respective educational methods.

K. Ardalan, *Case Method and Pluralist Economics*,
https://doi.org/10.1007/978-3-319-72071-5_4

with the lecture methodology, the discussions in this chapter elaborate more on the case methodology.

1 Value-Free Education vs. Value-Laden Education

The lecture methodology provides objective/value-free knowledge; the case methodology provides holistic education, i.e., provides both objective/value-free knowledge and subjectivity/value-laden education. The lecture methodology pursues technical knowledge; the case methodology pursues technical knowledge in relation to lived experience and action. For instance, the lecture methodology turns the study of literature into the study of structural patterns, or turns the study of philosophy into the technical analysis of linguistics and logical intricacies. These are not regarded as holistic learning by the case methodology because the scientific discoveries which they produce do not cast much light on either the nature or the proper use of human experience. That is, science can say how to make a bomb or save a life, but it cannot say whether either should be done.

The lecture methodology values knowledge for its own sake, whether that knowledge lays claim on scientific certainty or understanding images, ideas, aesthetic forms, and so forth. A mind loaded with some knowledge is able to acquire more knowledge faster than a mind with lesser knowledge. Thus, learning is added to learning with no end.

The case methodology values holistic education and its use in human life. Knowledge should shape the experience of learning. In this way, the case methodology has satisfactory answers for students when they ask: Why all of this learning? Where is this learning going? What is the use of this learning? They realize that education is not merely an academic exercise and that they do not have to embrace vocational or professional studies in order to see practical ends stand clearly in view.

In short, according to the lecture methodology we live in order to learn, but according to the case methodology we learn in order to live.

The case methodology involves not only the state of mind, feelings, scientific truth, bodies of knowledge, but also action. For the case methodology, the subject matter is human experience (i.e., intellectual, emotional, social, cultural), which addresses issues related to action, such as how to act and how to live.

In order to teach students how to think about right action, the lecture methodology teaches them absolutes, so that they will know not only how to think, but also what to think and what to do. For the case methodology, this does not involve a thought process, but it involves memorization which precedes experience, precludes thinking, and prevents learning.

For the case methodology, thinking about right action is quite the opposite because thinking is complicated, difficult, and active. It requires examination of all facts, ideas, experiences, and choices with due consideration of value judgment. It involves examination of the ideal ends of action, the relative goods in human experience, the costs and rewards of obligation, the effects of action on both the actor and others, the relation of thought to feeling, and the merits of claims to truth.

Such examinations constitute thinking about the right action. Of course, such examinations performed by different people do not lead to their agreement on their answers. Similarly, not everyone who performs such examinations will act on the answers given. But without such examinations, no one can be expected to act properly. That is, thinking about right action is a necessary but not a sufficient condition for acting properly. Mere thinking does not lead to action, but the action cannot occur without it.

In the case methodology, teachers train students to think by asking value-charged questions, and lead students from thinking to acting by showing the benefits of such thinking in experience.

The case methodology challenges thought in the context of practical experience. In any given case, whether it is from law, business, ethics, or teaching, the underlying assumption is that experience is the matrix of thought, and the end of thought is action. A case always requires a decision for an action to be made. The case methodology is based in actuality and directed towards it.

In the case methodology, teachers use case-books for thinking and right action, and transform education into the study of lived experience and the preparation for right action. Then students come to know the case methodology as the compelling authority of the useful, since its worth is confirmed by the rewards of experience.

In the case methodology, even if students cannot act properly, their minds are prepared to think about action and to see the uses in experience of acting in one way rather than another. Students habitually and regularly think about the ends and means of action and then act to achieve the best ends. Such students, in effect, have learned virtue, grace, how to live well, or any other form of right action. Such students have learned how to learn from experience and how to act on the basis of that learning.

2 Knowledge Is Facts vs. Knowledge Is Wisdom and Facts

The educational objectives of the lecture methodology and the case methodology are different. In the lecture methodology, the educational objective is the transfer of factual knowledge from the teacher to the students. In the case methodology, the educational objectives are developing students' judgment and wisdom. Teachers using the lecture methodology wonder how cases can be used when there are so much theoretical and substantive materials to impart. Teachers using the case methodology do not believe in imparting knowledge because teaching is not a transfer process.

In the case methodology, the educational goal is not to strictly involve students' minds with textbooks facts, which they forget soon after they graduate, rather the educational goal is to instill practical knowledge and the habit of logical and correct reasoning in every subject.

The case methodology is based on the idea that wisdom cannot be told. There are few truths, facts, or fixed rules to be learned in administration. This is because managerial situations and circumstances are unique and varied. Therefore, learning how to deal with new circumstances is more important. Consequently, the case methodology adheres to the clinical approach of learning by doing.

In the lecture methodology, students are trained to believe that the solution to human problems is found in logical statements and propositions. Furthermore, students' formal education is intellectual, i.e., they learn abstract concepts, general propositions, and answers.

According to the case methodology, logic and mathematics do not exhaust the nature of reality. The case methodology emphasizes both quantitative and qualitative assessments. It encourages the students to play with numbers so that they get a better understanding of the entire situation. Meanwhile, it warns students that they should not get lost in detailed numerical analysis with little reflection on the actual meaning of the numbers. It emphasizes that students should know why they do the calculation which they do, i.e., what they intend to do with the result, and how they plan to interpret it. It suggests that students improve their business intuition by guessing the answer before they perform the calculation. It recommends that students freely use their visual sense when they try to interpret numbers, e.g., to draw a diagram to facilitate their interpretation.

In the case methodology, students are made aware that case alternatives should be evaluated on both quantitative and qualitative grounds. Sometimes, quantitative (including the financial) side indicates that a particular idea is positive, while the qualitative side does not support that proposition strongly. In such situations, judgment determines what should be done given both the quantitative and the qualitative factors.

In the lecture methodology, students graduate with the impression that their education has provided them with a body of specific knowledge, a set of formulae, correct answers, and ready-made patterns of behavior that enable them to be successful administrators. Students who graduate from a case methodology program do not look for the easy answers. They do not expect business problems to lend themselves to oversimplification, and to one simple, right method of analysis which at the end arrives at the only correct answer.

In the case methodology, on the contrary, students develop skills to analyze a situation, to formulate a plan of action, and to carry that plan into action through the people in their organization or in their community. They are aware that the knowledge of a few formulae and the ability to manipulate a calculator are not enough to produce a really good executive. They know that average-grade technicians who can come up with the right answers to routine problems and procedures are not highly paid while people with qualities of judgment and leadership are highly paid.

In the lecture methodology, teachers use textbooks. They are mostly concerned with the textbook techniques but are not explicit about the conceptual framework of the subject matter they teach. In the case methodology, in contrast, the objectives are for the students to understand and be able to use the conceptual framework of the subject matter they teach. Furthermore, the teacher makes sure to use that framework on a daily basis. They do this because a business manager is more involved with the basic conceptual framework of the subject matter than its techniques. Case teachers think of management as being largely a matter of practice.

In the case methodology, teachers build up a sequence of experiences in which they get the students involved. Then, the teachers use their knowledge and understanding of the conceptual framework of the subject matter in asking questions and calling upon students for reactions. In this way, the students gradually gain a working capacity in applying the fundamentals.

3 Teaching vs. Learning

There is a distinction between the lecture methodology and the case methodology regarding what teachers know about how students learn. In the lecture methodology, the idea of teaching is disconnected from the idea of learning. Teaching is conveying information, that is, teaching is organizing and communicating content. In order to discover whether students have learned, teachers see how well students are able to report back what teachers have told them, that is, teachers are not concerned with how students learn. In the case methodology, on the other hand, knowledge of teaching is dependent on the understanding of how students learn. Teaching is engaging students in learning, that is, teaching is involving students in the active construction of knowledge. Teachers need to know not only the subject matter, but also how students learn and how to transform them into active learners.

In the case methodology, context sets the frame of reference for thinking about effective teaching. That is, learning is contextual. There are at least three dimensions to the context: (1) new knowledge is acquired when prior knowledge is extended and revised; (2) new ideas gain meaning when their coherent relationship is presented; and (3) knowledge becomes usable when its applications to concrete problem-solving situations are shown.

In the case methodology, valuable student learning opportunities are provided by the group discussion process. This is because in practice, final decisions regarding business problems are reached only after discussions take place among groups, whether small or large. Each case class is essentially a practical experience in group behavior and the way business decisions are arrived at through group discussions. Each case class provides a learning experience regarding how to listen to the views of others, how to express one's view, and how to persuade others to one's point of view. It also provides an opportunity to improve one's judgment by being appreciated as well as humiliated by own peers. Furthermore, it also provides an invaluable opportunity to experience how useful is the rigorous logical analysis of the problem (which is what the lecture methodology teaches), and how judgment needs to be made in weighing the factors which have no common denominator.

According to the case methodology students think and learn most while they are involved with the conditions of the problem at hand, seek alternatives, and find their solution. If they cannot find their solution (together with the teacher and other students), they will not learn, no matter how accurately they can recite some correct answer (which is what the lecture methodology teaches).

In the lecture methodology, education consists of the cumulative and unending acquisition of factual knowledge. Educational growth consists of mechanically, i.e., in isolation, adding information, skills, or educative expressions to students' repertoire over time.

In the case methodology, education consists of the cumulative and unending acquisition, combination, and reordering of individual experiences. Educational growth consists of combining the understanding of past experiences with the understanding of present experiences in order to be able to understand future experiences. That is, educational growth requires continual and cohesive reorganization and reformulation of past experiences in the light of new experiences.

In the case methodology, students discover and develop their own unique framework for approaching, understanding, and dealing with business problems.

4 Subject-Matter Logic vs. Combined Pedagogical Logic and Subject-Matter Logic

In the case methodology, when planning a course, a mixture of the pedagogical logic and the subject-matter logic must be considered. Furthermore, since the purpose is the student's achievement of the course goals, ultimately the pedagogical logic of experience must carry a higher priority than the subject-matter logic.

In the lecture methodology, the subject-matter logic drives the course. Teachers prepare their lecture in a relatively short period of time and have full control over the sequence and timing of activities in class. They can interject humor, at a predetermined time, to keep students interested, and can put something slightly outrageous to get the attention of a student who is dozing. Teachers can relatively easily anticipate most of the questions which may be asked and prepare to answer them in a way which allows them to gain students' respect.

In the case methodology, teachers spend a lot of time on their case preparation because they want to be ready to go wherever the discussion goes. They are not in control because the vehicle is the students' vehicle. It is much more difficult to influence the process of the case methodology in a way which is productive. In any case, teachers put much preparation effort in the course in order to prevent things from getting out of hand.

In the case methodology, when developing the class plan, there is a continuum of high to low structure, from which a teacher can choose depending on the following influential factors: the kind of case, the position in the course, the type of student involved, and the teacher's orientation and experience.

Too much structure constrains students, and too little structure frustrates students. Teachers need to try hard to strike a balance between when structure is needed and when it is not. Teachers may allow students to roam within 15-min blocks but not for an hour. So, teachers plan sections of the class in general terms, but they do not specify where the class will be within each section, i.e., they do not specify that the class will go from point A to B to C. This is what the students determine in class through the class process. Teachers have a genuine interest in what happens in the classroom, in students, and in the learning process.

In the case methodology, teachers provide the impromptu services which the group discussion requires. They keep the class process orderly. They ask questions which reveal the relevance of the ongoing discussion and enhance group thinking. They weave together the threads of individual contributions into a pattern which can be perceived by themselves and their students. They track time and note whether the discussion is not moving fast enough to make efficient use of class time or is too fast to allow the comprehension of a large section of the class. They manage an essentially undirected activity while stay out of the way. They do not prevent the class from making discoveries, which may be new even to them. Teachers examine their class rather than their subject matter because unpredictable developments are the distinguishing feature of real learning.

5 Learning the Content vs. Learning the Combined Process and Content

In the lecture methodology, course priority is given to the objective that certain concepts are fully understood. Usually, there is extensive involvement in the technical details of analysis, which allows teachers to be portrayed as smart people. Teachers expect students to go through detailed numerical calculations. In a real business situation, such students do not know who they are and what role they have to play. They tend to spend a lot of time and energy with numbers and they expect those numbers to tell them the answer because to them the answer is in the numbers. When they cannot come up with an answer, they think the reason is that they do not know how to deal with numbers.

In the case methodology, course priorities are both process and content based. That is, course priority is given to a review of course objectives, case objectives, plans for a particular class within the sequence of all classes, and the importance of having a certain class and a certain case within a certain course. The priority planning is important because with scarce class time higher priority topics receive higher preference. Priority is not only given to making sure that certain concepts are fully understood, but also to problem identification and analysis, alternative generation, decision-making, implementation planning, sorting or specification of information, and proper application of relevant theory to practice. In the first few classes in a case course, priority is given to familiarizing the class with the discussion process and the teacher's expectations regarding proper student preparation and class participation.

In the case methodology, the central focus is on the learning process. It involves constant reinforcing, apprenticeship, discussing together, working together, and over time arriving at a cohesive central understanding. The goal is to teach students to follow a consistent path and a consistent objective.

In the case methodology, in the first year of the program, teachers mostly emphasize process learning. They teach a certain amount of content, but of crucial importance is really that mental process. Teachers help students to develop a disciplined mental approach to an unstructured problem. They make sure that students can formulate what the problem is, otherwise they cannot analyze it. When students are able to define the problem, then they can select the proper tool. The aim is to prepare students in such a way that they will be able to make decisions in business.

In the case methodology, each case is turned into an experience. Students take the role of the manager in the case. Rather than spending a lot of time and energy dealing with numbers and expect those numbers to tell the answer, teachers take a case and teach it entirely without numbers. They ask students to get inside the case as an experience, start anywhere in the case, see how all matters will work themselves out, and see how they will come up with their own way of solving the business problem. That is, case problem solving is seen as a process and managed as a process.

In the case methodology, the success of the process of case discussion is dependent on an intricate integration of course objectives (substantive knowledge as well as analytical and clinical skills), case problems, and student and section learning needs. The process requires teacher's mastery of case teaching skills and techniques. The process involves complex teacher's tasks and the way those complex tasks help unleash students' learning power.

In the case methodology, often process-based cases are superimposed on knowledge-based content. They primarily focus on the dynamics of individual and group discussions and interactions, but include large enough data on the knowledge requirement of the course that one would appreciate the academic circumstances in which the case problem developed.

6 Generalized Learning vs. Specific Application in Specific Social Context Learning

In the case methodology, teachers use cases with the clear purpose that business education is not to teach truths (whether there are or are not such things as truths), but to teach students how to think when confronted with new situations.

In the lecture methodology, students are trained in an environment of certainty where they follow set generalized rules in order to arrive at the answer. When such students confront a real business case, the business environment does anything but to give them a feeling of certainty, which is strangely disconcerting. They are confronted with an absence of professional dicta, and a lack of answers which students can report. Moreover, they need to decide what problems they feel are important, and what they would do. They realize that today's problems cannot necessarily be solved by yesterday's solutions. That is, whenever they feel that they have arrived at generalizations or principles which apply in all situations, they confront a new situation with a new set of variables which defy such application. They claim that they have insufficient evidence or data on which basis to make a decision, and therefore in a real business situation they cannot make a decision. Preconceived notions and handed-down attitudes which are examined in the context of reality and with a focus on effectiveness can be seen for what they are. In a specific business situation, the manager is not expected to deliver commentaries on the generalities. Such generalized knowledge is associated with the scientist whose aim is to discover and make verifiable propositions about a certain class of phenomena. The situational orientation of business cases reminds students of the vast gap between simplified, global prescriptions and what can be done by a specific manager, at a specific time, on a specific issue.

In the case methodology, students are trained to play the role of a real manager in a real business situation. They impose a meaningful framework on the unruliness of the case facts. They search for the key pieces of data, distinguishing central facts from peripheral ones. They organize the conflicting explanations and alternatives presented to them, and arrive at a reasonable recommendation for action. They express their views, feelings, reactions, attitudes, and prejudices which are reinforced or rejected by their colleagues. They have the opportunity to re-evaluate and re-appraise their recommendation, character, and personality.

In the case methodology, the emphasis is on the primacy of situational analysis. The goal of the case discussion is to help students to develop the capacity to deal with situation-specific problems. Based on experience gained in many case discussions, students derive generalizations, but they are stated tentatively, tested frequently, and always used with care.

In the case methodology, the emphasis is on the imperative of combining analysis and action, i.e., combining knowledge and practitioner's duty to act. The case methodology seeks to combine these two activities. Although knowledge is always partial relative to the complexities of an administrative problem and never capable of providing complete solution, the manager's task is to apply it in a specific administrative situation.

In the case methodology, the emphasis of teaching objectives is on the balance of substance and process. There are two kinds of knowledge which are different but related. One is the kind of knowledge which is associated with the work of scientists and scientific methodology. The other is the kind of knowledge which is associated with the practitioners of a skill in relation to the class of phenomena that they work with. The difference between the two kinds of knowledge becomes apparent when the aim of scientists is contrasted with the aim of practitioners of a skill. The aim of the scientists is to discover and make verifiable propositions about a certain class of phenomena; the aim of the practitioners is the immediate control of the phenomena with which they work. The knowledge which practitioners acquire from the practice of skills often remains intuitive and implicit, but it serves their immediate purpose well. For instance, skilled carpenters who work with different kinds of wood have acquaintance with their properties. They know what each type of wood can be used for. However, they do not have the kind of analytical knowledge which scientists seek, such as the relative tensile strengths of different materials.

In the case methodology, the focus is on understanding the specific context. It deals with the examination of the unique circumstances that differentiate one situation from others. The managers' choice of the problems to work on, and the way and the order in which they deal with them, depend on the type of industry in which their company operates. Other equally important factors are the key challenges facing the particular manager, at the particular time, with particular resources, and with particular limitations.

In the case methodology, an understanding of appropriate boundaries is considered important. This is because problems which are confronted by the manager are not clear cut. Certain boundaries are defined by external forces, others by organizational structure and financial limits. Managers need to have skills to define the boundaries of any issue such that a balance is struck between the need for breath (i.e., to include all essential factors) and the need for depth (i.e., to enhance the likelihood for constructive improvement).

In the case methodology, there is an appreciation for the sensitivity to the interrelationships and the connectedness of all organizational functions and processes. Managers must recognize that the specific issue, with which they are dealing, influences and is influenced by the general situation. The manager must think about the organization holistically and behave accordingly.

In the case methodology, there is encouragement for examining and understanding any administrative issue from a multi-dimensional perspective. Manager must consider not only the present circumstance of an issue but also its history and future. They must accept that any problem may be understood differently by different individuals and groups, and that such understanding change dramatically within the organizational hierarchy. Presidents and foremen have different agendas. Managers must be aware of this multidimensional context and have the capacity to deal with the inevitable conflicts it creates.

In the lecture methodology, the whole of the educational process is devoted to applying rigorously defined methods to find answers to questions or problems carefully posed by others. When such students first encounter a real business case, they become uncomfortable, confused, and ineffectual.

In the case methodology, students learn a more generalized approach to problem-solving or decision-making, which involves not only the application of valuable analytical techniques for choice-making, but also the identification of problems and prescription of possible solutions.

In the case methodology, there is a genuine effort to promote students' ability to analyze and evaluate the circumstances of the problems, to make decisions, and to construct programs of action for their implementation, which are appropriate for the particular situation at hand. This process is inductive rather than deductive. The purpose is the development of students' proficiency in analyzing administrative problems, reaching decisions regarding desirable actions, and formulating programs to effect the decision. In this process, the purpose is not the development of generalizations or principles, even though such development may be a useful pedagogical device to provide ideas for consideration when another problem is encountered.

In the case methodology, students apply the problem-solving model, which consists of the following steps:

(a) What are the objectives of the organization?
(b) What is the problem?
(c) What are the key relevant facts and information?
(d) What are the alternatives?
(e) What are the decision criteria?
(f) What is the analysis of the alternatives in view of the decision criteria?
(g) Which alternative should be recommended?
(h) What should be the plan of action for implementation (when and how)?
(i) What results should be expected? and
(j) What is the overall evaluation?

Two objectives lie behind encouraging students to go through such steps routinely. First, it helps students to take charge of active class participation. Second, it helps students to develop managerial, decision-making skills. Case teachers point out that while every case is different, it is the process of learning how to learn which is generalizable.

In the case methodology, a major portion of the case normally deals with the background of the organization as well as the industry. This provides the context for the issue and it relates to contingency theory. This section is very important and is one of the prime reasons for using cases. In a business case, there are a variety of potential options for decision, and the preferred one depends on circumstances. Since standard universal solutions do not exist, there is a need for cases. This is very similar to what happens in the field of medicine. There does not exist one particular medicine which cures every kind of headache. The doctor's analytical skills are needed to choose among treatment options based on the patient's personal health, age, economic, social, and cultural factors.

After the background information, a case usually provides details about the immediate issue. The immediate issue refers to the specific decision, problem, challenge, or opportunity which is faced by the decision-maker in the case. Since, in reality, cases do not exactly repeat themselves, the purpose of being concerned with the immediate issue is to develop a better understanding of its basic, underlying issues. Basic issues tend to be usually present and common. Learning how to appropriately deal with the details is valuable because it helps students in developing an approach which is generalizable to an array of other situations. In the case data analysis, considerable effort is devoted to interpreting the information contained in the case, drawing appropriate inferences, and making logical deductions.

The identification of constraints and opportunities implied by the case situation are also necessary because they affect the analysis and the recommendations. Constraints and opportunities are not always explicit in the case, often they are implied by the environmental context, or the date and location of the case.

7 Teacher- and Subject-Matter-Centered Education vs. Learner-Centered Education

In the case methodology, the student plays the key role in the learning process. Course goals are developed and established in terms of the student, not in terms of the teacher or the subject matter. Teachers have a sincere interest in helping students to learn.

In the lecture methodology, what is important is the list of topics that the teacher wants to cover. Teachers take the center stage and display their professional expertise. What they teach or what they assign is treated as equivalent with student learning.

In the case methodology, the focus of teachers is on the student developing personally rather than the courses they teach. The focus is on the learning process, not the teaching system. The focus is on learning with cases, not teaching with cases. Each student enters the class with a particular personal background and ambitions and gains in the class what is most appropriate for that student. It is a fairly personalized approach.

In the case methodology, course development is based on the nature of the students the teacher has. For instance, there is a difference between students in the undergraduate program and the students in the MBA program. Course objectives for these two groups of students are different. This is because in contrast to MBA students undergraduate students lack career identification and are conditioned as students. When case-methodology teachers take these factors into account, the content of their course drops considerably relative to what lecture-methodology teachers plan to accomplish during the same time in a course of the same title. With undergraduate students, the case-methodology teachers assign less weight to the amount of substance students learn relative to the MBA students. With undergraduate students, the significant challenge for the teacher is getting their attention to who is a manager and how they, as individuals, identify with that person.

In the case methodology, the whole process of learning is based on the idea that students learn better by being actively involved in their own learning. This implies that the participatory aspect of the case methodologies gives the case its greatest powers.

In the case methodology, case assignments are used to bridge instructor's case analysis and student's case analysis; and to bridge instructor's expectations for class discussion and student's learning progress. In the case discussion, the teacher might record ideas on the board, and students are responsible for evaluating them. One of the main goals is to train students to perform their analysis of the case, to find solutions to problems, and to make decisions.

In the case methodology, students are required to participate. This is because, in a business meeting, if a business graduate does not participate, that student does not play a role, would not be promoted, and would not succeed.

In the case methodology, the minimum requirement is for the student to attend class regularly. The class can be regarded as a company. As manager, the teacher wants to be informed in advance if a student will be absent. Thus, the student is responsible to inform the teacher. The teacher is more interested in being notified rather than be given the reasons for the absence. The teacher recognizes that students have various and changing priorities. It is in managing these priorities that students develop and learn to live with the consequences of their decisions.

In the case methodology, students are encouraged to think about and practice several interpersonal dimensions of participation. They learn how to tell someone that his/her analysis is lousy without turning off the person or creating personality clashes. They learn how to tell someone that he/she is wasting class time with his/her personal anecdotes. They learn how to make sure that they understand the arguments as they develop in class. They learn how to break into an argument effectively. Of course, these are not easy to learn. These involve a sense of timing, indicate a willingness to assume responsibility for control, and represent active involvement in the class.

In the case methodology, real education is regarded as the process of drawing out the student's mind. What is important is not what students dig out, but is the power that they develop by digging. Students are expected to do things by themselves, because there are neither answers in the back of the book nor, for the most part, there are any books at all. Teachers do not tell students; they expect students to study the case and then tell them. Then, teachers subject students to questioning, probing, and challenging, with insistence on respects for facts, logic, and consistency. In this way teachers hold students responsible for organizing the pertinent facts, determining the matters at issue, formulating critical questions, reaching answers to those questions by weighing evidence and pros and cons, and finally deciding what they would do if they were the person who had to make the decision.

The move from the lecture methodology to the case methodology is not only a matter of teaching, but also a matter of un-teaching. It is a change of culture, a change of mind-set.

8 Conclusion

This chapter discussed how, within the framework of the four paradigms, foundational philosophies underlie educational philosophies, and each educational philosophy favors a certain educational methodology, which in turn implies a certain way or method of education. More specifically, this chapter discussed how each foundational philosophy implies the specification of the course goals, objectives, and contents.

References

Ardalan, Kavous. 2003a. The Lecture-versus-Case Controversy: Its Philosophical Foundation. *Southwestern Economic Review* 30 (1): 99–118.

———. 2003b. Alternative Approaches Utilized in the Case Method: Their Philosophical Foundations. *Academy of Educational Leadership Journal* 30 (3): 103–120.

———. 2006. The Philosophical Foundation of the Lecture-versus-Case Controversy: Its Implications for Faculty Teaching, Research, and Service. *International Journal of Social Economics* 33 (3): 261–281.

———. 2008. The Philosophical Foundation of the Lecture-versus-Case Controversy: Its Implications for Course Goals, Objectives, and Contents. *International Journal of Social Economics* 35 (1/2): 15–34.

———. 2013. The Philosophical Foundation of the Lecture Method of Instruction and the Case Method of Instruction: Implications for Examinations. *Contemporary Issues in Education Research* 6 (1): 1–7.

———. 2015. Chapter 3: Using Entertaining Metaphors in the Introduction of the Case Method in a Case-Based Course. In *Exploring Learning and Teaching In Higher Education*, ed. Mang Li and Yong Zhao, 69–96. New York, NY: Springer.

Barnes, Louis B., Abby J. Hansen, and C. Roland Christensen. 1994. *Teaching and the Case Method: Text, Cases, and Readings*. Boston, MA: Harvard Business School.

Barrow, Robin, and Patricia White, eds. 1993. *Beyond Liberal Education: Essays in Honor of Paul H Hirst*. New York, NY: Routledge.

Barrow, Robin, and Ronald Woods. 1989. *An Introduction to Philosophy of Education*. New York, NY: Routledge.

Blake, Nigel, Paul Smeyers, Richard Smith, and Paul Standish, eds. 2002. *The Blackwell Guide to the Philosophy of Education*. New York, NY: Blackwell.

Brosio, Richard A. 1998. The Continuing Correspondence between Political Economy and Schooling: Telling the News. *Journal of Thought* 33 (3): 85–105.

Burrell, Gibson, and Gareth Morgan. 1979. *Sociological Paradigms and Organizational Analysis*. Hants, England: Gower Publishing.

Cahn, Steven M., ed. 1996. *Classic and Contemporary Readings in the Philosophy of Education*. New York, NY: McGraw-Hill College Division.

———., ed. 2009. *Philosophy of Education: The Essential Texts*. New York, NY: Routledge.

Carr, David. 2003. *Making Sense of Education: An Introduction to the Philosophy and Theory of Education*. New York, NY: Routledge.

Chambliss, J.J., ed. 1996. *Philosophy of Education: An Encyclopedia*. New York, NY: Garland Publishers.

Christensen, C. Roland, and David A. Garvin, eds. 1991. *Education for Judgment*. Cambridge, MA: Harvard Business, School Press.

Cromer, Alan H. 1997. *Connected Knowledge: Science, Philosophy, and Education*. Oxford, England: Oxford University Press.

Curren, Randall R., ed. 2003. *Companion to the Philosophy of Education*. New York, NY: Blackwell.

———., ed. 2007. *Philosophy of Education: An Anthology*. Malden, MA: Blackwell.

Dooley, Arch R., and Wickham Skinner. 1977. Casing Casemethod Methods. *Academy of Management Review* 2 (2): 277–289.

Ellis, Arthur K., John J. Cogan, and Kenneth R. Howey. 1991. *Introduction to the Foundations of Education*. Upper Saddle River, NJ: Prentice Hall.

Erskine, James A., Michiel R. Leenders, and Louise A. Mauffette-Leenders. 2003. *Teaching with Cases*. 3rd ed. London, ON, Canada: Ivey Business School, University of Western Ontario, Erskine Associate Inc., and Leenders and Associates Inc..

Freedman, James O. 1996. *Idealism and Liberal Education*. Ann Harbor, MI: University of Michigan Press.

Gragg, Charles I. 1954. Because Wisdom Can't Be Told. In *The Case Method at the Harvard Business School*, ed. Malcolm P. McNair. New York, NY: McGraw-Hill.
Gutek, Gerald Lee. 2000a. *Philosophical and Ideological Perspectives on Education*. 3rd ed. New York, NY: Allyn & Bacon.
———. 2000b. *Historical and Philosophical Foundations of Education: Selected Readings*. Upper Saddle River, NJ: Prentice Hall, College Division.
———. 2003. *Philosophical and Ideological Voices in Education*. 1st ed. New York, NY: Allyn & Bacon.
Hancock, Ralph C., ed. 1999. *America, the West, and Liberal Education*. New York, NY: Rowman & Littlefield.
Hare, William, and John P. Portelli, eds. 2001. *Philosophy of Education: Introductory Readings*. 3rd ed. New York, NY: Detseling Enterprises.
Hickman, Larry, and Thomas M. Alexander, eds. 1998. *The Essential Dewey: Pragmatism, Education, Democracy*. Bloomington, IN: Indiana University Press.
Kimball, Bruce A., and Robert Orrill, eds. 1995. *The Condition of American Liberal Education: Pragmatism and a Changing Tradition*. New York, NY: College Entrance Examination Board.
Larochelle, Marie, Nadine Bednarz, and Jim Garrison, eds. 1998. *Constructivism and Education*. Cambridge, England: Cambridge University Press.
Marples, Roger, ed. 1999. *The Aims of Education*. New York, NY: Routledge.
Mauffette-Leenders, Louise A., James A. Erskine, and Michiel R. Leenders. 2007. *Learning with Cases*. 4th ed. London, ON, Canada: Ivey Publishing, Ivey Business School, University of Western Ontario.
McLaren, Peter. 1998. Revolutionary Pedagogy in Post-Revolutionary Times: Rethinking the Political Economy of Critical Education. *Educational Theory* 48 (4): 431–462.
Morgan, Gareth. 1983. *Beyond Method: Strategies for Social Research*. Beverley Hills, CA: Sage.
———. 1985. Qualitative and Action Based Research. In *Actes du Colloque, Perspective de Recherche Pour lo Praticien*, ed. Y. Allaire, M. Landry, H. Mintzberg, and G. Morgan, 81–187. Rouyn-Noranda, QC, Canada: University of Quebec at Abitibi-Temiscaminque.
Noddings, Nel. 2016. *Philosophy of Education*. Boulder, CO: Westview Press.
Orrill, Robert, ed. 1999. *Education and Democracy: Re-Imaging Liberal Learning in America*. New York, NY: College Entrance Examination Board.
Ozmon, Howard A. 2011. *Philosophical Foundations of Education*. 7th ed. New York, NY: Pearson.
Philosophy of Education Society. 2003. *Philosophy of Education 2002*. New York, NY: Philosophy of Education Society Press.
Popkewitz, Thomas S., and Lynn Fendler, eds. 1999. *Critical Theories in Education: Changing Terrains of Knowledge and Politics*. New York, NY: Routledge.
Power, Edward J. 1995. *Educational Philosophy: A History from the Ancient World to Modern America*. New York, NY: Garland Publishers.
Reynolds, John I. 1978. There's Method in Cases. *Academy of Management Review* 3 (1): 129–133.
Rocha, Samuel D. 2014. *A Primer for Philosophy and Education*. Eugene, OR: Cascade Books.
Rorty, Amelie Oksenberg, ed. 1998. *Philosophers on Education: Historical Perspectives*. New York, NY: Routledge.
Sadovnik, Alan R., Susan Semel, and Peter Cookson. 2000. *Exploring Education: An Introduction to the Foundations of Education*. 2nd ed. New York, NY: Allyn & Bacon.
Schrag, Francis. 1995. *Back to Basics: Fundamental Educational Questions Reexamined*. San Francisco, CA: Jossey-Bass Education Series.
Siegel, Harvey. 2012. *The Oxford Handbook of Philosophy of Education*. Oxford, England: Oxford University Press.
Talisse, Robert B., and D. Micah Hester. 2002. *On the Philosophy of Education*. New York, NY: Wadsworth Publishing.
Winch, Christopher, and John Gingell. 1999. *Key Concepts in the Philosophy of Education*. New York, NY: Routledge.

Educational Methodologies: Implications for the Role of Teachers and Students

This chapter discusses the implications of the first three chapters with respect to the role of teachers and students. For this purpose, this chapter brings major aspects of the first three chapters to the forefront, and elaborates on their connections and implications for the way educational methodologies are applied.[1]

The first three chapters, in essence, discussed that, within the framework of the four paradigms, foundational philosophies underlie educational philosophies, and each educational philosophy favors a certain educational methodology.[2] In other words, as one moves from the objective to the subjective end of the spectrum in Exhibit 1.1 of Chap. 1, the in-class instructional methodology favored changes from totally having a lecture-oriented educational methodology to completely having a discussion-oriented educational methodology, e.g., a case-oriented educational methodology. This chapter discusses how these educational methodologies, in turn, determine the way such educational methodologies are applied to determine the type of the role of teachers and students. In order to show this, this chapter focuses on certain aspects of the applications of the lecture methodology and the case methodology and compares them. Since most readers are familiar with the lecture methodology, the discussions in this chapter elaborate more on the case methodology.

---

[1] For this literature see Ardalan (2003a, 2003b, 2006, 2008, 2013, 2015), Barnes et al. (1994), Barrow and White (1993), Barrow and Woods (1989), Blake et al. (2002), Brosio (1998), Burrell and Morgan (1979), Cahn (1996, 2009), Carr (2003), Chambliss (1996), Christensen and Garvin (1991), Cromer (1997), Curren (2003, 2007), Dooley and Skinner (1977), Ellis et al. (1991), Erskine et al. (2003), Freedman (1996), Gragg (1954), Gutek (2000a, 2000b, 2003), Hancock (1999), Hare and Portelli (2001), Hickman and Alexander (1998), Kimball and Orrill (1995), Larochelle et al. (1998), Marples (1999), Mauffette-Leenders et al. (2007), McLaren (1998), Morgan (1983, 1985), Noddings (2016), Orrill (1999), Ozmon (2011), Philosophy of Education Society (2003), Popkewitz and Fendler (1999), Power (1995), Reynolds (1978), Rocha (2014), Rorty (1998), Sadovnik et al. (2000), Schrag (1995), Siegel (2012), Talisse and Hester (2002), and Winch and Gingell (1999). This chapter is based on Erskine et al. (2003), and Mauffette-Leenders et al. (2007).

[2] The difference between "educational method" and "educational methodology" should be kept in mind. The former refers to a tool, whereas the latter signifies an approach, an orientation, and a way of thinking about how to generate and apply respective educational methods.

K. Ardalan, *Case Method and Pluralist Economics*,
https://doi.org/10.1007/978-3-319-72071-5_5

1 Passive Students vs. Active Students

In the lecture methodology, teaching is telling, knowledge is facts, and learning is recall. Teachers deliver content, in the form of factual information. Students receive it. Learning is satisfactorily completed when the student transfers the disciplinary knowledge back to the teacher at the required moment. The lecture methodology constructs formal learning such that it discourages social interaction. It emphasizes individual cognition over social interaction, abstract manipulation of symbols over concrete application in practical settings, and generalized learning over specific social context application learning. Consequently, learning progressively diminishes student's competencies for the real social life.

In the case methodology, human learning, i.e., the acquisition and application of knowledge, is regarded as fundamentally a social act. The social dimension of learning is critical to the practical application of knowledge. For instance, children acquire language through social interactions with adults and other children. Carpenters, bookmakers, chefs, surgeons, experimental scientists, and practitioners of other occupations which require strategies for decision making, acquire most of their practical knowledge from observing and interacting with other skilled practitioners.

In the case methodology, teaching is considered a transformation vocation. The teacher should not only transmit information, but also transform students from passive recipients of teacher's knowledge into active constructors of their own and others' knowledge. Of course, the teacher cannot transform students without their own active participation. Teachers should create the pedagogical, social, and ethical conditions in which students take charge of their own learning, individually and collectively.

In the case methodology, discussion is a systematic way of constructing a context for learning from the knowledge and experience of students, in addition to the disciplinary knowledge. Collectively, students should take responsibility for determining the direction of the discussion. Teachers should enable that responsibility. Teachers believe that learning occurs when students actively form the relationship of new knowledge to its intellectual and social context.

In the case methodology, students are responsible for performing a thorough analysis of the case in hand. They are expected to be prepared for presenting or communicating their analysis to their classmates in a similar fashion to what they would if they were in a managerial position in the real world. They are expected to define and change their analysis under the critical examination of their classmates and teacher. Their role varies according to whether they are offering their analysis or criticizing a classmate's. But they are always expected to remain actively involved, especially when there is disagreement on the definition of the problem or its solution.

In the case methodology, students are required to participate in class discussion, are expected to define problems and develop their solutions, and are expected to develop their problem-solving skills. If students rely on their classmates and the teacher to do the case analysis and problem-solving exercise, they miss one of the fundamental intended benefits of the case methodology. Moreover, they do not develop communication and interpersonal skills which are required in a real-life managerial position.

The transition from the lecture methodology to the case methodology involves a basic change in culture. It involves a move from the individual, competitive model of the lecture methodology to teamwork with cooperation. Furthermore, it involves a move from a conception of curriculum as discrete pieces of factual information of the lecture methodology to synthetic, analytic structures for ideas.

2 Teacher Responsible vs. Student Responsible

In the case methodology, it is not the teacher, but the student who is responsible for the exploration and argumentation of both the analysis and the plan of action. The focus is on students' learning through their joint, co-operative effort, rather than on the teacher's views conveyed to the students (this is what is done in the lecture methodology). The teacher has important roles to play, but it does not include telling the students the facts (this is what is done in the lecture methodology). Teachers ask questions to guide students' discussion into unconsidered but important areas. Teachers manage the progress of discussion according to the time available. When other students do not challenge superficial thinking of a student, teachers lead the student along the path of his/her thinking until he/she sees the consequences of his/her thinking.

In the case methodology, each student is expected to contribute to the learning of the class: (a) by actively participating; (b) by taking risks; (c) by teaching others; and (d) by learning from the teacher and classmates.

In the case methodology, each student is expected to take a series of steps in the following order:

1. Before Class: Each student receives the case and the reading assignments, reads and prepares individually, participates in a small group discussion of the case.
2. During Class: Each student asks questions on reading assignments, participates in class discussion of the case by sharing his/her insight and listening carefully to the insight of others.
3. After Class: Each student reviews his/her preparation along with the class discussion and notes the concepts learned.

In the case methodology, each student is expected to perform the following activities:

1. To prepare, through reading of materials and analysis of the case under consideration.
2. To offer viewpoints where these differ from the class in order to:

   (a) Improve his/her thinking and skills at analysis.
   (b) Improve the class discussion of the case.

3. To develop both his/her theoretical and conceptual model(s) of the topic and the field under study, and his/her skill of problem-solving.
4. To try to make inferences or generalizations on the basis of each case discussed.

In the case methodology, small group discussions are considered very beneficial. Each student brings some insight into the group discussion, which consequently covers a variety of points faster than the individual, surpasses each separate individual preparation, and reduces the total preparation time. They also learn that it is a good managerial skill to recognize good ideas when presented.

Small group discussions give the student the opportunity to learn to work with others. Students learn to use resource persons more effectively and to appreciate the ideas of others. Small-group skills are particularly useful in practice because much of a manager's time is spent on task forces and committees.

In the case methodology, teachers may ask students to form their own groups for an initial probationary period, during which they work on a case to decide whether they want to change membership, with no questions asked.

In the case methodology, in small group discussions, each student is expected to check his/her insights, assumptions, and preparation against those of others; to clarify understanding; to listen attentively and critically to others; and to argue for his/her positions developed during the individual preparation stage.

In the case methodology, in group and class discussions, students are expected to participate based on the willingness to give and take. Class discussion involves a lot of new ideas which would take a much longer time for a student to uncover alone. The synergy generated by class discussion shows how far the class can go beyond the analysis reached by each student in isolation. It is almost impossible for any student preparation or small group discussion to reach the level of understanding which is achievable by class discussion.

In the case methodology, the purpose of the class discussion is not just to arrive at a thorough understanding of the case and an optimal resolution of the problem, which is expected in the lecture methodology. The class discussion also expects students to practice in the large group to share their individual preparations and small group discussions with the rest of the class and to be evaluated by them and the instructor.

In the case methodology, teachers do not expect that only right answers be part of class discussions. From a pedagogical perspective, wrong answers can provide valuable insights. Mistakes are expected to occur and have to occur for true learning to occur.

In the case methodology, discussion is based on the idea of the reciprocity between students and teachers. That is, the roles of teacher and student are reversible. Students teach each other, and they teach the teacher. Teachers learn through class discussion, not only by being exposed to students' understandings of the subject, but also by accumulating knowledge about teaching.

The case methodology presents many ideas regarding participatory, student-oriented, active-learning arrangements. The case methodology involves student participation in discussing the analysis and solution of relevant and practical problems. The case methodology deals with the testing of theory in practice. The move from the lecture methodology to the case methodology involves the move from the position of students as simple recipients of knowledge to participatory education.

3 Student as an Outsider vs. Student as an Outsider and Insider

In the lecture methodology, the purpose is to find the most efficient solution to the company's problems. In the case methodology, it is important that every student tries to solve the problem because it is only through participation that students can become part of that process.

In the lecture methodology, students do not role play and they do not know who they are in relation to the problem. They spend a lot of time and energy with numbers and expect those numbers to lead them to the answer because they believe the answer is in the numbers. If they do not find the answer, it is because they do not know how to deal with numbers.

In the case methodology, the case is translated into an experience. Students take the role of the manager in the case. To show the importance of qualitative aspects of the situation, case teachers discuss a case without reference to numbers. They ask the students to regard the case as an experience, get inside it, start somewhere, and find your solution to the problem.

In the case methodology, the group discussion process provides students with valuable practical learning opportunities. In practice, business problems are decided on after they are discussed among smaller or larger groups. Each case class is a practical experience both in group's behavior and group discussions in arriving at business decisions. Each case class provides a learning experience in how to listen to the views of others, how to express one's view, and how to persuade others to one's point of view. It gives opportunities to express one's view and gain confidence in one's own judgment, and at times become humiliated. It also provides students with the opportunity to learn how far one can proceed by rigorous logical analysis of some aspects of the problem (which is what the lecture methodology teaches) and to what extent judgment has to be used in order to weigh many factors which have no common denominator.

In the case methodology, the basic idea is that students think and learn most when they wrestle with the conditions of the problem, and seek and find their own solution. If they cannot find their own solution (with the help of the teacher and other students) they do not learn, not even if they can accurately recite some correct answer.

In the case methodology, education is regarded as consisting of the cumulative and unending acquisition, combination, and reordering of individual experiences, i.e., learning experiences should not be described in isolation. Educational growth is considered to consist of combining past experiences with present experiences in order to understand future experiences. That is, students must continually and cohesively reorganize and reformulate past experiences with new experiences.

In the case methodology, students routinely apply the classical problem-solving model of case analysis: problem, causes, analysis, alternatives, evaluation, decision, and implementation. There are two major benefits for students when they go through these steps routinely. First, they assume the active participation role in the case. Second, they develop the managerial, decision-making skills.

In the case methodology, the student takes the place of the decision-maker in the case, without assuming the personality and gender of the individual in the case. Thus, the student brings his/her personal skills, background, and biases to the situation at hand. In the individual preparation stage, the student faces the problem, takes advantage of opportunities, and makes a decision. The student's acceptance of this role and the assumption of responsibilities are major challenges in the use of cases. It is very comfortable to be an observer of and commentator about the situation, which is the role of students in the lecture methodology. The student benefits more if the acceptance of the ownership of the situation and the assumption of the role take place earlier.

In the case methodology, a standard case assignment question is as follows: "If you were in John Doe's position in this organization, what would be your analysis of the situation described, and what action would you take and why?" If no assignment questions are provided with the case, the student is expected to ask him- or her-self that question.

In their case analysis, students take the role of the focal person in the case. They do not change their age, gender, personality, or experience, but imagine themselves in the shoes of John Doe. The student brings his/her values, age, gender, background, theoretical and practical understanding, training, expertise, and culture into the position. The background of the organization and the problem remain as identified in the case, but the task facing John Doe has now become that of student's.

Fundamental to the case learning process is the student's acceptance of the ownership of the problem. Questions such as "If the student were a consultant to John Doe, what would the student recommend?" and "What is the student's assessment of this organization's situation" distant the student from the role the student should play. That is, the student is turned into a spectator, commentator, or bystander, rather than a problem-solver or decision-maker.

In the case methodology, students are enabled to discover and develop their unique framework for approaching, understanding, and dealing with business problems.

4 Theoretical Exposure vs. Theoretical and Practical Exposure

Integration of theory with practice has been one of the enduring questions in business education. In the lecture methodology, the teacher's goal is to teach the theory. In the case methodology, the teacher's goal is to integrate theory and practice. The case methodology is based on the principle of growth through experience, that is, practice makes perfect and permanent.

In the case methodology, teacher's emphasis is on relating analysis and action. The lecture methodology's goal has been to know, while the practitioner's necessity has been to act. The case methodology's goal has been combine these two activities. This is because the application of knowledge has been the manager's primary task. Knowledge has always been partial to the complexities of administrative problems and has never been capable of providing complete solutions.

In the case methodology, teachers believe that learning is contextual in at least the following three ways: (1) New knowledge is acquired by extending and revising prior knowledge; (2) New ideas gain meaning when they are presented in a coherent relationship to one another; and (3) Knowledge becomes usable when it entails applications to concrete problem-solving situations.

In the case methodology, teachers use cases as an effective way of bringing actual experience into the classroom which leads to rich educational discussion. It is learning by doing, learning from others, and teaching others. It is a learning which remains deeply ingrained in students. The routine exercise to identifying, analyzing, and solving problems in different settings converts students to professionals for their field of work. Students experience the world of management, i.e., a rehearsal of life.

Typically, a case is a partial, historical, and clinical record for the study of a business situation, which involves an opportunity, a challenge, a decision confronted actually by a practicing administrator or managerial group. Furthermore, a case also provides information about the surrounding facts, opinions, and prejudices upon which executive decisions have to depend. Normally, it is written from the viewpoint of the decision-maker and the student is expected to play the role of the decision-maker. Students analyze, discuss, and decide on these real and company-specific cases with due consideration of the complexity and ambiguity of the practical world.

In the case methodology, teacher's emphasis is on the primacy of situational analysis. This situational orientation focuses on what can be said to a specific manager, at a specific time, and on a specific issue, which stands in contrast to the generalized prescriptions of the lecture methodology. From the experience accumulated after many case discussions, the student derives generalization, but they are stated tentatively, tested frequently, and used carefully.

In general, teachers set priorities for their courses. This means that, during the limited class time, topics with higher priority will receive preference over others. In the case methodology, this starts with a review of course objectives, case objectives, plans for this particular class within the sequence of all classes, and the importance of having this class and this case within this class. In teaching with cases, priority is not only given to making sure that certain concepts are fully understood, but also to sorting or specification of information, problem identification and analysis, proper application of relevant theory to practice, alternative generation, decision-making, and implementation planning. Initially, priority is given to familiarizing students with the discussion process and the teacher's expectations regarding proper student preparation and participation in class. Priorities are, therefore, multidimensional, and are both process and content based. In the lecture methodology, priority is given only to making sure that certain concepts are fully understood.

In the case methodology, teachers help students to develop a disciplined mental approach to an unstructured problem. Students learn to distinguish and define the problem and select the proper tool. In the lecture methodology, teachers place too much emphasis on the technical details in class. This allows knowledgeable teachers to gain the respect of students, but, many students do not know how to define the problem in tackling a managerial issue.

In the case methodology, teachers aim at preparing students for decision making in business. Therefore, they do not expect students to perform detailed numerical calculations which are not necessary. This is in contrast to the lecture methodology.

In the lecture methodology, students graduate with the impression that their education has provided them with any body of specific knowledge, any set of formulae, any answers, or any patterns of behavior that enable students immediately to become successful administrators. In the case methodology, students are trained to analyze a situation, to formulate a program of action, and to effectively implement that program through the people in their organization. These students are aware that business problems do not lend themselves to one simple, right method of analysis which arrives at the end at the only correct answer. This is in contrast to the lecture methodology. Business and social communities vitally need qualities of judgment and leadership.

In the case methodology, teachers place students in cases which involve serious and important experiences for them in their careers, including activities which they must perform well in their careers. In designing their new case course, teachers get excited, concerned, worried, enthusiastic, and very much involved with problems that they see in business, in the economy, and with managers who are struggling and attempting to cope.

As an example, consider the Human Resources course. A teacher, who uses either the case methodology or the lecture methodology, knows that the conceptual theoretical knowledge for human resources management is in the library. But only the case teacher asks: What are some companies doing about it? What are some managers of human resources doing about it? What is their role? What is their opportunity?

As another example, consider the Investment Management course. There are at least two ways to organize the course. One way is to decide on the textbooks and the literature, which is what both the lecture methodology teacher and the case methodology teacher would do. However, the case teacher is aware that the investment textbooks do not have much to offer about the management of investments. The case teacher, therefore, adds a second way of organizing the course by talk to people in the investment business. In this way, the case teacher gets an accurate picture of what issues leading practitioners wrestle with, specific examples, possible cases, as well as recommendations of who else the case teacher should talk to about the business in general. Then the case teacher decides on the organization of the course.

In the lecture methodology, the proper relationship of theory and practice is as follows. Rigorous professional practice is essentially technical. Its rigor is defined by the use of describable, testable, replicable techniques derived from scientific research, based on knowledge which is objective, consensual, cumulative, and convergent. Accordingly, rigorous management requires the use of management science.

In the lecture methodology, practice is technical only when certain things are kept isolated from one another. Deciding and doing must be kept separate from one another. Means and ends must be kept separate from one another. Research and practice must be kept separate from one another. Research can generate new knowledge only in the protected setting of the scholar's study or in the carefully controlled environment of a scientific laboratory.

In the case methodology, managers convert an uncertain situation into a solvable problem. They construct not only the means to be used but also the ends to be achieved. That is, ends and means are reciprocally determined. In the unstable world of practice, where methods and theories developed and applicable in one context are not suitable in another, practitioners function as researchers and invent the techniques and models which are appropriate for the situation at hand. The world of practice is notoriously unprotected and uncontrollable. The lecture methodology's view of practice leads to the dilemma of rigor or relevance.

In the lecture methodology, professional rigor and rigorous practice depend on well-formed problems of instrumental choice which require research-based theory and technique to obtain their solutions. In the case methodology, real-world problems are not well-formed. They are messy, indeterminate, problematic situations. The term practice takes full account of the competencies practitioners display in situations of uncertainty, complexity, and uniqueness. Case teachers and students should analyze how skilled practitioners build up repertoires of exemplars, images, and strategies of description in terms of which they learn to see novel, one-of-a-kind phenomena.

5 Competitive Education vs. Collaborative Education

In the case methodology, discussion forms the basis of learning. Cases provide the focus for the exchange of ideas and the joint stakeholders are instructors and students. The class discussion requires individual preparation and small group discussion as prerequisites. Small groups—alternatively referred to as study groups, learning teams, syndicates, or break-out groups—give students the opportunity to discuss their insights about the case.

In the case methodology, the climate of case discussion is one of collaboration, not competition, which prevails in the lecture methodology. All class participants share their ideas and insights, which become public knowledge. The students learn to be flexible in the give and take and exchange of ideas.

In the case methodology, the class discussion reflects the collective efforts of all students, helped by a teacher, which provides the opportunity for further improvement of each student's learning. The group synergy is achieved by the commitment of the whole class to the best utilization of the limited class time and to the collective search for superior insights.

In the case methodology, at the core of the case discussion process there is a fundamental insight that teaching and learning are inseparable as both are parts of a single continuum of reciprocal giving and receiving. In class discussion, students share the task of teaching with the teacher and one another, that is, all teach, and all learn.

In the case methodology, class discussion is based on the idea of learning by teaching, adding to the collective wisdom of the whole class, comparing self preparation and delivery with a sample of colleagues one may professionally work with in a future career. Students' performance in the case classroom is a reliable indication of their performance in the real organization. Performance means being active in contributing, listening, questioning, and responding.

In the case methodology, case discussions provide a safe environment for the students' evolving ideas. This is because the case methodology emphasizes cooperation and values contributions. Not all opinions are equally correct as most of the discussions tend toward a consensus that finds some approaches to be more correct than others. Of course, class discussion reaches its goals only when all contributors' ideas are explored.

In the case methodology, students learn through case discussion by listening, talking, and reflecting. The effective participation in a case discussion requires listening and thinking at the same time. Meaningful contributions relate to both the case content and the discussion process. The way a student expresses his/her ideas significantly affects its acceptance.

In the case methodology, active listening requires understanding not only what is being said but also what it being meant. Listening should accompany an open mind. Preconceptions and experiences greatly limit the capacity to hear and understand. It takes a lot of time and effort to really hear and understand someone's spoken words and implied feelings. The goal should be listening for the total meaning, which includes both the verbal and non-verbal components of the message, i.e., both the content and the underlying attitudes and values which are conveyed.

In the case methodology, active listening has an evaluative component. Students compare their peers' views with their own ideas and positions. Students tend to determine whether they agree with their peers' views or not and explain why. These encourage students to further participate in the discussion.

In the case methodology, class discussion allows students to reflect on their own preparation in comparison with the class position at the end of the class period. Students determine whether they agreed or disagreed with others and why. Students realize whether they did well or poorly in their individual preparation and in their small group discussion and why.

In the case methodology, in their discussions, students share their analysis, subject their ideas to open debate, take risks, and critique others' positions in a positive manner. Students regard participation not as a problem, but as an opportunity with high pay-off which allows them to develop a set of skills for effectiveness and success in their chosen profession. The process of case discussion is similar to real life public and private meetings which are conducted after the business issue has been discussed by smaller units such as project teams, taskforce, or committees.

In the case methodology, small groups provide opportunities to increase student's performance and to improve student's learning. Small group working sessions, when properly undertaken, constitute an enriching component of the case learning experience.

In the case methodology, ideally, each discussion group should contain a variety of skills, cultures, experiences, and expertise. The variety of perspectives from members with diverse backgrounds enriches the group discussions. A balanced distribution of members with quantitative and qualitative skills improves the overall learning in the group discussions.

In the case methodology, each small group develops its own rules of conduct, standards of participation, and expectations of members' behavior.

In the case methodology, each student arrives at his/her own decisions based on both the individual preparation as well as the small group discussion. It is not always necessary for a group discussion to achieve consensus or a group position. That is, students do not need to agree with each other on the solution of the case. In real life, consensus becomes important because then key stakeholders would support the implementation of major decisions. In small group discussion, diversity of opinions and options enriches student learning but with insufficient availability of time group's ability to achieve consensus becomes limited.

In the case methodology, case discussion allows each student to influence the outcome. Students who plan and regularly hold short small group meetings to exchange views on each case will acquire superior learning, better team management skills, and increased self-confidence.

In the case methodology, many factors influence the level of student's participation: the teaching style and skills of the teacher; student's own personality, background, experience, and culture; course content; and the cases themselves.

In the case methodology, students in case classes have the opportunity to stretch, test, push, fend, and grow such that they will be prepared for the challenges ahead in the professional world.

In the case methodology, the program involves a culture which is fundamentally different from the culture of the lecture methodology. The case methodology involves a change in culture away from the individual, competitive model of the lecture methodology to one in which students succeed through teamwork. Furthermore, the case methodology involves a change in culture away from a conception of curriculum as discrete bits of factual information of the lecture methodology to one in which students are introduced to powerful synthetic, analytic structures for ideas.

6 Knowledge vs. Combined Knowledge and Skills

In the lecture methodology, students study by themselves and take examinations. In the case methodology, the ability to communicate well, whether with another person or with a group, is considered more important than the ability to write a good examination. This is what the business world prefers as well.

In the case methodology, the goal is the development of analytical and decision-making skills rather than the acquisition of knowledge of management theories and techniques, which is the goal in the lecture methodology. Of course, such knowledge is important and its acquisition is more effective through lectures and readings.

In the case methodology, students develop their critical thinking skills because they believe that these skills, and not the sole pursuit of management theories, that differentiate between managers in successful and less successful organizations.

In the case methodology, students develop skills such as oral communication, debating, persuasion, resolving issues, and time management. They gain a sense of confidence in themselves and in relating to their peers. Their exposure to a variety of business situations broadens their views and skills.

In the case methodology, students develop presentation skills. They learn that in any presentation there are certain common elements. They learn that their presentation is not just for content but also for style of delivery, eye contact, poise, timing, linking between various presenters, and use of visual aids. They become aware of the importance of mannerism and asking for feedback. They improve their presentation skills through rehearsal and gain confidence.

The overriding goal for an educational experience is that students who go through it change in certain desirable ways. There is a broad range of learning goals to choose from. The case methodology provides the students with the opportunity to develop a wide range of skills as follows:

Acquire knowledge
Develop concepts
Understand techniques
Acquire skill in the use of a technique, concept, or knowledge
Acquire skill in analysis of complex and unstructured problems
Acquire skill in synthesis of plans for action and implementation
Grow in ability to listen
Grow in ability to form trustworthy relationships
Develop certain attitudes, e.g.,

    Responsibility—for own decision, for outcomes
    Skepticism
    Criticism—of self, of status quo
    Confidence—"can do"

Develop ability to communicate—briefly, effectively, persuasively
Develop certain qualities of mind, e.g.,

    Distinguishing between hopes, beliefs, inferences, facts

Clarity of objectives and purposes
Analysis
Self-starting—initiative
A set of standards—moral, business, institutional

Develop judgment and wisdom, e.g.,

To foresee implications, outcomes
To place situations in a long range, broad perspective
To generalize—accurately from specifics at the level of detail, to perceive trends and develop useful concepts

The above is in line with Bloom's Taxonomy of learning outcomes:

Evaluation:	Form criteria, make judgments, detect fallacies, evaluate, decide
Synthesis:	Produce a new communication not clearly evident before (requires originality or creativity).
Analysis:	Identify components, how they are related and arranged; distinguishing fact from fiction.
Application:	Apply understandings to solve new problems in new situations when no directions or methods of solution are specified.
Comprehension:	Change the information to a more meaningful parallel form, paraphrase, interpret, infer, imply, extrapolate when told to do so (lowest level of understanding).
Knowledge:	State terms, specific facts, definitions, categories, ways of doing things (No evidence of understanding is required. The learner needs only to "boomerang" back information given).

In the case methodology, students are expected to analyze and evaluate the circumstances of the problems, to make decisions, and construct programs of action for their execution appropriate for the particular situations. The process is inductive rather than deductive. Students are expected to become proficient in analyzing administrative problems, reaching decisions for desirable actions, and formulating programs for effecting the decision. They are expected to realize that the purpose is not the development of generalizations or principles even though such development may provide ideas for consideration in dealing with a specific situation.

The case methodology is excellent for developing a variety of ideas, a depth of understanding of factors involved in administrative problems, considerable skill in the analysis of these factors, significant skill in thinking of and appraising alternative courses of action, reaching a sensible decision among them, and in planning to make the decision effective.

7 Conclusion

This chapter discussed how, within the framework of the four paradigms, foundational philosophies underlie educational philosophies, and each educational philosophy favors a certain educational methodology, which in turn implies a certain way or method of education. More specifically, this chapter discussed how each foundational philosophy implies the specification of the role of teachers and students.

References

Ardalan, Kavous. 2003a. The Lecture-versus-Case Controversy: Its Philosophical Foundation. *Southwestern Economic Review* 30 (1): 99–118.

———. 2003b. Alternative Approaches Utilized in the Case Method: Their Philosophical Foundations. *Academy of Educational Leadership Journal* 30 (3): 103–120.

———. 2006. The Philosophical Foundation of the Lecture-versus-Case Controversy: Its Implications for Faculty Teaching, Research, and Service. *International Journal of Social Economics* 33 (3): 261–281.

———. 2008. The Philosophical Foundation of the Lecture-versus-Case Controversy: Its Implications for Course Goals, Objectives, and Contents. *International Journal of Social Economics* 35 (1/2): 15–34.

———. 2013. The Philosophical Foundation of the Lecture Method of Instruction and the Case Method of Instruction: Implications for Examinations. *Contemporary Issues in Education Research* 6 (1): 1–7.

———. 2015. Chapter 3: Using Entertaining Metaphors in the Introduction of the Case Method in a Case-Based Course. In *Exploring Learning and Teaching In Higher Education*, ed. Mang Li and Yong Zhao, 69–96. New York, NY: Springer.

Barnes, Louis B., Abby J. Hansen, and C. Roland Christensen. 1994. *Teaching and the Case Method: Text, Cases, and Readings*. Boston, MA: Harvard Business School.

Barrow, Robin, and Patricia White, eds. 1993. *Beyond Liberal Education: Essays in Honor of Paul H Hirst*. New York, NY: Routledge.

Barrow, Robin, and Ronald Woods. 1989. *An Introduction to Philosophy of Education*. New York, NY: Routledge.

Blake, Nigel, Paul Smeyers, Richard Smith, and Paul Standish, eds. 2002. *The Blackwell Guide to the Philosophy of Education*. New York, NY: Blackwell.

Brosio, Richard A. 1998. The Continuing Correspondence between Political Economy and Schooling: Telling the News. *Journal of Thought* 33 (3): 85–105.

Burrell, Gibson, and Gareth Morgan. 1979. *Sociological Paradigms and Organizational Analysis*. Hants, England: Gower Publishing.

Cahn, Steven M., ed. 1996. *Classic and Contemporary Readings in the Philosophy of Education*. New York, NY: McGraw-Hill College Division.

———., ed. 2009. *Philosophy of Education: The Essential Texts*. New York, NY: Routledge.

Carr, David. 2003. *Making Sense of Education: An Introduction to the Philosophy and Theory of Education*. New York, NY: Routledge.

Chambliss, J.J., ed. 1996. *Philosophy of Education: An Encyclopedia*. New York, NY: Garland Publishers.

Christensen, C. Roland, and David A. Garvin, eds. 1991. *Education for Judgment*. Cambridge, MA: Harvard Business School Press.

Cromer, Alan H. 1997. *Connected Knowledge: Science, Philosophy, and Education*. Oxford, England: Oxford University Press.

Curren, Randall R., ed. 2003. *Companion to the Philosophy of Education*. New York, NY: Blackwell.

———., ed. 2007. *Philosophy of Education: An Anthology*. Malden, MA: Blackwell.

Dooley, Arch R., and Wickham Skinner. 1977. Casing Casemethod Methods. *Academy of Management Review* 2 (2): 277–289.

Ellis, Arthur K., John J. Cogan, and Kenneth R. Howey. 1991. *Introduction to the Foundations of Education*. Upper Saddle River, NJ: Prentice Hall.

Erskine, James A., Michiel R. Leenders, and Louise A. Mauffette-Leenders. 2003. *Teaching with Cases*. 3rd ed. London, ON, Canada: Ivey Business School, University of Western Ontario, Erskine Associate Inc., and Leenders and Associates Inc..

Freedman, James O. 1996. *Idealism and Liberal Education*. Ann Harbor, MI: University of Michigan Press.

Gragg, Charles I. 1954. Because Wisdom Can't Be Told. In *The Case Method at the Harvard Business School*, ed. Malcolm P. McNair. New York, NY: McGraw-Hill

Gutek, Gerald Lee. 2000a. *Philosophical and Ideological Perspectives on Education*. 3rd ed. New York, NY: Allyn & Bacon.

———. 2000b. *Historical and Philosophical Foundations of Education: Selected Readings*. Upper Saddle River, NJ: Prentice Hall, College Division.

———. 2003. *Philosophical and Ideological Voices in Education*. 1st ed. New York, NY: Allyn & Bacon.

Hancock, Ralph C., ed. 1999. *America, the West, and Liberal Education*. New York, NY: Rowman & Littlefield.

Hare, William, and John P. Portelli, eds. 2001. *Philosophy of Education: Introductory Readings*. 3rd ed. New York, NY: Detseling Enterprises.

Hickman, Larry, and Thomas M. Alexander, eds. 1998. *The Essential Dewey: Pragmatism. Education, Democracy*. Bloomington, IN: Indiana University Press.

Kimball, Bruce A., and Robert Orrill, eds. 1995. *The Condition of American Liberal Education: Pragmatism and a Changing Tradition*. New York, NY: College Entrance Examination Board.

Larochelle, Marie, Nadine Bednarz, and Jim Garrison, eds. 1998. *Constructivism and Education*. Cambridge, England: Cambridge University Press.

Marples, Roger, ed. 1999. *The Aims of Education*. New York, NY: Routledge.

Mauffette-Leenders, Louise A., James A. Erskine, and Michiel R. Leenders. 2007. *Learning with Cases*. 4th ed. London, ON, Canada: Ivey Publishing, Ivey Business School, University of Western Ontario.

McLaren, Peter. 1998. Revolutionary Pedagogy in Post-Revolutionary Times: Rethinking the Political Economy of Critical Education. *Educational Theory* 48 (4): 431–462.

Morgan, Gareth. 1983. *Beyond Method: Strategies for Social Research*. Beverley Hills, CA: Sage.

———. 1985. Qualitative and Action Based Research. In *Actes du Colloque, Perspective de Recherche Pour lo Praticien*, ed. Y. Allaire, M. Landry, H. Mintzberg, and G. Morgan, 81–187. Rouyn-Noranda, QC, Canada: University of Quebec at Abitibi-Temiscaminque.

Noddings, Nel. 2016. *Philosophy of Education*. Boulder, CO: Westview Press.

Orrill, Robert, ed. 1999. *Education and Democracy: Re-Imaging Liberal Learning in America*. New York, NY: College Entrance Examination Board.

Ozmon, Howard A. 2011. *Philosophical Foundations of Education*. 7th ed. New York, NY: Pearson.

Philosophy of Education Society. 2003. *Philosophy of Education 2002*. New York, NY: Philosophy of Education Society Press.

Popkewitz, Thomas S., and Lynn Fendler, eds. 1999. *Critical Theories in Education: Changing Terrains of Knowledge and Politics*. New York, NY: Routledge.

Power, Edward J. 1995. *Educational Philosophy: A History from the Ancient World to Modern America*. New York, NY: Garland Publishers.

Reynolds, John I. 1978. There's Method in Cases. *Academy of Management Review* 3 (1): 129–133.

Rocha, Samuel D. 2014. *A Primer for Philosophy and Education*. Eugene, OR: Cascade Books.

Rorty, Amelie Oksenberg, ed. 1998. *Philosophers on Education: Historical Perspectives*. New York, NY: Routledge.

Sadovnik, Alan R., Susan Semel, and Peter Cookson. 2000. *Exploring Education: An Introduction to the Foundations of Education*. 2nd ed. New York, NY: Allyn & Bacon.

Schrag, Francis. 1995. *Back to Basics: Fundamental Educational Questions Reexamined*. San Francisco, CA: Jossey-Bass Education Series.
Siegel, Harvey. 2012. *The Oxford Handbook of Philosophy of Education*. Oxford, England: Oxford University Press.
Talisse, Robert B., and D. Micah Hester. 2002. *On the Philosophy of Education*. New York, NY: Wadsworth Publishing.
Winch, Christopher, and John Gingell. 1999. *Key Concepts in the Philosophy of Education*. New York, NY: Routledge.

Educational Methodologies: Implications for Examination

This chapter discusses the implications of the first three chapters with respect to the type of examination. For this purpose, this chapter brings major aspects of the first three chapters to the forefront, and elaborates on their connections and implications for the way educational methodologies are applied.[1]

The first three chapters, in essence, discussed that, within the framework of the four paradigms, foundational philosophies underlie educational philosophies, and each educational philosophy favors a certain educational methodology.[2] In other words, as one moves from the objective to the subjective end of the spectrum in Exhibit 1.1 of Chap. 1, the in-class instructional methodology favored changes from totally having a lecture-oriented educational methodology to completely having a discussion-oriented educational methodology, e.g., a case-oriented educational methodology. This chapter discusses how these educational methodologies, in turn, determine the way such educational methodologies are applied to determine the type of examination. In order to show this, this chapter focuses on certain aspects of the applications of the lecture methodology and the case methodology and compares

[1]For this literature see Ardalan (2003a, 2003b, 2006, 2008, 2013, 2015), Barnes et al. (1994), Barrow and White (1993), Barrow and Woods (1989), Blake et al. (2002), Brosio (1998), Burrell and Morgan (1979), Cahn (1996, 2009), Carr (2003), Chambliss (1996), Christensen and Garvin (1991), Cromer (1997), Curren (2003, 2007), Dooley and Skinner (1977), Ellis et al. (1991), Erskine et al. (2003), Freedman (1996), Gragg (1954), Gutek (2000a, 2000b, 2003), Hancock (1999), Hare and Portelli (2001), Hickman and Alexander (1998), Kimball and Orrill (1995), Larochelle et al. (1998), Marples (1999), Mauffette-Leenders et al. (2007), McLaren (1998), Morgan (1983, 1985), Noddings (2016), Orrill (1999), Ozmon (2011), Philosophy of Education Society (2003), Popkewitz and Fendler (1999), Power (1995), Reynolds (1978), Rocha (2014), Rorty (1998), Sadovnik et al. (2000), Schrag (1995), Siegel (2012), Talisse and Hester (2002), and Winch and Gingell (1999). This chapter is based on Ardalan (2013), Erskine et al. (2003), and Mauffette-Leenders et al. (2007).

[2]The difference between "educational method" and "educational methodology" should be kept in mind. The former refers to a tool, whereas the latter signifies an approach, an orientation, and a way of thinking about how to generate and apply respective educational methods.

K. Ardalan, *Case Method and Pluralist Economics*,
https://doi.org/10.1007/978-3-319-72071-5_6

them. Since most readers are familiar with the lecture methodology, the discussions in this chapter elaborate more on the case methodology.

1 Textbook vs. Cases

The lecture methodology requires textbooks, whereas the case methodology uses descriptions of specific business situations.

In the case methodology, the focus is on the personal development of the individual rather than the course theoretical knowledge. It is a learning process, not a teaching system. It is learning with cases, not teaching with cases. Different students come with different background and ambitions, and each one gets what is most appropriate for that individual. It is a fairly individualized approach.

In the case methodology, which is a Socratic method and has been used since antiquity, the role of books, lectures, and essays is reduced to a minimum. Through the skilful questioning of the teacher, knowledge originates from the students and becomes engraved in the student's minds.

In the lecture methodology, the educational goal is for students to learn textbooks facts. However, students may forget those facts as soon as they graduate. In the case methodology, the educational goal is to instill in students practical knowledge and, more importantly, to provide the opportunity for them to develop the skill of logical and correct reasoning in every subject.

In the lecture methodology, the use of textbooks leads students to believe that whenever they apply the techniques stated in the textbook they will be able to solve real-world problems. In the case methodology, teachers believe that textbook techniques may not work since the practical world is much more complex.

In the lecture methodology, teachers use textbooks. They do not explicitly teach the conceptual framework of their subject matter, but they teach the textbook techniques. In the case methodology, teachers' concerns are for the students to understand and be able to apply the conceptual framework of their subject matter and, therefore, teachers consistently use that framework. They do this because a business manager is far more involved with the conceptual framework of the subject matter than with its techniques.

In the case methodology, teachers arrange a sequence of experiences involving students. Then, teachers use their knowledge of the conceptual framework to ask questions and call on students for reactions. In this way, students gradually acquire a working capacity to deal with the fundamental concepts. In the lecture methodology, teachers follow the textbook outline and hope that the students will somehow obtain a working understanding of what the teacher teaches.

In the case methodology, the emphasis is on relating analysis and action. While the lecture methodology's emphasis is to know, the practitioner's necessity is to act. The case methodology combines these two activities. The manager's primary task is the application of knowledge, which is partial to the complexities of administrative problems and does not produce complete solutions.

In the case methodology, the emphasis is on situational analysis. It shows the vast gap which exists between global prescriptions of the lecture methodology and what a specific manager needs, at a specific time, with respect to a specific problem. The case methodology helps students to develop the capacity to deal with specific situations, which is in contrast to the lecture methodology's emphasis on the provision of generalized statements. In the case methodology, students gather experience in many case discussions and derive generalization, which are stated tentatively, tested frequently, and used carefully.

In the case methodology, the emphasis is on promoting the ability of the students to analyze and evaluate the circumstances of the problems in particular situations and to make decisions and to construct plans of action for their implementation. The process is inductive rather than deductive. The development of generalizations or principles is useful in providing ideas for consideration in handling a specific situation.

In the case methodology, it is believed that logic and mathematics do not exhaust the nature of reality and therefore it is not believed that if students only read one more textbook they would have the solutions to problems. In the lecture methodology, it is believed that the solutions to human problems are found in logical statements and propositions and therefore students' formal education is primarily intellectual, i.e., they learn abstract concepts, general propositions, and answers.

2 Single Answer vs. Multiple Answers

In the lecture methodology, the educational process is devoted to applying rigorously defined methods to questions or problems carefully posed by others in order to find answers. In the case methodology, students learn a generalized approach to problem-solving or decision-making which involves not only the application of analytical techniques for choice-making, but also identification of problems and recommendation of solutions.

In the case methodology, education is regarded as a process of drawing out the student's mind. In the lecture methodology, education is regarded as transferring teacher's ideas and textbook contents to the student's mind. In the case methodology, value is given not in what students dig out, but in what they gain by digging. In the case methodology, students are expected to find things out for themselves because there are no answers in the back of the book, and in most cases there are no books at all. In the lecture methodology, teachers tell students. In the case methodology, teachers expect students to study the case and then tell teachers, and then teachers ask questions from students while probing, challenging, and insisting on respecting facts, logic, and consistency. In this way teachers help students to sort out the relevant facts, define the problems, formulate critical questions, evaluate answers to those questions by weighing evidence and pros and cons, and decide as if they were in charge.

In the case methodology, students are involved in class discussion of possibilities, probabilities, and expedients: the possibilities of the combination of very intricate facts, the probabilities of human reactions, and the expedients most likely to bring about the responses in others that lead to a definite end. The purpose of business education is not to teach truths (if there are such things as truths, as the lecture methodology claims the existence of truth) but to teach students to think and decide when they face new situations. Indeed, there is rarely a single case with at least two intelligent solutions.

In the lecture methodology, students are educated in an environment of certainty with set rules for arriving at the answer. In the case methodology, the atmosphere of the classroom lacks certainty. There is an absence of subject matter rules and principles with no answers which students can record in their notebook. Students are asked what problems they feel are important and what they would do to solve them. They note that today's problems may not be solved by yesterday's solutions. Whenever they feel that they have arrived at generalizations or principles which are applicable to all situations, they confront a situation which denies such analysis. They are expected to do the best they can with whatever evidence or data are available, even if they are insufficient, like a real manager in a real business situation, it is their duty to impose a meaningful framework on the unruliness of the case facts. They have to search for the key relevant data by distinguishing central facts from peripheral ones. They have to evaluate the conflicting explanations and alternatives presented to them and make a meaningful recommendation for action. When they express their views, feelings, reactions, attitudes and prejudices and see them reinforced or rejected by their peers; they re-evaluate and re-appraise their character and personality.

In the case methodology, the central focus is on the learning process. It is implemented through persistent reinforcing, apprenticeship, working and discussing together, and gradually reaching a cohesive central tendency. The aim is for students learning to follow a consistent path to an objective.

In the case methodology, multidimensionality is one of the major aspects of cases and students look at everything simultaneously and talk about anything that needs to be changed, improved, or modified. Although the case provides the students and the teacher with the same amount of information for their decision making, they voice different opinions and suggest different solutions.

A lecture teacher prepares an analysis of the case from a scientific point of view that is totally exhaustive, mutually exclusive, and gives a clear breakdown, ensures the class gets there, and forces the students into his/her assumptions and framework. A case teacher not only prepares the case content but also sets his/her class plan in terms of the behavioral, conceptual, and analytical teaching objectives.

In the case methodology, teachers do not believe that a high level of technical penetration is so important because teaching analysis of numbers specifically turns the goal of teaching to achieving the right numerical answer. They identify the students with the manager or decision maker in the situation who needs to define the problem, find possible options, and decide. With respect to the decision, students should determine the approach and set of attitudes towards the problem in the case which would lead them to the solution so that the activities with the highest pay-off would be recognized. The students need to properly conceive of the situation along with a global framework of policy, strategy, and tactics. Then they can classify the problem and perform the numerical analysis if necessary.

In the case methodology, teachers believe that learning begins with the differences of opinion. Usually, several different alternatives are suggested during the discussion of the case. By the end of the discussion, no single decision may be reached and no attempt may be made to come to a specific decision. Afterwards, students will think further about the case discussion and come to their own conclusions.

In the case methodology, differences of opinion are the norm. Usually, there are more than just one single acceptable answer to a complex business situation. In a case discussion, most aspects of the case are discussed and each student is exposed to other viewpoints. The teacher may test the consensus on a controversial point by having a show-of-hands vote. The teacher and the students acknowledge that the minority may be right.

In the case methodology, learning flourishes when it is anchored in a climate of genuine respect, trust, and openness to diversity. In case discussions, students note that, as human beings, they usually see only what they want to see or what they are accustomed to seeing. At the end of the case discussion a consensus about the best alternative or decision may not emerge, because more than one alternative may be fully reasonable.

The lecture methodology is very powerful in the transfer of knowledge from the teacher to the students. The case methodology is very powerful in promoting critical thinking (in the liberal arts setting), problem-solving (in the professional school setting), sensitivity, cooperation, and desire for discovery.

In the case methodology, students see in partnership both the teaching/learning process and their own selves. Students take responsibility of their own education by deepening their personal involvement, participating in quality discussion, and making an emotional investment in the outcome of the course. This responsibility not only stimulates them to develop, but also enhances the effectiveness of the teachers. In discussing cases, diversity in backgrounds, personalities, questions posed, learning styles, frames of inquiry, and spectrums of interpretation ensures that the class does not search for the only path to the only answer. In this way, the powerful energy of experience and creativity of students will be unleashed.

3 Rigidity vs. Flexibility

In the case methodology, teachers help students to explore unfamiliar situations, to experience decision-making under uncertainty, and to practice the art and science of management, or other professions.

In the case methodology, it is not the teachers but students who are responsible for exploration and argumentation of both analysis and plan of action. Therefore, the focus is on students' learning through their joint, co-operative effort. In the lecture methodology, teachers convey their views to the students and telling the students the answers. In the case methodology, the role of teachers is an important one. They guide the discussion, through their questioning, to important areas which have not been discussed by students. They manage the limited class time by tracking the progress of discussion. They challenge superficial thinking when other students do not, by questions leading the students along the path of their proposal until they notice the consequences of their proposal.

In the case methodology, students learn to accept compromise and accommodation. In the lecture methodology, students learn to search for the perfect solution. In the case methodology, students learn to view action as a spectrum of potential possibilities. In the lecture methodology, students learn to view action as a few go or no-go intervention points. In the case methodology, students learn that almost all management challenges are based in the human and organizational context. Technical, financial, or conceptual issues are closely related to people in the action stage. The issues can be dealt with only when the human issues are simultaneously dealt with as well.

In the case methodology, a major section of the case explains the background of the organization and the industry. This section defines the context for the problem. Normally, there are several alternatives for making a decision and the preferred one depends on circumstances. This is because no standard universal solution exists. A similar practice is followed in medicine. Different people with headache cannot be cured by prescribing one particular medicine. The doctor's analytical skills distinguish among treatment options by looking at the patient's personal health, age, economic, social, and cultural factors.

In the lecture methodology, teachers organize their courses with an overall framework regarding a manager who in dealing with a particular topic has to think about, has to worry about, and how they are related to each other and to other areas in the business. In the case methodology, teachers believe that most areas of business are not that clear-cut. That is, the world is so complex that denies one global solution. Similar to psychologists and sociologists, they do not use one overall framework, but many frameworks.

Teachers set priorities for their courses. This is because class time is a scarce resource and more important topics receive preference over others. In both the lecture methodology and the case methodology, priority is given to students' understanding of certain concepts. In the case methodology, teachers review course objectives, case objectives, plans for a particular class within all classes, and the importance of having a particular class and a particular case within a particular course. In addition, in the case methodology, priority is given to distinguishing relevant information, proper application of relevant theory to practice, problem identification and analysis, alternative generation, decision-making, and implementation planning. In the first few classes, priority is given to familiarizing students with the discussion process and the teacher's expectations regarding student preparation and participation in class. In the case methodology, therefore, priorities are multidimensional, i.e., they are both process and content oriented.

In the case methodology, teachers provide the necessary services which group discussions require. They keep discussions orderly. They ask questions which are related to the ongoing discussion and enhance group thinking. They combine individual contributions into a pattern which their class can understand. They manage class time in order to avoid a discussion which is either too slow and is not utilizing well the available time, or too fast and is not allowing enough comprehension on the part of a major portion of students. They have control over the undirected class discussion, but at the same time allow the class to make its discoveries, which may be new even to the teachers. Since unpredictable developments are the hallmark of real learning, teachers examine their class rather than their subject matter.

In the lecture methodology, teachers can prepare a good lecture in a few hours and have control over the order and timing of what is to occur. Teachers include humor to keep students interested. Teachers know when to add something unusual to get the attention of a student whose mind is not in the class. Teachers anticipate most of students' questions and prepare the answers beforehand and maintain their self-respect in view of the students' questions. In the case methodology, teachers spend a lot of time on their case preparation. This is because they want to be prepared to go wherever the discussion goes. That is, teachers are not in control because the vehicle is the students' vehicle. It is much more difficult to influence the process of the case discussion productively.

In the case methodology, the class plan has a continuum from high to low structure. Several factors influence the choice of a teacher on this continuum: the type of the case, the position in the course, the type of student involved, and the teacher's orientation and experience.

In the case methodology, teachers believe that the world of business is not divided into separate compartments, but in the lecture methodology, teachers believe as if it were. A case is more than just a linear programming application, or a break-even analysis problem, it has other dimensions. Furthermore, there are many factors in the case discussion which make the case itself not so dominant. The case needs to be seen in context, that is, not only in terms of the theoretical coverage, but also in other dimensions.

In the case methodology, teachers stress both quantitative and qualitative assessments. As in the lecture methodology, teachers recommend that the students perform numerical analysis in order to acquire a better understanding of the situation. However, in contrast to the lecture methodology, case teachers warn students against becoming overwhelmed by detailed numerical analysis because it may prevent them from reflecting on the actual meaning of the numbers. Case teachers suggest that students should know why they do the calculation, what they intend to do with the result, and how they plan to interpret it. They also suggest that students develop their business intuition by guessing at the answer before they perform the calculation. They further suggest that students use their visual sense when searching for numerical meaning by drawing a graph in order to facilitate their interpretation.

In the case methodology, students who transfer from or come with a background in sciences face difficulty. This is because they have been trained and conditioned into rigidity, which is the norm in the lecture methodology. In contrast, in the case methodology, it is learning to become non-rigid.

In the case methodology, there are several steps in the case analysis which bring into sharp focus the flexibility of the case methodology in contrast to the rigidity of the lecture methodology. Students generate alternatives based on their creativity. They know that if an alternative is overlooked then all further work towards making the decision ignores that alternative's potential. Therefore, students not only consider constraints and opportunities that they have identified in the preceding data analysis phase but also their own knowledge or past experience and the theories learned from their readings. They come up with realistic and plausible alternatives based on their analysis and understanding of the issues involved. They look for alternatives in addition to those already specified in the case. Students are aware that the list of alternatives may contain the status quo as well as combinations of individual alternatives.

In the case methodology, students select the decision criteria by considering both quantitative as well as qualitative criteria. They base their selection of the most appropriate decision criteria for a given case on both what they believe are the objectives or the strategy of the organization and what they believe are important to them as the decision makers. That is, they select realistic decision criteria.

In the case methodology, students analyze, evaluate, and compare alternatives by following the standard approach of listing the key advantages and disadvantages of each alternative. Then, they weigh these pros and cons to select the best course of action. They compare and contrast each alternative, in light of the decision criteria they have selected, in order to make the best decision, which can be quite challenging. When they have selected multiple decision criteria, they decide based on the weighting of each criterion against the others. For instance, in most cases, there are concerns about the short and the long term. Both short- and long-term considerations are relevant in analyzing alternatives, predicting corresponding outcomes, and planning and implementing action. The alternatives may be as follows: (1) One with quick and highly beneficial results but average long-term consequences, or (2) Another with good long-term prospects but average immediate pay-offs. Students decide with respect to the actions which need to be taken in both the short term and the long term. Indeed, the frequent exercise of judgment based on the case situation and students' experience makes learning in the case methodology so unique.

In the case methodology, students predict outcomes by the assessment of the results and consequences of available alternatives. Students face the issue of uncertainty in such predictions which forces them to assign probabilities to various random events which impact the outcomes.

In the case methodology, students do quantitative versus qualitative analysis and are aware that most alternatives may be evaluated on both quantitative and qualitative grounds. When the quantitative side (including the financial) suggests that a particular alternative is favorable, the qualitative side may not necessarily support the alternative strongly. In such situations judgment determines where the balance should lie.

In the case methodology, students are aware that selecting the preferred alternative is the ultimate point in case analysis, i.e., they need to address the case issues and make a decision. Decision-making becomes complex when students are faced with several issues, multiple objectives, and diverse decision criteria. Therefore, there is rarely only one desirable course of action to a case. What becomes important is students' analysis, their use of the available information, and their justification for selecting a certain alternative. That is, what becomes important is the path to their answer which students create.

In the case methodology, students learn through the group discussion process. In practice, the final decisions regarding business problems are reached only after discussions take place among smaller and larger groups. Each case class is both a group discussion in arriving at a business decision and a practical experience in group's behavior. Each case class provides an opportunity to listen to the views of others and to express and persuade others to one's point of view. It provides an opportunity to gain confidence in one's own judgment, while become humiliated some of the times. It shows to what limited extent one can move forward through the rigorous logical analysis of one or another dimension of the problem (which is the teaching of the lecture methodology) and to what extent judgment comes into play when many diverse factors must be weighed.

In the case methodology, students think and learn when tackling the conditions of the problem at hand in order to find their own way out. They may not be able to devise their own solution even if they can reproduce some correct answer (which is the teaching of the lecture methodology). The case methodology provides the opportunity for students to develop their own framework for approaching, understanding, and dealing with business problems.

4 Certainty vs. Ambiguity

The lecture methodology is efficient and economical in the use of time, energy, and the patience of instructor and students. Students seem to possess sureness, precision, and grasp of materials which is remarkable for the relatively short time they spend on acquiring their knowledge.

The case methodology trains students to act, rather than training them to know. This is because businesspeople must be able to act in the face of problems arising in new situations in a continually-changing environment. That is, education consists of acquiring skills necessary to act in new situations.

In the lecture methodology, students are trained under more structure. This makes it easier for them to go through the course but not an easier way to learn. Such students become frustrated when they move from the lecture methodology to the case methodology. This is because the case methodology brings more realism to the classroom. In the case methodology, students learn to tolerate incompleteness of information and ambiguity of situations. They learn how to face multi-dimensional issues and formulate action plans. They learn to recognize what the problem is in order to select the appropriate tool. The students who come into the case methodology from a lecture methodology background, most often face difficulty in making such recognition. This must be because they are trained to be too much involved in the technical details of problems. In the case methodology, on the other hand, students learn to develop a disciplined mental approach to an unstructured problem. Students are trained in such a way that they are able to make decisions in practical business situations. Therefore, students are not expected to go through unnecessary detailed numerical calculations, which is in contrast to the lecture methodology.

In the case methodology, starting with the first course, students face uncertainty, difficulty, complexity, which they have to make some order out of it. According to the problem-solving framework, the teacher may decide not to distribute the course syllabus, but rather talk about it. That is, the teacher may decide not to present the course and then implement, but rather expect students to derive the course concepts and the course framework from the discussion. The students might not know where the class is leading to until the class actually implements it, which is an exercise in making sense of uncertainty. The teacher may distribute the course syllabus in the class close to the end of the course and explain what the class has done, what cases have been used, what the class has done with respect to those cases, and where the class has reached. That is, after the fact, the teacher describes what the course was. Indeed, the teacher describes what the students have learned and how they have learned it and the students realize what they have been doing after they have done it.

In the case methodology, students experience considerable confusion, frustration, and anxiety. This is because cases can be long and complex, with or without assigned questions, and with or without right answers. Moreover, cases are open-ended and may provide limited or overwhelming amount of information. Furthermore, students have limited experience with the issue, industry, or product at stake.

In the case methodology, usually cases provide limited information which requires students to make assumptions. This reflects real business situations in which managers do not possess all the information they need, or are not able to acquire it, before making decisions. Frequently, managers are forced to make decisions based on partial information and, of necessity, make assumptions. Students analyze cases based on the information available in the case and can use their own background and experience to provide the political, economical, social, and technological context of the case. Most often, students recognize that they do not have enough information to assess the situation and experience the need to make assumptions. The case methodology provides students with ample opportunity to develop their skills in making sound assumptions, which is a delicate matter. Students should be aware when they are making an assumption. The assumptions should be plausible and realistic in the light of the information provided in the case. That is, students need to make sensible inferences tied to known facts. They should be able to justify it and explain the rationale behind it by reference to the evidence, knowledge, or experience which they base it on. Students should be cognizant of hidden assumptions, which are made implicitly or without awareness.

In the case methodology, it is almost always necessary to make some assumptions due to the lack of sufficient information. Consequently, assumptions become an integral part of any case analysis and action plan. Students may disagree on their assumptions. Teachers spend some time in class to make sure that the case analysis and alternatives are based on reasonable assumptions, given the case circumstances.

In the case methodology, students are expected to be explicit about their assumptions. Most often they make different assumptions, which is not necessarily a cause for concern. The role of assumptions becomes prominent when different assumptions lead to differing decisions. In case discussions, student experience some initial confusion, some initial wrestling, but the decision-making is critical. When students differ on the critical components, they should talk about their differences.

In the case methodology, teachers usually instruct the group that will formally present the case to distribute a list of its assumptions one class meeting before the presentation. Each student uses these assumptions, together with facts given in the case, to prepare for the discussion of the case in class. Given the same set of premises, the focus in this phase of class discussion is on the use of sound logic, which examines inferential reasoning. In another phase of class discussion, priority is given to an in-depth examination of the distributed assumptions. The discussion focuses on whether each assumption is necessary and whether it is sufficiently reasonable given the circumstances in the case. All cases are culture bound and given the right set of assumptions, each point of view holds a certain amount of truth.

In the case methodology, there are uncertainties for the teacher as well, which is in contrast to the lecture methodology. Class meetings do not follow a standard process or procedure. Teachers focus on managing the participative process and reinforce process variability from the start. Teachers manage the discussion process with a reference base from which variations can be contrasted. Variation may depend on the objectives of the class, the type of case, the place of this class in the sequence of classes, what happened in previous classes, other classes in other courses which are taken simultaneously by the students, the teaching style and mood of the instructor, the mood of the students, the time of year, the weather, the political and economic news, and so on. Teaching with cases is hard for teachers who prefer to imitate a standard objective model but delightful for innovative teachers.

In the case methodology, every class involves the opportunity for new intellectual adventure, risk taking, and new learning. The teacher might have discussed the case in previous courses, but previous teaching notes have limited current value. This is because with a new group of students there will be a unique class dynamic under different time circumstances with new questions.

5 Objective Exams vs. Combined Objective and Subjective Exams

In the lecture methodology, teaching is telling, knowledge is facts, and learning is recall. Teachers deliver content in the form of factual information and students receive it. Learning is satisfactorily completed when the student successfully transfers the material back to the teacher at the specified time.

In the lecture methodology, distinction among students is based on objective criteria because of its emphasis on factual information. Students who understand the material at some minimally acceptable level succeed and those who do not fail. The assessment tools include true-false questions, multiple-choice questions, objective exercises, and objective exams.

In the lecture methodology, students study by themselves and take examinations. In the case methodology, as in the business world, the ability to communicate with others is considered far more important than the ability to write a good examination.

In the case methodology, the focus is on the development of analytical and decision-making skills. In the lecture methodology, the focus is on the acquisition of knowledge in the form of management theories and techniques. Of course, acquiring such knowledge is important, but its acquisition is likely to be more effective through lectures or readings.

In the case methodology, assignments are used as a vehicle to bridge instructor case analysis and student case analysis and to bridge instructor expectations for learning and student class discussion progress. Students are encouraged to go beyond the assigned questions when preparing their case analysis because it is a useful problem-solving skill with high pay-offs.

In the case methodology, cases reflect reality, with all of its deceptions, contradictions, discrepancies of perception, and general resistance to orderly analysis. Cases have a core of ambiguity which generates a great deal of energy and liveliness in class discussions. Cases are controversial and study questions are open-ended, which frequently involve judgment. They help students clarify their own and each other's hidden assumptions. Cases encourage students to improve and defend their positions. Cases lure biases into the light for examination and assessment and avoid complacency.

In the case methodology, teachers do not offer students a code of rules or techniques. Each case is a slice of real life and the lessons it suggests varies for each student.

In the case methodology, complexity and uncertainty are dealt with, but not by applying specialized knowledge of well-defined tasks. That is, artistry is not reducible to the exercise of known routines. Similarly, problem finding does not belong to a body of knowledge concerned exclusively with problem solving. Among competing paradigms of professional practice, one cannot rely on professional expertise. The competencies central to professional practice are separate from their underlying model of professional knowledge.

In the case methodology, students who graduate are aware that their education has not provided them with a body of specific knowledge, a set of formulae and answers, and ready-made patterns of behavior that enables them immediately to become successful administrators. They are aware that this is the norm under the lecture methodology. In the case methodology, students develop skills to analyze a situation, to formulate a plan of action, and to implement it through the people in their organization or in their community. Students trained with the case methodology are aware that business problems do not have one easy, simple, right method of analysis which leads to only one correct answer, as in the lecture methodology.

They are aware that companies hire at an average pay level many average-grade technicians who can calculate the right answers to the problems that lend themselves to exact routines and procedures. They are aware that companies pay a very high price for qualities of judgment and leadership ant that they cannot develop those qualities if they look for easy answers and oversimplify the world they live in, as in the lecture methodology.

6 Objective Grading vs. Combined Objective and Subjective Grading

In the lecture methodology, teachers develop grading schemes with specific grades for every step taken. In the case methodology, teachers do not adhere to such grading schemes. They would like to know if the student makes sense and how well the case discussion is developed. If the student does not make sense, then no amount of individual points makes the whole discussion acceptable.

In the case methodology, student evaluation is much more difficult because of the lack of any precise grading scheme against which to measure the student's performance. The measurement of the student performance vis-a-vis the teacher's objective is extremely subjective. It is one of the risks that both the teacher and students take. In the lecture methodology, the teacher enters students' answers into a computer and they will be graded as right or wrong, and the teacher has a very precise numerical grade for each student.

In the case methodology, most cases do not have right or wrong answers. The quality of students' case analysis depends largely on their decision-making skills. It is their ability to distinguish the important from the urgent, the short term from the long term, the immediate from the basic, and the preferred from the less desirable which shows their insight that creates the power of persuasion that produces superior grades.

In the case methodology, students' grades are determined based on objective and subjective criteria. For instance, in their case analysis, students should identify their key assumptions by reference to the information provided in the case, knowing that different sets of sound assumptions are made by different students on the basis of the same case information. Moreover, students should demonstrate that the correct methodology is used when an analytical tool is applied. Furthermore, students should demonstrate that their arguments for or against any alternative solution are consistent not only with their assumptions and calculations but also with the prior interpretations of the case information.

In the case methodology, for instance, if there are 10 points allocated for a recommendation, the teacher may assign a grade between 7 and 10, depending on how the student's paper impresses the teacher. In this way, the teacher reduces some of the subjectivity in grading by specifying numbers.

In the case methodology, teachers create their grading scheme by first developing a framework of what they expect based on what they consider important. Then, they read several students' papers to recognize their analytical framework in order to develop a grading scheme. For example, the final grading scheme states that the implementation is worth 10 points: Idea X is worth 2 points, and idea b is worth 2 points, etc. such that all add up to 10. Teachers make a subjective evaluation of students' handling of the implementation with some reference to the list of ideas.

In the case methodology, in contrast to the lecture methodology, grading is both objective and subjective. Despite teachers' efforts to develop grading scheme, much of the grading remains subjective. For example: (1) Some teachers allows students to select the weights for different components of evaluation. This gives students an opportunity to exploit their strengths, balance project work loads, etc. (2) Most teachers who believe in the discussion/involvement format and the students' contribution to each other's learning argue for grading participation, which is very subjective. (3) Most teachers' grades are curved, which represents the teacher's expectation of a typical student achievement. Different teachers have different shapes for the curve in mind. The grade distributions at grade conference time at the end of the term show how different teachers' curves can be.

In the case methodology, teachers use a student peer evaluation system for their group work. They ask students to assign anonymously a letter grade to each of their group peers. Teachers list for them the criteria which they have to consider in assessing their peer contributions to the group. Then, teachers incorporate the individual aggregate score in making grade decision.

In the case methodology, teachers assign participation grades to students. At the end of every class meeting they go through the class list. They determine whether the student participated, and decide on the quality of the discussion of those who participated. The teachers do this even though they know it is not overly scientific. Then, at the end of the course, they add up the quantities and rank students. Then they look at each individual student and readjust this ranking by whether they feel a student has fewer entries, but those few are of high quality. The teachers' final decision is a subjective one. They ask how good the student is. The teachers may not allow participation grades to fail a student. However, they may allow it to drop the student's grade. If a student had outstanding participation and one bad examination, the teachers may reduce the weight of that examination. It seems that the teachers are scientific by grading students after each class, but at the end of the course it is their subjectivity which determines the course grade.

7 Conclusion

This chapter discussed how, within the framework of the four paradigms, foundational philosophies underlie educational philosophies, and each educational philosophy favors a certain educational methodology, which in turn implies a certain way or method of education. More specifically, this chapter discussed how each foundational philosophy implies the specification of the type of examination.

References

Ardalan, Kavous. 2003a. The Lecture-versus-Case Controversy: Its Philosophical Foundation. *Southwestern Economic Review* 30 (1): 99–118.

———. 2003b. Alternative Approaches Utilized in the Case Method: Their Philosophical Foundations. *Academy of Educational Leadership Journal* 30 (3): 103–120.

———. 2006. The Philosophical Foundation of the Lecture-versus-Case Controversy: Its Implications for Faculty Teaching, Research, and Service. *International Journal of Social Economics* 33 (3): 261–281.

———. 2008. The Philosophical Foundation of the Lecture-versus-Case Controversy: Its Implications for Course Goals, Objectives, and Contents. *International Journal of Social Economics* 35 (1/2): 15–34.

———. 2013. The Philosophical Foundation of the Lecture Method of Instruction and the Case Method of Instruction: Implications for Examinations. *Contemporary Issues in Education Research* 6 (1): 1–7.

———. 2015. Chapter 3: Using Entertaining Metaphors in the Introduction of the Case Method in a Case-Based Course. In *Exploring Learning and Teaching In Higher Education*, ed. Mang Li and Yong Zhao, 69–96. New York, NY: Springer.

Barnes, Louis B., Abby J. Hansen, and C. Roland Christensen. 1994. *Teaching and the Case Method: Text, Cases, and Readings*. Boston, MA: Harvard Business School.

Barrow, Robin, and Patricia White, eds. 1993. *Beyond Liberal Education: Essays in Honor of Paul H Hirst*. New York, NY: Routledge.

Barrow, Robin, and Ronald Woods. 1989. *An Introduction to Philosophy of Education*. New York, NY: Routledge.

Blake, Nigel, Paul Smeyers, Richard Smith, and Paul Standish, eds. 2002. *The Blackwell Guide to the Philosophy of Education*. New York, NY: Blackwell.

Brosio, Richard A. 1998. The Continuing Correspondence between Political Economy and Schooling: Telling the News. *Journal of Thought* 33 (3): 85–105.

Burrell, Gibson, and Gareth Morgan. 1979. *Sociological Paradigms and Organizational Analysis*. Hants, England: Gower Publishing.

Cahn, Steven M., ed. 1996. *Classic and Contemporary Readings in the Philosophy of Education*. New York, NY: McGraw-Hill College Division.

———., ed. 2009. *Philosophy of Education: The Essential Texts*. New York, NY: Routledge.

Carr, David. 2003. *Making Sense of Education: An Introduction to the Philosophy and Theory of Education*. New York, NY: Routledge.

Chambliss, J.J., ed. 1996. *Philosophy of Education: An Encyclopedia*. New York, NY: Garland Publishers.

Christensen, C. Roland, and David A. Garvin, eds. 1991. *Education for Judgment*. Cambridge, MA: Harvard Business School Press.

Cromer, Alan H. 1997. *Connected Knowledge: Science, Philosophy, and Education*. Oxford, England: Oxford University Press.

Curren, Randall R., ed. 2003. *Companion to the Philosophy of Education*. New York, NY: Blackwell.

———., ed. 2007. *Philosophy of Education: An Anthology*. Malden, MA: Blackwell.

Dooley, Arch R., and Wickham Skinner. 1977. Casing Casemethod Methods. *Academy of Management Review* 2 (2): 277–289.

Ellis, Arthur K., John J. Cogan, and Kenneth R. Howey. 1991. *Introduction to the Foundations of Education*. Upper Saddle River, NJ: Prentice Hall.
Erskine, James A., Michiel R. Leenders, and Louise A. Mauffette-Leenders. 2003. *Teaching with Cases*. 3rd ed. London, ON, Canada: Ivey Business School, University of Western Ontario, Erskine Associate Inc., and Leenders and Associates Inc..
Freedman, James O. 1996. *Idealism and Liberal Education*. Ann Harbor, MI: University of Michigan Press.
Gragg, Charles I. 1954. Because Wisdom Can't Be Told. In *The Case Method at the Harvard Business School*, ed. Malcolm P. McNair. New York, NY: McGraw-Hill.
Gutek, Gerald Lee. 2000a. *Philosophical and Ideological Perspectives on Education*. 3rd ed. New York, NY: Allyn & Bacon.
———. 2000b. *Historical and Philosophical Foundations of Education: Selected Readings*. Upper Saddle River, NJ: Prentice Hall, College Division.
———. 2003. *Philosophical and Ideological Voices in Education*. 1st ed. New York, NY: Allyn & Bacon.
Hancock, Ralph C., ed. 1999. *America, the West, and Liberal Education*. New York, NY: Rowman & Littlefield.
Hare, William, and John P. Portelli, eds. 2001. *Philosophy of Education: Introductory Readings*. 3rd ed. New York, NY: Detseling Enterprises.
Hickman, Larry, and Thomas M. Alexander, eds. 1998. *The Essential Dewey: Pragmatism, Education, Democracy*. Bloomington, IN: Indiana University Press.
Kimball, Bruce A., and Robert Orrill, eds. 1995. *The Condition of American Liberal Education: Pragmatism and a Changing Tradition*. New York, NY: College Entrance Examination Board.
Larochelle, Marie, Nadine Bednarz, and Jim Garrison, eds. 1998. *Constructivism and Education*. Cambridge, England: Cambridge University Press.
Marples, Roger, ed. 1999. *The Aims of Education*. New York, NY: Routledge.
Mauffette-Leenders, Louise A., James A. Erskine, and Michiel R. Leenders. 2007. *Learning with Cases*. 4th ed. London, ON, Canada: Ivey Publishing, Ivey Business School, University of Western Ontario.
McLaren, Peter. 1998. Revolutionary Pedagogy in Post-Revolutionary Times: Rethinking the Political Economy of Critical Education. *Educational Theory* 48 (4): 431–462.
Morgan, Gareth. 1983. *Beyond Method: Strategies for Social Research*. Beverley Hills, CA: Sage.
———. 1985. Qualitative and Action Based Research. In *Actes du Colloque, Perspective de Recherche Pour lo Praticien*, ed. Y. Allaire, M. Landry, H. Mintzberg, and G. Morgan, 81–187. Rouyn-Noranda, QC, Canada: University of Quebec at Abitibi-Temiscaminque.
Noddings, Nel. 2016. *Philosophy of Education*. Boulder, CO: Westview Press.
Orrill, Robert, ed. 1999. *Education and Democracy: Re-Imaging Liberal Learning in America*. New York, NY: College Entrance Examination Board.
Ozmon, Howard A. 2011. *Philosophical Foundations of Education*. 7th ed. New York, NY: Pearson.
Philosophy of Education Society. 2003. *Philosophy of Education 2002*. New York, NY: Philosophy of Education Society Press.
Popkewitz, Thomas S., and Lynn Fendler, eds. 1999. *Critical Theories in Education: Changing Terrains of Knowledge and Politics*. New York, NY: Routledge.
Power, Edward J. 1995. *Educational Philosophy: A History from the Ancient World to Modern America*. New York, NY: Garland Publishers.
Reynolds, John I. 1978. There's Method in Cases. *Academy of Management Review* 3 (1): 129–133.
Rocha, Samuel D. 2014. *A Primer for Philosophy and Education*. Eugene, OR: Cascade Books.
Rorty, Amelie Oksenberg, ed. 1998. *Philosophers on Education: Historical Perspectives*. New York, NY: Routledge.
Sadovnik, Alan R., Susan Semel, and Peter Cookson. 2000. *Exploring Education: An Introduction to the Foundations of Education*. 2nd ed. New York, NY: Allyn & Bacon.

Schrag, Francis. 1995. *Back to Basics: Fundamental Educational Questions Reexamined.* San Francisco, CA: Jossey-Bass Education Series.

Siegel, Harvey. 2012. *The Oxford Handbook of Philosophy of Education.* Oxford, England: Oxford University Press.

Talisse, Robert B., and D. Micah Hester. 2002. *On the Philosophy of Education.* New York, NY: Wadsworth Publishing.

Winch, Christopher, and John Gingell. 1999. *Key Concepts in the Philosophy of Education.* New York, NY: Routledge.

Educational Methodologies: Implications for Student-Teacher Relations

This chapter discusses the implications of the first three chapters with respect to student-teacher relations. For this purpose, this chapter brings major aspects of the first three chapters to the forefront, and elaborates on their connections and implications for the way educational methodologies are applied.[1]

The first three chapters, in essence, discussed that, within the framework of the four paradigms, foundational philosophies underlie educational philosophies, and each educational philosophy favors a certain educational methodology.[2] In other words, as one moves from the objective to the subjective end of the spectrum in Exhibit 1.1 of Chap. 1, the in-class instructional methodology favored changes from totally having a lecture-oriented educational methodology to completely having a discussion-oriented educational methodology, e.g., a case-oriented educational methodology. This chapter discusses how these educational methodologies, in turn, determine the way such educational methodologies are applied to determine the type of student-teacher relations. In order to show this, this chapter focuses on certain aspects of the applications of the lecture methodology and the case methodology and compares them. Since most readers are familiar with the lecture methodology, the discussions in this chapter elaborate more on the case methodology.

---

[1] For this literature see Ardalan (2003a, 2003b, 2006, 2008, 2013, 2015), Barnes et al. (1994), Barrow and White (1993), Barrow and Woods (1989), Blake et al. (2002), Brosio (1998), Burrell and Morgan (1979), Cahn (1996, 2009), Carr (2003), Chambliss (1996), Christensen and Garvin (1991), Cromer (1997), Curren (2003, 2007), Dooley and Skinner (1977), Ellis et al. (1991), Erskine et al. (2003), Freedman (1996), Gragg (1954), Gutek (2000a, 2000b, 2003), Hancock (1999), Hare and Portelli (2001), Hickman and Alexander (1998), Kimball and Orrill (1995), Larochelle et al. (1998), Marples (1999), Mauffette-Leenders et al. (2007), McLaren (1998), Morgan (1983, 1985), Noddings (2016), Orrill (1999), Ozmon (2011), Philosophy of Education Society (2003), Popkewitz and Fendler (1999), Power (1995), Reynolds (1978), Rocha (2014), Rorty (1998), Sadovnik et al. (2000), Schrag (1995), Siegel (2012), Talisse and Hester (2002), and Winch and Gingell (1999). This chapter is based on Erskine et al. (2003), and Mauffette-Leenders et al. (2007).

[2] The difference between "educational method" and "educational methodology" should be kept in mind. The former refers to a tool, whereas the latter signifies an approach, an orientation, and a way of thinking about how to generate and apply respective educational methods.

K. Ardalan, *Case Method and Pluralist Economics*,
https://doi.org/10.1007/978-3-319-72071-5_7

1 Students' Anonymity vs. Knowing Students' Names and Backgrounds

In the lecture methodology, there is relatively less need for the teachers to know their students in the class. This is because all of the grades are based on written assignments, written term work, mid-term examination, and final examination. Moreover, the interactions or the contacts in class are at a minimum level. In the case methodology, since case discussions require a more personal approach, the instructors must develop their own means for identifying students.

In the case methodology, teachers believe that the first class meeting is the most important class in the whole course. They look for the answers to the following questions: Who are these students? Where do they come from? What is their prior knowledge? What do they know about my subject? What do they think interpersonal behavior is going to be like? What kinds of questions are running through their minds? The answers to these questions are important because the teacher wants to start where the students are and take them where the teacher wants them to go.

In the case methodology, there is no place for anonymity because without personal identification it is impossible to run a suitable course. The teacher quickly learns the names of the students and provides means for the students to become acquainted with one another. The teacher may ask students to sit at the same place for a few weeks so that their names can be more quickly learned.

In the case methodology, the teachers know their students as soon as the course starts. That is, they are able to identify the students by name in and out of class. Moreover, they have background information on each student such that appropriate resource people can be called on at the appropriate time in the class to contribute to class discussion. In the case methodology, students are not anonymous and none of them can hide in the classroom. Both the teacher and the students know everyone in the class. For this purpose a number of common aids are available:

1. Personal data forms
2. Name cards
3. Photos
4. Layout sheets or seating charts
5. Sitting in the back of the class
6. Participation in social activities
7. Personal visits in the office
8. Study group visits.

In the case methodology, teachers believe that it is very important to know the students in the classroom because when they teach with cases they work with all the experiences that the students bring to the class. The lack of identification translates into a barrier to communication. Case teachers expect students to have their name plates because it increases free interchange and heightens the students' sense of responsibility for participation in class discussion.

In the case methodology, some teachers intentionally arrive early in class. Then they can see who comes in with whom, who talks with whom, who is shunned, and who is looked up to by the peers. The teacher may watch how each student moves, walks, holds him- or her-self, and seats him- or her-self. Later in the course, when a student is holding him- or her-self differently, slumping his/her shoulders, or dragging his/her feet, the teacher makes him or her feel easy in class and talks with him or her after class to find out if there is any problem and how the teacher may help. Some teachers chat with a few students to stay current with the gossip of class news, and to show their interest in how the class is doing and how they get along.

2 Classroom Is a Podium and Rows of Seats vs. Classroom Is a Round Table

In the lecture methodology, classrooms in most educational institutions and seminar rooms outside educational institutions are designed as a rectangular room with a podium or desk at one end of the room and rows of seats and benches across from it. For the lecture methodology such an arrangement is functional because it involves a one-way communication and the primary task of the student is to listen to the speaker. It may not be the best arrangement because it is often difficult to see the speaker from the back row.

In the case methodology, the above-mentioned layout has many difficulties. This is because case discussion involves two-way communications and it is difficult for a student sitting in the back row to talk to the backs of the heads of the students sitting in the front rows. It is also difficult for students at the front of the class to turn around and see the student who is contributing at the back of the class. Moreover, this layout places too much emphasis on the teacher and too little emphasis on the students.

In the case methodology, the physical layout of the classroom is extremely important. For effective class participation and class discussion, the teacher needs to be able to identify the student who is talking and students need to be able to identify and face other students who are contributing to the class discussion. Physical facilities must be conducive to the discussion of cases. The layout of the classroom should encourage, not discourage, class participation and class discussion.

In the case methodology, classrooms should have excellent acoustics with swivel seats arranged in semicircular tiers such that a student contributing to the class discussion in the front row, or in the far end of the back row, can face the rest of the class and can easily be heard.

In the case methodology, the ideal layout for a small group is a round table or a circular seating arrangement. This layout allows everyone to be able to see each other and facilitates face to face communication. Unfortunately, as the class size increases the circular arrangement loses its disadvantages. This is because there is a limit to the size of the table, and the distance between participants increases rapidly, which hinders class communication.

In the case methodology, when the class size is large, other class layout options need to be examined. Possible alternatives are various row seating arrangements, preferably ramped, in amphitheatre style. Chairs should be moveable or rotatable so that students in the front row can turn around and see the students behind them. The table in front of each student should have enough space so that the student is able to feel comfortable and is able to spread on it case and reference materials. Curved benches are preferred to long straight benches because the curve helps each student to see others seated in the same row. Similarly, it is preferred for each additional row to be at a sufficiently higher level than the previous ones.

In the lecture methodology, classroom layout is not designed for a seminar context. There are individual desks, movable, and scattered in the classroom. Usually, they are not in a reasonable configuration when the class starts.

In the case methodology, teachers arrange for the physical facilities and classroom layout to be conducive to class participation and class discussion. Otherwise, the physical layout becomes a barrier to communication.

3 Teacher as a Lecturer vs. Teacher as a Facilitator

In the lecture methodology teaching is telling, knowledge is facts, and learning is recall. Teachers deliver content through their lecture and students receive it; and learning is satisfactorily completed when the student successfully transfers material back to the teacher at the specified time.

In the case methodology, the teacher leads the discussion of real business situations. The teacher works with students as a guide and not as oracle. The teacher does not approve, disapprove, or make judgments, but raises questions.

In the case methodology, real education is regarded as a process of drawing out the student's mind, not of pouring the teacher's ideas in the student's mind, which is what is done in the lecture methodology. That is, it is the power that students develop by digging which is important, not what they dig out. In the case methodology, students are expected to analyze cases by themselves as there are no answers in the back of the book and in some classes there is not even any textbook. The teachers do not tell students but expect students to analyze the case and tell the teachers and then teachers ask students questions. Teachers insist on the consistent application of logic to the facts of the case at hand. Teachers expect students to distinguish the pertinent facts, define the problem, determine the matters at issue, formulate questions, discuss the answers to those questions by weighing pros and cons, and finally decide what they would do if they were the person who had to make the decision.

In the case methodology, students, not the teacher, are responsible for exploration and argumentation of the case analysis and plan of action. That is, students' learning takes place through their joint, co-operative effort, rather than through the teacher's lecture. The role of the teacher is not to tell the students the answers but it is: (1) To guide their discussion to important but unconsidered aspects of the case; (2) To relate the progress of discussion to the time available; (3) To challenge a student's superficial thinking when other students do not, by posing questions which would lead the student through the path of his/her proposal until its consequences are exposed and understood.

In the case methodology, the teacher clearly states that students are responsible for good class discussions and that the teacher is a facilitator. The teacher stays out of class discussion and acts as a facilitator to make things happen. The students do the talking, the thinking, and the deciding. The teacher skillfully decides when to enforce his/her own rules in class.

In the case methodology, teachers assist the students to become independent thinkers and doers. Teachers help students to develop their logic by friendly questioning and encouraging support from other students. If a student makes an illogical comment, the teacher asks other students to express their viewpoints. Teachers express their opinions at the students' request. Teachers summarize the class discussions, which are especially useful at the end of a discussion or when the teachers find it useful to change the course of the class discussion.

In the case methodology, teachers manage the class discussion such that: (1) Every student has the opportunity to participate in the discussion; (2) No student is allowed to monopolize the discussion; and (3) The class logically moves from the statement and evaluation of the issues to a consensus solution.

In the case methodology, the teacher facilitates the class discussion and provides opportunities for students to maximize their learning. There is no one best way of teaching cases. Some teachers tend to be more directive and others more non-directive. Teachers follow different approaches and complement each other.

In the case methodology, teaching is regarded as a transformation process. Teaching is not only the transfer of information, but also the transformation of students from passive recipients of others' knowledge to active constructors of their own and others' knowledge. This transformation requires the active participation of students. Teaching is creating the pedagogical, social, and ethical environment in which students become responsible for their learning, both individually and collectively.

In the case methodology, the educational goal is not for students to memorize all the textbooks facts which they may forget soon after they graduate, but rather to learn practical knowledge and apply logical and correct reasoning in every subject.

In the lecture methodology, teachers use textbooks and are not explicit about the conceptual framework of the subject matter they teach but are concerned with the textbook techniques. In the case methodology, the teacher is concerned with students' understanding and applying the conceptual framework of the subject matter and therefore uses that framework frequently. This is because, business managers are more involved with the conceptual frameworks than with the techniques.

In the case methodology, the teacher involves the students in a sequence of experiences and asks them questions related to the conceptual framework of the subject matter so that they gradually acquire a working capacity of the fundamentals. In the lecture methodology, the teacher follows the textbook outline and hopes that the students somehow get a working understanding of the subject matter.

In the case methodology, the teacher develops the course based on the type of the students in class. For instance, the teacher considers undergraduates and MBAs to be different and therefore sets different course objectives. In general, undergraduates lack career identification and act as young students. The teacher believes that these factors are more important than the list of topics that a teacher in the lecture methodology wants to cover. The case teacher accounts for these more important factors and reduces the content of the course. The teacher does not worry as much about the substance of an undergraduate course as that of an MBA course. The teacher spends time with the undergraduate students to show who and what a manager is and how the students should identify with that person.

In the case methodology, the teachers provide the necessary services which group discussions require. They maintain orderly class discussions. They ask challenging questions to advance group thinking and reveal the relevance of the discussion up to that point. They combine individual contributions into a pattern which the class can perceive. They manage the class time such that they avoid a discussion which either is not moving fast enough to efficiently use the available class time or is moving too fast to be comprehensible by half of the class. In such occasions, they exercise control over the undirected class discussion, but at the same time they stay out of the way to allow the class to make its discoveries, which may be new to the teachers as well. The teachers examine their class rather than their subject matter because unpredictable developments distinguish real learning.

In the case methodology, the teachers spend a lot of time on their case preparation so that they would be able to allow the class discussion to follow its unpredictable path. In the lecture methodology, the teachers prepare their lecture in a relatively short period of time, have complete control over the sequence of steps which are to be taken in class, know when to interject humor to maintain students' interest, know when to include something outrageous to get the attention of a student who is daydreaming, and anticipate questions which students may ask. The lecturer can prepare in advance to answer those questions in class and gain students' high respect. In the case methodology, the teachers are not in control because students drive the class discussions and it is only occasionally when the teachers influence the discussion process to make it more productive, which is a difficult task.

In the case methodology, the class plan may take a position on a continuum from high to low structure. The teacher's decision as to where on this continuum the class plan should be depends on several factors: the kind of case, the position in the course, the type of student involved, and the teacher's orientation and experience.

In the case methodology, in contrast to the lecture methodology, teachers face a good deal of uncertainty because what happens in the classroom is not a standard process or procedure. Teachers manage the participative process and reinforce process variability from the start of the course, but they have a reference base to which variations can be contrasted. Variation may depend on the objectives of the class, the type of case, the place of a class in the sequence of classes, what happened in previous classes or other classes in other courses which are taken simultaneously by the students, the teaching style and mood of the instructor, the mood of the students, the time of year, the weather, the political and economic news, and so on. Teachers who would like to imitate an objective model (i.e., lecturer) find case teaching very unfortunate, but innovative teachers find it delightful.

In the case methodology, when teachers prepare for their classes, they consider the following topics: identification of the educational objectives, identification of the case issues, suggested student assignment, suggested questions to be asked during the class discussion, and comments regarding the analysis and solution. The quality of Teaching Notes varies considerably with case authors. Particularly useful are teacher's comments regarding what actually happened in class when a certain case was discussed. Such comments are written within the context of a particular course, therefore these same conditions may not pertain to another course. That is, the transplantation of a case from an environment and one course to another environment and another course may not produce satisfactory results. Therefore, each teacher should develop his/her own teaching notes and be prepared for variations.

In the case methodology, the teachers avoid a rigid approach to cases. They believe that novelty and innovation are the hallmark of learning and that rigidity ruins the desire for participation. The teachers aim to lead a stimulating class discussion.

In the case methodology, discussion is based on the core idea of reciprocity between students and teachers, in which the roles of teachers and students are easily reversible. Students no only teach each other, but also they teach the teacher, by revealing their understandings of the subject. Teachers learn not only by being exposed to students' understandings of the subject, but also by gaining experience in the practice of teaching.

4 Teacher-Student Separation vs. Teacher-Student Unity

In the lecture methodology, primacy is given to the teacher. The teacher's presentation of the subject matter drives the classroom activity and the class plan; and the students play a subordinate role. In the case methodology, a major change is involved in the teacher's role, classroom activities, students' responsibilities, and teacher-student relationships. There is a strong emphasis on student involvement and self-teaching because it is recognized that significant learning comes from the creative efforts of the individual learner.

In the case methodology, class discussions become most useful when the teacher avoids the relative certainty of planned lectures and the teacher-dominated class activities and embraces the uncertainty of hard-to-plan, free-flowing class discussions which are driven by student ideas, follow unusual paths, and reach unexpected end points. Lecture methodology teachers feel most uncomfortable in a case methodology environment.

In the lecture methodology, the teacher has power over the student, which reflects a master-apprentice relationship with great efficiency when the transfer of knowledge is the primary objective. However, when the objective is critical thinking (in the liberal arts sense) or problem-solving (in the professional schools sense), or the development of qualities such as sensitivity, cooperation, and desire for discovery, then the discussion methodology is substantially advantageous. To achieve these complex, value-laden objectives, both teachers and students must modify their traditional roles, responsibilities, and relationships.

In the case methodology, partnership is a vehicle by which students observe not only the teaching/learning process but also themselves. Students deepen their personal involvement, take responsibility for the quality of the discussion, and make an emotional investment in the outcome of the course, to claim ownership of their own education. This ownership not only stimulates them to excel, but also enhances effectiveness of the teachers. When discussing cases, an appreciation of diversity (in backgrounds, personalities, questions posed, learning styles, frames of inquiry, and spectrums of interpretation) ensures that the class avoids the lecture-type single-track path to single-point destination. In this way, they unleash and then slowly harness a powerful energy of creativity that students often do not know they possess.

In the case methodology, class discussion elevates the collective wisdom of the whole group, and tests a student's preparation and delivery in comparison with a sample of the peer group the student may have in a future professional career. If the student can actively contribute, listen, question, and respond in the case classroom he/she can successfully do the same after graduation in the real organization.

In the case methodology, the teachers believe that student growth, not teacher's ego gratification, is the instructional goal. They have a sincere interest in helping students to learn. Their focus is on developing the student as opposed to displaying professional expertise of the teacher. In the lecture methodology, one is left with the impression that the teachers display their brightness, or that the teachers are insecure to the extent that they have to gain their status by demonstrating their intellectual superiority. Hence, the lecture methodology does not provide students with the same kind of experience that the case methodology does. In the case methodology, students are allowed considerable individual freedom to influence the outcome.

In the case methodology, the teacher's roles differ from those in the lecture methodology. First, the teacher's task is not to teach but to encourage learning. This shift affects a wide range of activities of the teacher such as preparing class material, planning class sessions, and measuring what the course has achieved. Second, the teacher must give up the role and status of a center-stage, intellectually superior authority figure and accept to be a member of a learning group, but with a unique position. Consequently, the teacher provides information, monitors the quality of student analysis and presentation, and facilitates the process of joint inquiry.

In the lecture methodology, the teacher has a dominating role and controls the class. The students' obligation is only to follow a predetermined teaching plan. The teacher decides which topics art to be taught and determines when they have been adequately covered. Students are rarely provided with the opportunity to initiate exploration for discovery. Students know that they have to work through the teacher's teaching plan. The lecture methodology is comfortable for the teacher, but it provides thin education for the students.

In the case methodology, the instruction is a learning process consisting of a complicated interaction of the case situation, individual student, overall class section, and discussion leader. It blends cognitive and affective learning modes.

In the case methodology, the fundamental insight at the core of the discussion process is that teaching and learning are inseparable parts of a reciprocal giving and receiving. Students share the task of teaching with the instructor and one another. All teach and all learn.

In the case methodology, the teacher believes that learning students' names is important and the student gets a sense of belonging and feels that the teacher cares.

In the case methodology, the responsibilities and authority are diffused. The teacher may be seen as a craftsperson, and may assume the role of a student.

In the case methodology, students' intellectual and emotional involvement explains its extraordinary power in creating a highly personal learning experience. That involvement stands in sharp contrast to the stereotypical lecture class. Case classes involve students in the give-and-take of class discussion, both mind and vocal cords. It provides students with the opportunity to practice managerial skills both in class and in other academic activities by taking responsibility for their own self-education and for the development of other students, because managers are both teachers and students in their everyday work. Case discussion reflects the actual administrative life and allows students to practice real-life administrative skills such as: observing, listening, diagnosing, deciding, and intervening in group processes to achieve desired objectives.

In the lecture methodology, classrooms in educational institutions and seminar rooms outside educational institutions are rectangular rooms which are set up with a podium or desk at one end of the room and rows of seats across it. For the lecture methodology's one-way communication, where the primary task of the student is to listen to the speaker, such an arrangement is functional.

In the case methodology, the above-mentioned layout creates many difficulties and severely limits group discussion. This is because case discussion requires two-way communication and it is difficult for a student who is sitting in the back row of the class to talk to the backs of the heads of the students who are sitting in the front rows of the class. In addition, it is difficult for students who at sitting in the front rows of the class to turn around and see the student who is contributing from the back of the classroom. Furthermore, the above-mentioned layout places an unnecessary emphasis on the teacher and too little emphasis on the students, which may be regarded as a military formation.

In the case methodology, the teachers believe that physical facilities are extremely imp. The ideal layout for a small class is a perfectly round table or a circular seating arrangement. The circle provides perfect sight lines to everyone and allows face to face communication. The circular layout of the classroom means equality of all participants. For larger classes, a U-shaped amphitheatre classroom would be suitable.

In the case methodology, scale and continuity are also important. The case methodology is most appropriate for classes consisting of 20–80 students. The case methodology is more useful when there is a stable membership because the class develops into a social organization and a group dynamic that can be very helpful.

In the case methodology, teachers prefer to minimize the number of objects at the front of the classroom which act as a barrier between the teacher and the students. For instance, they prefer not to have a podium, instead they prefer to have a flat table to place their materials on. They prefer not to have an overhead projector which sits on the table and obstructs the view, rather they prefer to have one which is built into the table. They prefer not to have objects that physically separate the teacher from the students. Teachers prefer classrooms which are architecturally designed to minimize the physical distance and to maximize the psychological togetherness between teacher and students, and encourage student-to-student rather than teacher-to-student interactions, which is the characteristic of the lecture methodology.

For the teacher, the move from the lecture methodology to the case methodology is significant. The teacher's new role changes from asking questions from a series of individual students to directing a process by which the class explores a complex case situation. Symbolically, in the lecture methodology, the teacher is treated as a king and placed on a platform separated from the students from where he/she overlooks students. In the case methodology, the teacher sits at a desk from where he/she looks up at the students. The power balance between teacher and students shifts perceptibly, by which students gain increased opportunity for personal learning and group contribution.

5 Conclusion

This chapter discussed how, within the framework of the four paradigms, foundational philosophies underlie educational philosophies, and each educational philosophy favors a certain educational methodology, which in turn implies a certain way or method of education. More specifically, this chapter discussed how each foundational philosophy implies the specification of the student-teacher relations.

References

Ardalan, Kavous. 2003a. The Lecture-versus-Case Controversy: Its Philosophical Foundation. *Southwestern Economic Review* 30 (1): 99–118.

———. 2003b. Alternative Approaches Utilized in the Case Method: Their Philosophical Foundations. *Academy of Educational Leadership Journal* 30 (3): 103–120.

———. 2006. The Philosophical Foundation of the Lecture-versus-Case Controversy: Its Implications for Faculty Teaching, Research, and Service. *International Journal of Social Economics* 33 (3): 261–281.

———. 2008. The Philosophical Foundation of the Lecture-versus-Case Controversy: Its Implications for Course Goals, Objectives, and Contents. *International Journal of Social Economics* 35 (1/2): 15–34.

———. 2013. The Philosophical Foundation of the Lecture Method of Instruction and the Case Method of Instruction: Implications for Examinations. *Contemporary Issues in Education Research* 6 (1): 1–7.

———. 2015. Chapter 3: Using Entertaining Metaphors in the Introduction of the Case Method in a Case-Based Course. In *Exploring Learning and Teaching In Higher Education*, ed. Mang Li and Yong Zhao, 69–96. New York, NY: Springer.

Barnes, Louis B., Abby J. Hansen, and C. Roland Christensen. 1994. *Teaching and the Case Method: Text, Cases, and Readings*. Boston, MA: Harvard Business School.

Barrow, Robin, and Patricia White, eds. 1993. *Beyond Liberal Education: Essays in Honor of Paul H Hirst*. New York, NY: Routledge.

Barrow, Robin, and Ronald Woods. 1989. *An Introduction to Philosophy of Education*. New York, NY: Routledge.

Blake, Nigel, Paul Smeyers, Richard Smith, and Paul Standish, eds. 2002. *The Blackwell Guide to the Philosophy of Education*. New York, NY: Blackwell.

Brosio, Richard A. 1998. The Continuing Correspondence between Political Economy and Schooling: Telling the News. *Journal of Thought* 33 (3): 85–105.

Burrell, Gibson, and Gareth Morgan. 1979. *Sociological Paradigms and Organizational Analysis*. Hants, England: Gower Publishing.

Cahn, Steven M., ed. 1996. *Classic and Contemporary Readings in the Philosophy of Education*. New York, NY: McGraw-Hill College Division.

———., ed. 2009. *Philosophy of Education: The Essential Texts*. New York, NY: Routledge.

Carr, David. 2003. *Making Sense of Education: An Introduction to the Philosophy and Theory of Education*. New York, NY: Routledge.

Chambliss, J.J., ed. 1996. *Philosophy of Education: An Encyclopedia*. New York, NY: Garland Publishers.

Christensen, C. Roland, and David A. Garvin, eds. 1991. *Education for Judgment*. Cambridge, MA: Harvard Business School Press.

Cromer, Alan H. 1997. *Connected Knowledge: Science, Philosophy, and Education*. Oxford, England: Oxford University Press.

Curren, Randall R., ed. 2003. *Companion to the Philosophy of Education*. New York, NY: Blackwell.

———., ed. 2007. *Philosophy of Education: An Anthology*. Malden, MA: Blackwell.

Dooley, Arch R., and Wickham Skinner. 1977. Casing Casemethod Methods. *Academy of Management Review* 2 (2): 277–289.

Ellis, Arthur K., John J. Cogan, and Kenneth R. Howey. 1991. *Introduction to the Foundations of Education*. Upper Saddle River, NJ: Prentice Hall.

Erskine, James A., Michiel R. Leenders, and Louise A. Mauffette-Leenders. 2003. *Teaching with Cases*. 3rd ed. London, ON, Canada: Ivey Business School, University of Western Ontario, Erskine Associate Inc., and Leenders and Associates Inc..

Freedman, James O. 1996. *Idealism and Liberal Education*. Ann Harbor, MI: University of Michigan Press.

Gragg, Charles I. 1954. Because Wisdom Can't Be Told. In *The Case Method at the Harvard Business School*, ed. Malcolm P. McNair. New York, NY: McGraw-Hill.

Gutek, Gerald Lee. 2000a. *Philosophical and Ideological Perspectives on Education*. 3rd ed. New York, NY: Allyn & Bacon.

———. 2000b. *Historical and Philosophical Foundations of Education: Selected Readings*. Upper Saddle River, NJ: Prentice Hall, College Division.

———. 2003. *Philosophical and Ideological Voices in Education*. 1st ed. New York, NY: Allyn & Bacon.

Hancock, Ralph C., ed. 1999. *America, the West, and Liberal Education*. New York, NY: Rowman & Littlefield.

Hare, William, and John P. Portelli, eds. 2001. *Philosophy of Education: Introductory Readings*. 3rd ed. New York, NY: Detseling Enterprises.

Hickman, Larry, and Thomas M. Alexander, eds. 1998. *The Essential Dewey: Pragmatism, Education, Democracy*. Bloomington, IN: Indiana University Press.

Kimball, Bruce A., and Robert Orrill, eds. 1995. *The Condition of American Liberal Education: Pragmatism and a Changing Tradition*. New York, NY: College Entrance Examination Board.

Larochelle, Marie, Nadine Bednarz, and Jim Garrison, eds. 1998. *Constructivism and Education*. Cambridge, England: Cambridge University Press.

Marples, Roger, ed. 1999. *The Aims of Education*. New York, NY: Routledge.

Mauffette-Leenders, Louise A., James A. Erskine, and Michiel R. Leenders. 2007. *Learning with Cases*. 4th ed. London, Ontario, Canada: Ivey Publishing, Ivey Business School, University of Western Ontario.

McLaren, Peter. 1998. Revolutionary Pedagogy in Post-Revolutionary Times: Rethinking the Political Economy of Critical Education. *Educational Theory* 48 (4): 431–462.

Morgan, Gareth. 1983. *Beyond Method: Strategies for Social Research*. Beverley Hills, CA: Sage.

———. 1985. Qualitative and Action Based Research. In *Actes du Colloque, Perspective de Recherche Pour lo Praticien*, ed. Y. Allaire, M. Landry, H. Mintzberg, and G. Morgan, 81–187. Rouyn-Noranda, QC, Canada: University of Quebec at Abitibi-Temiscaminque.

Noddings, Nel. 2016. *Philosophy of Education*. Boulder, CO: Westview Press.

Orrill, Robert, ed. 1999. *Education and Democracy: Re-Imaging Liberal Learning in America*. New York, NY: College Entrance Examination Board.

Ozmon, Howard A. 2011. *Philosophical Foundations of Education*. 7th ed. New York, NY: Pearson.

Philosophy of Education Society. 2003. *Philosophy of Education 2002*. New York, NY: Philosophy of Education Society Press.

Popkewitz, Thomas S., and Lynn Fendler, eds. 1999. *Critical Theories in Education: Changing Terrains of Knowledge and Politics*. New York, NY: Routledge.

Power, Edward J. 1995. *Educational Philosophy: A History from the Ancient World to Modern America*. New York, NY: Garland Publishers.

Reynolds, John I. 1978. There's Method in Cases. *Academy of Management Review* 3 (1): 129–133.

Rocha, Samuel D. 2014. *A Primer for Philosophy and Education*. Eugene, OR: Cascade Books.

Rorty, Amelie Oksenberg, ed. 1998. *Philosophers on Education: Historical Perspectives*. New York, NY: Routledge.

Sadovnik, Alan R., Susan Semel, and Peter Cookson. 2000. *Exploring Education: An Introduction to the Foundations of Education*. 2nd ed. New York, NY: Allyn & Bacon.

Schrag, Francis. 1995. *Back to Basics: Fundamental Educational Questions Reexamined*. San Francisco, CA: Jossey-Bass Education Series.

Siegel, Harvey. 2012. *The Oxford Handbook of Philosophy of Education*. Oxford, England: Oxford University Press.

Talisse, Robert B., and D. Micah Hester. 2002. *On the Philosophy of Education*. New York, NY: Wadsworth Publishing.

Winch, Christopher, and John Gingell. 1999. *Key Concepts in the Philosophy of Education*. New York, NY: Routledge.

Educational Methodologies: Implications for Faculty Teaching, Research, and Service

This chapter discusses the implications of the first three chapters with respect to faculty teaching, research, and service. For this purpose, this chapter brings major aspects of the first three chapters to the forefront, and elaborates on their connections and implications for the way educational methodologies are applied.[1]

The first three chapters, in essence, discussed that, within the framework of the four paradigms, foundational philosophies underlie educational philosophies, and each educational philosophy favors a certain educational methodology.[2] In other words, as one moves from the objective to the subjective end of the spectrum in Exhibit 1.1 of Chap. 1, the in-class instructional methodology favored changes from totally having a lecture-oriented educational methodology to completely having a discussion-oriented educational methodology, e.g., a case-oriented educational methodology. This chapter discusses how these educational methodologies, in turn, determine the way such educational methodologies are applied to determine the type of faculty teaching, research, service. In order to show this, this chapter focuses on certain aspects of the applications of the lecture methodology and the case methodology and compares them. Since most readers are familiar with the lecture methodology, the discussions in this chapter elaborate more on the case methodology.

---

[1] For this literature see Ardalan (2003a, 2003b, 2006, 2008, 2013, 2015), Barnes et al. (1994), Barrow and White (1993), Barrow and Woods (1989), Blake et al. (2002), Brosio (1998), Burrell and Morgan (1979), Cahn (1996, 2009), Carr (2003), Chambliss (1996), Christensen and Garvin (1991), Cromer (1997), Curren (2003, 2007), Dooley and Skinner (1977), Ellis et al. (1991), Erskine et al. (2003), Freedman (1996), Gragg (1954), Gutek (2000a, 2000b, 2003), Hancock (1999), Hare and Portelli (2001), Hickman and Alexander (1998), Kimball and Orrill (1995), Larochelle et al. (1998), Marples (1999), Mauffette-Leenders et al. (2007), McLaren (1998), Morgan (1983, 1985), Noddings (2016), Orrill (1999), Ozmon (2011), Philosophy of Education Society (2003), Popkewitz and Fendler (1999), Power (1995), Reynolds (1978), Rocha (2014), Rorty (1998), Sadovnik et al. (2000), Schrag (1995), Siegel (2012), Talisse and Hester (2002), and Winch and Gingell (1999). This chapter is based on Ardalan (2006), Erskine et al. (2003), and Mauffette-Leenders et al. (2007).

[2] The difference between "educational method" and "educational methodology" should be kept in mind. The former refers to a tool, whereas the latter signifies an approach, an orientation, and a way of thinking about how to generate and apply respective educational methods.

K. Ardalan, *Case Method and Pluralist Economics*,
https://doi.org/10.1007/978-3-319-72071-5_8

1 Faculty Teaching: Science of Teaching vs. Art of Teaching

This sub-section shows that the sequence of foundational philosophy, educational philosophy, and educational methodology underlies the way teachers view an instructional method in practice. In order to show this, the sub-section focuses on how teachers view the lecture or case methods of instruction depending on which philosophy they believe in. More specifically, the functionalist paradigm views teaching as science whereas the interpretive paradigm views teaching as an art. Since most readers are familiar with the lecture methodology, the discussions in this section elaborate on the case methodology.

According to the case methodology teaching is essentially a transformation vocation. The aim of teaching is not only to transmit information (as in the lecture methodology), but also to transform students from passive recipients of the teacher's knowledge into active constructors of their own and other students' knowledge. The teacher cannot transform without the student's active participation, of course. Teaching is fundamentally about creating the pedagogical, social, and ethical conditions under which students agree to take charge for their own learning, individually, and collectively.

The case teachers regard teaching as an art rather than a science (as in the lecture methodology). The classroom process requires teachers to bring with them a complex tactile familiarity so that in the moment they can synthesize it, largely unconsciously, and respond partly in awareness on the basis of intuitive skill in the moment as they see it. They have no more than that available to them because there are contingencies in that moment which are simply beyond cognition. The issue for them is how to get ready to be there in that moment. The teacher cannot go into the classroom with a role that is consistent for every person, every course, or every institution.

In a case discussion, the teacher performs a large number of tasks. The objectives are multiple and varied. The teacher is not only concerned with the relevant tasks and problems of the case discussion but also with all of the normal tasks and objectives of any teacher in any circumstances, including the lecture methodology. This translates into a very complex task, and consequently, a continual influx of trade-off decisions right on the spot in the classroom. The difficulty is that many of the tasks have conflicting aims. For example, any time taken by the teacher to speak (as is done extensively in the lecture methodology) has to be taken from the students' participative time. A teacher who uses a great deal of control for the sake of efficiency (which is the norm under the lecture methodology) may take away from the student the responsibility for learning. A teacher who plays an active role in cutting off discussion and orchestrating discussion (as in the lecture methodology) may not encourage the class to do its own discipline. A teacher who wishes to use up time to discuss theory in class (as in the lecture methodology) may not permit the students sufficient time to do problem solving or decision making or implementation planning. The teacher must, therefore, know how to manage trade-offs. These are far from simple and can only be resolved in a total program and course philosophy.

There is a large number of variations around the main theme that exists in the teaching with cases. There is a variety of case teaching styles and no one style is better or worse than another, nor that in certain circumstances, a certain style is preferable. However, style is an important element in teaching with cases because it ties the various roles together in a logical whole. The teacher identifies and considers suitable styles. The teacher identifies these options and experiments to find a way suitable for his/her own situation. There is a difference between teaching with cases a particular way out of ignorance versus out of choice. The variation in case use frequently observed in practice stems largely from a fundamental difference in the perceived objectives held by each instructor. Teachers complement each other. It would be very boring if all teachers did the inevitable thing in the classroom. Then teachers become teaching machines.

Teaching with cases cannot be separated from its surrounding environment. Not only do objectives for using cases vary, but so do, for example, students, teachers, class times, facilities, and environmentalists. In one way this lack of standardization is unfortunate. It makes the process uncertain. In another, it increases the challenge to perform the task well and gives the individual teacher an opportunity to custom build an approach suitable to his/her unique situation. There are, of course, many different ways of using cases and it is unlikely that one comes close to capturing all.

In the case methodology, the classroom is a new experience each time, which is one of the reasons teachers can teach the same case many times. One of the major abilities of case teachers is experience and confidence, a confidence to abandon a pre-set perception of how things should go.

In the case methodology, students are presented with an array of different styles and approaches. This is very useful to the students because they would have to experience different styles and to learn in spite of the differences. A teacher may feel free to choose his/her own style and not be perceived as too far out by the students.

In the case methodology, in contrast to the lecture methodology, there are uncertainties for the teacher as well as the students. What happens in the classroom is by no means a standard process or procedure. The focus of teaching with cases lies on managing the participative process. Case teachers usually reinforce process variability at the start. From a discussion standpoint it is useful to have a reference base from which variations can be contrasted. Variation may depend on the subject matter, the objectives of the class, the type of case, the place in the sequence of classes, what happened in previous classes, or other classes in other courses taken simultaneously by the same students. In addition, variation among classes may depend on the teaching style of the teacher, the mood of the instructor, the mood of the students, the chemistry of the class, physical facility, the time of year, the weather, the political and economic news, and surely, other factors a teacher may be able to identify under the circumstances. Case classes often appear to be disorderly and lacking in substance to a casual observer. Good discussions unfold in unexpected ways that are different from a teaching plan. That there is no such a thing as a standard case class which can be used as an objective model is unfortunate for those who seek imitation, and delightful for innovative teachers. In teaching with cases, considerable coordination is required to make sure that the whole makes sense.

In designing a new course, the case teachers get excited, concerned, worried, enthusiastic, and very much involved with problems that they see in business, in the economy, and with managers who are struggling and attempting to cope.

For instance, consider the Human Resources course. A teacher, whether using the case methodology or the lecture methodology, knows that the conceptual knowledge and the theoretical frameworks for better management of human resources are all in the library. But only the case teacher asks: So why does it not work? This and other issues are what the case teacher wants to address in a new course: What are some companies doing about it? What are some personnel managers, managers of human resources, doing about it? What is their role, their opportunity?

As for another example, consider the Investment Management course. A case teacher knows that there are at least two ways to organize the course. One way is to look at the textbooks and the literature, which is what the lecture methodology would dictate. However, a case teacher would soon find that the investment textbooks do not have much to do with management of investments. The second way, therefore, is to go talk to people in the investment business. In this way, the case teacher gets an accurate picture of what problems leading practitioners (that is, high-ranking practitioners who are at the leading edge) wrestle with, specific examples, possible cases, as well as recommendations of who else the case teacher should talk to about the business in general. The case teacher then decides how to organize the course.

In general, detailed course planning concerns itself with the sequence of individual sessions and the selection of materials. In the lecture methodology, the teacher is concerned about how to teach the theory. In the case methodology, the teacher is concerned about how to integrate theory and practice.

Under the lecture methodology, teachers use textbooks. They are not usually very explicit about the conceptual framework of the subject matter they teach but are mostly concerned with the textbook techniques. In the case methodology, the objectives are to get students to understand and be able to use some conceptual framework and the teacher's role from day to day is to be sure he/she uses that framework. This is because, a business manager is far more involved with the basic hypotheses of the conceptual framework of a course, than with the techniques. Case teachers think of management largely as a matter of practice.

The case methodology allows the teacher to build up a sequence of experiences in which they can get the students involved. Then, the teacher can use his/her knowledge of the conceptual framework in asking questions, using the blackboard, and calling upon students for reactions. So, the students gradually begin to get a working capacity to deal with the fundamentals. It sounds very simple but if a teacher is trained with the lecture methodology, then there is a tremendous act of faith required to jump into the case methodology of teaching, instead of hanging onto the security blanket of a textbook outline and hoping that the students will somehow get a working understanding of what the teacher talks about. In addition to the act of faith, there is a tremendous investment of time and effort required to make this switch.

A teacher who has been trained under the lecture methodology prepares an analysis of the case from a scientific point of view that is totally exhaustive, mutually exclusive, and gives a clear and penetrating breakdown, and that he/she wants to make sure the class gets there. That is, such a teacher tries to force students into his/her assumptions and framework. For a case teacher, just as important and maybe more important than the case content preparation is that he/she should know, in terms of the behavioral, conceptual, and analytical teaching objectives, what it is he/she is going after in the class.

Case teachers do not believe that it is so important that they get to a high level of technical penetration because if they force that level of analysis, then they are trying to teach analysis of numbers specifically and that the goal is achieving the right numerical answer. Case teachers identify the students with the manager or decision maker in the situation, and what the problem is, and what the options are. In terms of that decision, what approach or set of attitudes towards the problem in the case will lead him/her to the solution so that the activities with the highest pay-off can be recognized. Very often, it is getting the right question; if the students can conceive of the situation properly along with a global framework of policy, strategy, and tactics, they will be able to classify it as this or that kind of problem and then do the numbers if necessary.

This sub-section showed that the sequence of foundational philosophy, educational philosophy, and educational methodology underlay the way teachers view an instructional methodology in practice. In order to show this, the sub-section focused on how teachers view the lecture or case methodologies of instruction depending on which philosophy they believe in. More specifically, it was noted that the functionalist paradigm views teaching as science whereas the interpretive paradigm views teaching as an art.

Next, in a similar manner, it is shown that each foundational philosophy underlies how faculty view and perform their research.

2 Faculty Research: Scientific Research vs. Clinical Research

This sub-section shows that the sequence of foundational philosophy to the philosophy of science underlie the way teachers view their research methodology and perform research. In order to show this, the sub-section focuses on how teachers view research methodologies depending on which philosophy they believe in. More specifically, it is noted that the functionalist paradigm arrives at the scientific research methodology whereas the interpretive paradigm follows the clinical research methodology.

The case methodology meets both the teacher's teaching and research needs. The development of new field cases links teachers to the world of practice. It encourages them to be in touch with their professional counterparts, maintaining a dialogue that explores current problems and anticipates future issues. Clinical fieldwork provides a teacher with rich data from which to extract new hypotheses and modify current working generalizations.

Based on carefully designed research plans and intensive field research, cases have evolved into complex educational instruments. Their content has broadened to include internal company information as well as external industry data, and psychological, sociological, and anthropological observations as well as technical and economic material.

Under the lecture methodology, most teachers are not in touch with the raw data but only a second, third, and fourth abstraction of the data. In the case methodology, on the contrary, most teachers are actively in touch with their own raw material.

Any adequate use of a research methodology would highly benefit from a deep understanding of its underlying worldview. The rest of this sub-section, therefore, discusses the relationship between paradigms and research methodologies. It shows how fundamental, paradigmatic assumptions translate into the methodology of research. It discusses the functionalist and interpretive research methodologies, called scientific and clinical, respectively.

The methodology traditionally favored in the study of social sciences is called scientific. It is based on its paradigmatic assumptions, and, therefore, committed to the method of observation.

The scientific methodology consists of the following five principal stages[3]:

1. Observation,
2. Theory building,
3. Hypothesis: systematic doubt,
4. Experimental framework/design, and
5. Test: rejection, reformulation, or confirmation of the theory.

The scientific methodology begins with the observation of the phenomenon. It is based on the idea that the researcher observes what is "out there." Reality is the source of ideas, which is the basis for the development of theory. This is the process which is called theory building. The scientist makes sense of what is observed "out there" in the "real world."

The theory often starts as a very broad idea, which is rather imprecise. In the next stage, the scientist comes up with a hypothesis, or a set of hypotheses, which translates the theory into a testable form.

A hypothesis should have the crucial property of being refutable, i.e., the possibility that it is untrue. In other words, the development of a hypothesis is based on "systematic doubt," which is crucial for the scientific process. Without bringing doubt on research, it is not scientific. The scientist should try to refute, or disprove, his or her favored theory, perhaps not to reject it altogether, but to proceed in terms of a methodological process of rejection, reformulation, or confirmation of the theory.

The test of a hypothesis is based on the specification of the hypothesis in a testable form, so that it can be refuted. The testing, based on systematic doubt, leads to the rejection or confirmation of the hypothesis. But, to be scientific, confirmation should not be sought, but should come through the process of attempting to reject. This process is an open one: when the hypothesis is not confirmed, it is reformulated,

[3] See Ardalan (2003b), Morgan (1983, chapters 3–6), and Morgan (1985).

which, in turn, may lead to the reformulation of the theory. In other words, the results of the experiments may lead to the recommencement of the process.

The scientific methodology is an iterative process. It begins with stage 1, goes through the various steps to stage 5, and then goes back to stages 2 or 1. This is to obtain an improved understanding of the subject of study.

The model presented above represents the scientific methodology. Its aim is to generate ever better descriptions and explanations of reality.

The clinical methodology consists of the following five stages[4]:

1. Get inside: get deeply involved in the situation,
2. Adopt the role of a learner,
3. Map the system of symbols and their meanings,
4. Identify key themes and explanations, and
5. Test against opinion in the situation: reject, reformulate, or confirm themes and explanations.

The clinical methodology starts with the idea that, instead of observing reality from the outside, one should attempt to understand it from within. Whereas the scientist applying the scientific methodology observes the phenomenon from a distance, the clinical scientist makes direct and unstructured contact with it, with no preconception in terms of what is to be discovered. The clinical scientist becomes a participant in the situation to be investigated. In fact, one of the techniques in clinical research is called "participant observation," which is very flexible. The main goal is to understand how people construct their world.

The clinical scientist gets inside the situation to understand how it is put together from within. This is done without taking on the role of an expert, with a theory about how that phenomenon works, as is done in the scientific methodology. Rather, the clinical scientist takes on the role of a learner, who attempts to understand the situation being researched.

The next stage of research is mapping the rich fabric of the phenomenon: the symbols, the meanings, the rituals, the routines, the folklore, and the history, which the researcher documents. Actually, this process starts at the beginning of research, and continues throughout. Clinical methodology relies heavily on keeping rigorous documentation of the scientist's observations and actions within the phenomenon. The scientist keeps journals of his or her visits about; observation of events and situations; who interacts and talks with whom, conversations, and interviews. Such journals sensitively document from within, what people are seeing, and saying from their standpoint. Once the clinical scientist is well advanced with this mapping stage, he or she will have built a large file of documents containing explanations and descriptions of the pattern of symbols and meanings that seem relevant to the phenomenon.

The next stage of the research process is identifying the key themes and interpretations of the situation. This is similar to the theory building, stage 2, of the scientific methodology. In clinical methodology, it is delayed until stage 4. This is because it believes that the theory should not be brought in from the outside, but

[4] See Ardalan (2003b), Morgan (1983, chapters 9–11), and Morgan (1985).

should make sense from the inside. The clinical scientist attempts to explain how reality is constructed. Therefore, the methodology used should be compatible with the internal mechanisms of this reality construction process.

The next stage of research is to test the validity of the theory, by bringing systematic doubt into the explanations and themes. In other words, the clinical scientist tests whether the explanations produced from the situation make sense to the people in it. This is diametrically different from the scientific methodology, since the scientist applying the scientific methodology leaves the situation with the data. Often, the statistics collected are tested through mathematical statistical techniques to bring systematic doubt.

Clinical research is not the replication of what is obvious. It might be a new, novel insight, but one which makes sense to the members in the situation. The clinical research must employ a process of systematic doubt if it is to constitute a scientific one. An unfavorable test result leads to the reformulation of the initial insight, explanation, and theory. There is a feedback loop which goes from stage 5 to stage 4; in an iterative manner. The final outcome is an explanation which is consistent with the process of reality construction within the situation. This case study is the knowledge product of clinical research.

Scientific and clinical methodologies are totally different, because they view knowledge in totally different ways. A case study may produce an insight which can be generalized to other situations. The scientific methodology is concerned with generalizability of facts, laws, and relationships. The clinical scientist looks for the generalizability of insights.

In other words, the scientific methodology is appropriate only in situations where it is possible to adequately deduce reality through the use of independent and dependent variables, and the statistical relationships among them. Deductive logic, however, is based on the assumption that variables do not carry any context-related meanings. Such interpretations of variables are often made in the natural sciences, but the same stance cannot be taken in social research. Many aspects of the social world cannot be reliably captured in the form of variables with literal properties.

Of course, it should not be implied that scientific methodology should not be used in studying the social world. Whenever meanings of variables are stable, the scientific methodology is quite appropriate. However, it might first be necessary to use the clinical methodology to establish if meanings are stable and situation-independent. If they are not, understanding these phenomena might only be implemented through the clinical methodology.

This sub-section showed that the sequence of foundational philosophy to the philosophy of science underlie the way teachers view their research method and perform research. In order to show this, the sub-section focused on how teachers view research methodologies depending on which philosophy they believe in. More specifically, it was noted that the functionalist paradigm arrives at the scientific research methodology whereas the interpretive paradigm follows the clinical research methodology.

Next, in a similar manner, it is shown that each foundational philosophy underlies how faculty view and perform their service.

3 Faculty Service

This sub-section shows that the sequence of foundational philosophy to the educational philosophy underlie the way teachers view and perform their service. In order to show this, the sub-section focuses on how teachers view the nature of their service depending on which philosophy they believe in. More specifically, it is noted that the faculty who believe in the functionalist paradigm arrive at a different set of criteria for performing their service than their counterparts believing in the interpretive paradigm. Faculty services considered are: Student Admission, Program Development, Faulty Recruitment, and Scheduling.

Student Admission: Technical Qualification vs. General Qualifications

The case methodology promotes the idea of education being of a general nature rather than a specialized one, as is the norm under the lecture methodology. In their admission policy, case teachers look to see if an applicant is only highly focused on quantitative skills, and if so, the student will probably not do well with the case methodology. This is because such students have always been trained and conditioned into rigidity, as is the norm under the lecture methodology. In contrast, the case methodology is based on flexibility. Case teachers also like to watch where the applicants are from and who they are, to be certain that their culture can be modified to make the use of cases acceptable. This is a cultural, and not a grade issue. Case teachers invite applicants in the strong cultural risk areas to arrive early and are given a special introductory program, e.g., they come and sit in on case classes during the year. And, if there are doubts that they will be able to make it, teachers do not accept them. Case teachers also look for a high academic average. But, they do look for explanations as to why an applicant's average may not be as high as others. There may be compassionate, health, or other reasons for that. It is so easy merely to use cut-off averages, as is the norm under the lecture methodology.

In the admission policy of the case methodology there is a question of desirable attributes, or prerequisites, not only as to formal education, but also as to personal characteristics, like cultural background, values, leadership, independence, social and communication skills, work experience, age, health, sex, and entrepreneurial spirit.

The case methodology admits into the program a group of students with age, geography, and undergraduate background diversity. It might accept a little less grade performance in order to get a particular kind of student.

In the case methodology, the admissions process is not just setting a hurdle in terms of grades or GMAT scores: Case teachers compose a class. They look for students who have special achievement, special experiences, creativity, leadership in their background, something unique. Such students bring a tremendously interesting set of viewpoints to the discussion. Such students do very well in the case program; the others in the class do even better because such students are there.

Program Development: Technical Program vs. Integrative Program

The lecture methodology's curriculum of professional education still follows the hierarchy of professional knowledge. First, students are exposed to the relevant basic science, then to the relevant applied science, and finally to a practicum in which they are presumed to learn to apply classroom knowledge to the problems of practice.

In the case methodology, teachers should have a clear understanding of the objectives of the program in total, and then the objectives of parts of the program, before they can design, alter, or change the teaching methods, or the faculty, or anything else. There has to be a clear central thrust that everything fits and is consistent.

In the case methodology, the program concept focuses on the objective of developing the student as opposed to displaying professional expertise of the teacher, which is the norm under the lecture methodology.

In general, program planning is not an easy task. If cases are used in the program, special considerations need to be given to the faculty selection, the type of cases, the type of introduction to cases, the class composition, and the three prerequisites: facilities, participant identification, and materials.

The case methodology believes in the program integration, which implies that there should be a lot of interaction among teachers regarding what they would like to achieve, how well they are achieving it, and how the substance of each course is related to the others. It is a great idea if Finance can introduce investment analysis, and Operations can follow with a case dealing with an investment decision. Program integration is very difficult to achieve. In program design, frequent communication among teachers is primary, and implies that the institution fosters that kind of cooperativeness and interest in cooperation. The lecture methodology, on the other hand, fosters individualism to an extreme and in that methodology cooperation is not natural.

Most case teachers are involved in linking not only a point of discussion to another point, but a class to another class, a course section to another course section, a course to other courses, and even a course to a total program. In doing so, the teacher supplies the glue that makes the whole thing stick together.

The case methodology's educational goal is not to fill students' heads with textbooks facts that they may forget as soon as they graduate, but rather to instill practical knowledge and, above all, allow them to grow into the habit of logical and correct reasoning in every subject.

The case methodology aims to prepare students in such a way that they will be able to make decisions in business. Therefore, many case teachers do not expect students to go through detailed numerical calculations that may not be necessary, as is the situation under the lecture methodology.

Students need to know what the problem is in order to select the tool. Many students do not see the problem. This must be because sometimes there is too much involvement in the technical details in class, which is inherited from the lecture methodology. This methodology allows the teachers to get into the class and show how smart he/she is. The case methodology, on the other hand, emphasizes that teachers should help students develop a disciplined mental approach to an unstructured problem.

In the first year of most case programs, teachers emphasize process learning more than anything else. They teach a certain amount of content but the key is really that mental process. To get students to think what the problem is, because if they do not define the problem, they cannot analyze it.

The case methodology believes that the course development should also be based on the nature of the students the teacher has. An example is the difference between undergraduates and MBAs. In teaching them, case teachers have quite different objectives because with the undergraduates, their lack of career identification and their conditioning as students from the time they come in represent two major differences from MBAs. Case teachers think those are more important as opposed to a list of topics that the teacher might want to cover, as is the case under the lecture methodology. Once the case teachers take those things on, the content of what they will be doing drops considerably relative to what lecture-methodology teachers might try to accomplish in the same time when offering a course of the same title. With undergraduates, for example, the case teachers do not worry nearly as much about the substance of what students learn as with MBAs. Just getting their attention regarding who and what is a manager and how they, as individuals, identify with that person is a significant challenge.

In the case methodology, the program involves a basic change in culture, away from the individual, competitive model of the lecture methodology to one in which students can succeed only through teamwork, and away from a conception of curriculum as discrete bits of factual information of the lecture methodology to one in which students are introduced to powerful synthetic, analytic structures for ideas.

Faculty Recruitment: Theory Oriented vs. Application Oriented

In the case methodology, at the time of recruiting of a new teacher, the requirement is to see to what extent the candidate knows his/her subject matter, what type of research the candidate has done, what is the subject of his/her doctoral dissertation, and so on, to see if it is of a practical nature as opposed to a highly theoretical one, which is the norm under the lecture methodology.

In the case methodology, at the time of new hiring, teachers usually look for the experience or exposure to real life, a sensitivity to the way things actually work. This is because when a case problem is looked at in class, the theories, the concepts, or analytical techniques can be applied to it. Having gone through a good case program is often a good surrogate for experience. What often happens is that candidates coming through from a DBA or a Ph.D. program have not had a good case course themselves, as is the norm under the lecture methodology. They really do not have any role model to follow.

Most teaching job applicants come out of a lecture methodology doctoral dissertation with a narrow exposure. They have a strong theoretical but weak application background. If such an applicant is hired as a case teacher then he/she will be placed in an application-oriented environment which requires a comprehensive knowledge and overview. He/she must master 50–60 complex cases and begin to develop a teaching style. He/she must develop a relationship with students, make a living, and continue to produce on the research and publications front. This is a very full plate.

It is difficult for young teachers who have not taught with cases before. It is an anxiety inducing teaching process because they are not in control. A lecture is a lot easier. With cases, the teacher has to pull out concepts, modules, as things unfold. The teacher cannot just rely on abstract concepts. He/she has to be able to integrate practice and theory and it takes a lot of experience in both. It also takes a certain amount of tolerance with ambiguities. It takes a process awareness of the audience: how to call on and use people appropriately; an awareness of his/her body and where he/she is in the classroom; how that relates to what he/she is trying to do, and to the tone and content of the case.

The case methodology believes that it takes more confidence to be able to adopt a stance that concentrates on student development more than faculty expertise display, which is the norm under the lecture methodology. It is not easy for the teacher to stand up in front of a class and to resist expressing what he/she knows is a fantastic insight, or to admit to not knowing something that someone else in class might well know. It requires that the teacher depend on something else, something other than just his/her particular and intellectual expertise. If the teacher offers solutions, or if he/she insists that there is a right answer, it might seem easier for him/her to maintain his/her status with the group he/she is working with, which is the norm under the lecture methodology.

The case methodology recruits teachers who have the capability to live in such a world and to gain their status on other dimensions. The recruits must be intellectually active, keen and, in fact, expert. But they must also have sufficient personal security that they can let the development process take place.

Teachers do not change colleagues very often. The case methodology emphasizes that a teaching group is a social organization. It takes time to establish relationships and to understand what the others are doing. It is only by working with people that you know what they do and how they handle matters and how one can match them. At the same time, one has to be careful not to form little elite cliques of teachers which has its own problems.

It is very difficult to really understand good methods for socializing new teachers into the use of cases. This may be partly because a new teacher does not know what his/her style is going to be. Colleagues may provide comments that do not make sense to the new teacher.

New case teachers really need coaching. As new instructors, they need a criticizing session, a session on how their style is effective, ineffective, and what might be useful to modify. They can improve upon their style, especially for new recruits before they get set in their ways.

When the new teachers join the institution, they first have to understand how the institution operates and what participatory education is. New teachers, especially in the case methodology, need to be offered an orientation program, i.e., a basic minimum is necessary to inform the new teachers about the ways and processes of the new institution. Most of the time, this is done informally, although some institutions organize in the beginning of each academic year an orientation session for new faculty. Spouses are included in this orientation session where presentations are made on the background of the institution, how it relates to the overall institution, and also on its various programs and research activities. Some documentation about the use of cases should also be distributed in advance of this session.

In the case methodology, teachers who recruit new colleagues look for candidates who can not only integrate theory and practice but also integrate different dimensions of classroom process and their social life.

Scheduling: Atomistic Scheduling vs. Holistic Scheduling

In the case methodology, in contrast to the lecture methodology, teachers tell other teachers what they want to teach, so that they can take advantage of the synergy, and they schedule or reschedule according to how they can best build the totality. It is a focus on what happens to the student in total, as much as it is on who does what in each session.

When scheduling, case teachers not only talk about who is teaching what classes and when (which is the norm under the lecture methodology), but they also talk about which cases. Each teacher describes his/her cases. Each teacher gives a short summary of the teaching objectives, geographical location, type of industry or government sector, reading time, and the number of exhibits. This gives all other teachers a chance to talk about obvious days where there is too much reading or too much on certain types of products, industries, or geography. Then teachers do some trades. The other really important thing is that, as some teachers talk about their cases, others think about the synergies and interactions which may be generated among different cases used in different courses. In the case methodology, it helps if teachers can have materials especially designed for the students they teach.

In the case methodology, what makes the program more successful is the fit and sequencing of materials, so that it becomes a total package. It is not that teachers should put in pieces and run a number of cases, as opposed to running a course. Each piece by each teacher within the teaching group should have its own meaning which is obviously less than the total meaning. Not only every teacher should have material that has an integrity by itself, but also with those of other teachers. The attempt is both to integrate the material and to borrow from one another and support one another by that integration. This also brings a commitment of the members of the teaching group not to let the group down. The group creates a very high peer pressure, without almost knowing it, because if teachers are going to support other teachers, or refer to other teachers, then each teacher is going to try and do a much better job with his/her material.

In the case methodology, when scheduling courses, the decision as to what topics and which teacher teaches which time slot require attention not only to the obvious sequence dictated by the logic of topic and theoretical prerequisites, but also to such factors as mixing mathematical and non-quantitative sessions, as well as teacher personalities.

In the case methodology, teachers make up with especial care the different sections of the same course. Freshmen sections are balanced on the basis of age, sex, work experience, technical background, accounting skills, and military service. Later, when grades become available, teachers add the performance in each course and reshuffle sections so that every section has strong and weak students in each course.

This sub-section showed that the sequence of foundational philosophy to the educational philosophy underlie the way teachers view and perform their service. In order to show this, the sub-section focused on how teachers view the nature of their service depending on which philosophy they believe in. More specifically, it was noted that the faculty who believe in the functionalist paradigm arrive at a different set of criteria for performing their service than their counterparts believing in the interpretive paradigm. Faculty services considered were: Student Admission, Program Development, Faulty Recruitment, and Scheduling.

4 Conclusion

This chapter discussed how, within the framework of the four paradigms, foundational philosophies underlie educational philosophies, and each educational philosophy favors a certain educational methodology, which in turn implies a certain way or method of education. More specifically, this chapter discussed how each foundational philosophy implies the specification of the type of faculty teaching, research, and service.

References

Ardalan, Kavous. 2003a. The Lecture-versus-Case Controversy: Its Philosophical Foundation. *Southwestern Economic Review* 30 (1): 99–118.

———. 2003b. Alternative Approaches Utilized in the Case Method: Their Philosophical Foundations. *Academy of Educational Leadership Journal* 30 (3): 103–120.

———. 2006. The Philosophical Foundation of the Lecture-versus-Case Controversy: Its Implications for Faculty Teaching, Research, and Service. *International Journal of Social Economics* 33 (3): 261–281.

———. 2008. The Philosophical Foundation of the Lecture-versus-Case Controversy: Its Implications for Course Goals, Objectives, and Contents. *International Journal of Social Economics* 35 (1/2): 15–34.

———. 2013. The Philosophical Foundation of the Lecture Method of Instruction and the Case Method of Instruction: Implications for Examinations. *Contemporary Issues in Education Research* 6 (1): 1–7.

———. 2015. Chapter 3: Using Entertaining Metaphors in the Introduction of the Case Method in a Case-Based Course. In *Exploring Learning and Teaching In Higher Education*, ed. Mang Li and Yong Zhao, 69–96. New York, NY: Springer.

Barnes, Louis B., Abby J. Hansen, and C. Roland Christensen. 1994. *Teaching and the Case Method: Text, Cases, and Readings*. Boston, MA: Harvard Business School.

Barrow, Robin, and Patricia White, eds. 1993. *Beyond Liberal Education: Essays in Honor of Paul H Hirst*. New York, NY: Routledge.

Barrow, Robin, and Ronald Woods. 1989. *An Introduction to Philosophy of Education*. New York, NY: Routledge.

Blake, Nigel, Paul Smeyers, Richard Smith, and Paul Standish, eds. 2002. *The Blackwell Guide to the Philosophy of Education*. New York, NY: Blackwell.

Brosio, Richard A. 1998. The Continuing Correspondence between Political Economy and Schooling: Telling the News. *Journal of Thought* 33 (3): 85–105.

Burrell, Gibson, and Gareth Morgan. 1979. *Sociological Paradigms and Organizational Analysis*. Hants, England: Gower Publishing.

Cahn, Steven M., ed. 1996. *Classic and Contemporary Readings in the Philosophy of Education*. New York, NY: McGraw-Hill College Division.

———., ed. 2009. *Philosophy of Education: The Essential Texts*. New York, NY: Routledge.

Carr, David. 2003. *Making Sense of Education: An Introduction to the Philosophy and Theory of Education*. New York, NY: Routledge.

Chambliss, J.J., ed. 1996. *Philosophy of Education: An Encyclopedia*. New York, NY: Garland Publishers.

Christensen, C. Roland, and David A. Garvin, eds. 1991. *Education for Judgment*. Cambridge, MA: Harvard Business School Press.

Cromer, Alan H. 1997. *Connected Knowledge: Science, Philosophy, and Education*. Oxford, England: Oxford University Press.

Curren, Randall R., ed. 2003. *Companion to the Philosophy of Education*. New York, NY: Blackwell.

———., ed. 2007. *Philosophy of Education: An Anthology*. Malden, MA: Blackwell.

Dooley, Arch R., and Wickham Skinner. 1977. Casing Casemethod Methods. *Academy of Management Review* 2 (2): 277–289.

Ellis, Arthur K., John J. Cogan, and Kenneth R. Howey. 1991. *Introduction to the Foundations of Education*. Upper Saddle River, NJ: Prentice Hall.

Erskine, James A., Michiel R. Leenders, and Louise A. Mauffette-Leenders. 2003. *Teaching with Cases*. 3rd ed. London, ON, Canada: Ivey Business School, University of Western Ontario, Erskine Associate Inc., and Leenders and Associates Inc..

Freedman, James O. 1996. *Idealism and Liberal Education*. Ann Harbor, MI: University of Michigan Press.

Gragg, Charles I. 1954. Because Wisdom Can't Be Told. In *The Case Method at the Harvard Business School*, ed. Malcolm P. McNair. New York, NY: McGraw-Hill.

Gutek, Gerald Lee. 2000a. *Philosophical and Ideological Perspectives on Education*. 3rd ed. New York, NY: Allyn & Bacon.

———. 2000b. *Historical and Philosophical Foundations of Education: Selected Readings*. Upper Saddle River, NJ: Prentice Hall, College Division.

———. 2003. *Philosophical and Ideological Voices in Education*. 1st ed. New York, NY: Allyn & Bacon.

Hancock, Ralph C., ed. 1999. *America, the West, and Liberal Education*. New York, NY: Rowman & Littlefield.

Hare, William, and John P. Portelli, eds. 2001. *Philosophy of Education: Introductory Readings*. 3rd ed. New York, NY: Detseling Enterprises.

Hickman, Larry, and Thomas M. Alexander, eds. 1998. *The Essential Dewey: Pragmatism, Education, Democracy*. Bloomington, IN: Indiana University Press.

Kimball, Bruce A., and Robert Orrill, eds. 1995. *The Condition of American Liberal Education: Pragmatism and a Changing Tradition*. New York, NY: College Entrance Examination Board.

Larochelle, Marie, Nadine Bednarz, and Jim Garrison, eds. 1998. *Constructivism and Education*. Cambridge, England: Cambridge University Press.

Marples, Roger, ed. 1999. *The Aims of Education*. New York, NY: Routledge.

Mauffette-Leenders, Louise A., James A. Erskine, and Michiel R. Leenders. 2007. *Learning with Cases*. 4th ed. London, ON, Canada: Ivey Publishing, Ivey Business School, University of Western Ontario.

McLaren, Peter. 1998. Revolutionary Pedagogy in Post-Revolutionary Times: Rethinking the Political Economy of Critical Education. *Educational Theory* 48 (4): 431–462.

Morgan, Gareth. 1983. *Beyond Method: Strategies for Social Research*. Beverley Hills, CA: Sage.

———. 1985. Qualitative and Action Based Research. In *Actes du Colloque, Perspective de Recherche Pour lo Praticien*, ed. Y. Allaire, M. Landry, H. Mintzberg, and G. Morgan, 81–187. Rouyn-Noranda, QC, Canada: University of Quebec at Abitibi-Temiscaminque.

Noddings, Nel. 2016. *Philosophy of Education*. Boulder, CO: Westview Press.

Orrill, Robert, ed. 1999. *Education and Democracy: Re-Imaging Liberal Learning in America*. New York, NY: College Entrance Examination Board.

Ozmon, Howard A. 2011. *Philosophical Foundations of Education*. 7th ed. New York, NY: Pearson.

Philosophy of Education Society. 2003. *Philosophy of Education 2002*. New York, NY: Philosophy of Education Society Press.

Popkewitz, Thomas S., and Lynn Fendler, eds. 1999. *Critical Theories in Education: Changing Terrains of Knowledge and Politics*. New York, NY: Routledge.

Power, Edward J. 1995. *Educational Philosophy: A History from the Ancient World to Modern America*. New York, NY: Garland Publishers.

Reynolds, John I. 1978. There's Method in Cases. *Academy of Management Review* 3 (1): 129–133.

Rocha, Samuel D. 2014. *A Primer for Philosophy and Education*. Eugene, OR: Cascade Books.

Rorty, Amelie Oksenberg, ed. 1998. *Philosophers on Education: Historical Perspectives*. New York, NY: Routledge.

Sadovnik, Alan R., Susan Semel, and Peter Cookson. 2000. *Exploring Education: An Introduction to the Foundations of Education*. 2nd ed. New York, NY: Allyn & Bacon.

Schrag, Francis. 1995. *Back to Basics: Fundamental Educational Questions Reexamined*. San Francisco, CA: Jossey-Bass Education Series.

Siegel, Harvey. 2012. *The Oxford Handbook of Philosophy of Education*. Oxford, England: Oxford University Press.

Talisse, Robert B., and D. Micah Hester. 2002. *On the Philosophy of Education*. New York, NY: Wadsworth Publishing.

Winch, Christopher, and John Gingell. 1999. *Key Concepts in the Philosophy of Education*. New York, NY: Routledge.

Educational Methodologies: Implications for Institutional Mission and Administration

This chapter discusses the implications of the first three chapters with respect to institutional mission and administration. For this purpose, this chapter brings major aspects of the first three chapters to the forefront, and elaborates on their connections and implications for the way educational methodologies are applied.[1]

The first three chapters, in essence, discussed that, within the framework of the four paradigms, foundational philosophies underlie educational philosophies, and each educational philosophy favors a certain educational methodology.[2] In other words, as one moves from the objective to the subjective end of the spectrum in Exhibit 1.1 of Chap. 1, the in-class instructional methodology favored changes from totally having a lecture-oriented educational methodology to completely having a discussion-oriented educational methodology, e.g., a case-oriented educational methodology. This chapter discusses how these educational methodologies, in turn,

[1]For this literature see Alpert (1980), Aveni (2014), Baltmale (1975), Barnett (1988), Belford (1987), Bell (1975), Bergen (1994), Berube (2006), Bess (1975), Bilsky (1954), Breneman (1994), Bryant (1983), Calkins (1969), Carr (1990), Chopp et al. (2013), Cohen and Brawer (1982), Conn (1989), Conrad and Wyer (1982), Cross and Applebaum (1998), Curren (2007), Deresiewicz (2015), Draper (2015), Farnham and Yarmolinsky (1997), Feldman (1979), Ferrall (2011), Flynn (2004), Freeman (1996), Fry and Kolb (1979), Glyer and Weeks (1998), Gray (1981), Hancock (1999), Harbert (1983), Hayes (2015), Hersh (1997), Hitchcock (1972), Hoyt (1979), Hutton (2006), Keller (1986), Kenny (1993), Keohane (1988), Kimball (1990), Koblik and Graubard (2000), Kuss (1989), Lawrason (1984), Lee and Wallerstein (2015), Litz and Bloomquist (1980), McPherson (1998), Miles (1986), Morgan (1977), Murchland (1976), Noll and Ball (1979), Nussbaum (1997), Nuttall (1980), Olson (1975), O'Neill (1985), Pascarella et al. (2005), Patterson (1984), Plaza (1999), Ridley and Gallaer (1993), Rivera (1988), Roche (2010), Roth (2015), Rudolph (1962), Ryan (1980), Sagen (1979), Schaefer (1990), Schneider (2004), Selleck (1980), Simmons et al. (1979), Simpson (1980), Snow and Collini (1998), Stark and Lowther (1988), Stark et al. (1986), Tichenor (2001), Truxal (1986), Turner (1996), Viti (1984), Wicks (1980), Winter et al. (1981), Woodward et al. (1976), Wyman (1985), and Zakaria (2015). This chapter is based on Rudolph (1962) and Alpert (1980).

[2]The difference between "educational method" and "educational methodology" should be kept in mind. The former refers to a tool, whereas the latter signifies an approach, an orientation, and a way of thinking about how to generate and apply respective educational methods.

K. Ardalan, *Case Method and Pluralist Economics*,
https://doi.org/10.1007/978-3-319-72071-5_9

determine the way such educational methodologies are applied to determine the type of institutional mission and administration. It shows, in Sect. 1, that the lecture methodology leads to a preference for an educational institution that is more like a university, and it shows, in Sect. 2, that the case methodology leads to a preference for an educational institution that is more like a college.

1 Lecture Methodology and Preference for University-Like Institution

When the university was in the ascendancy relative to the old-time college, it pursued to insinuate its values into the lives of the colleges. The badge of the university organization men—who replaced the college professor—was a degree of Doctor of Philosophy, the Ph.D. The degree signified academic respectability; professional competence; and the assurance of a certain standard of training, experience, and exposure to the ideals, the rules, the habits of scientific Germanic scholarship. In 1884, Harvard had 189 faculty members of which only 19 professors had the Ph.D. degree; Michigan had 88 faculty members of which only 6 had the Ph.D. degree. This low proportion was indicative of the short supply. By the 1890s Johns Hopkins and the newer graduate schools of arts and sciences were trying to stay ahead of the race, and by then the faculty members with Ph.D. degrees were beginning to overtake their not similarly-trained colleagues. Between 1888 and 1895 faculty members with the doctorate constituted the majority at Brown, which appointed faculty members with the degree of Ph.D. from Hopkins, Clark, Yale, Chicago, Harvard, and Brown itself, as well as Freiburg, Strasburg, and Wurzburg. Between 1900 and 1903, at Illinois College, which is a small college, all faculty members were replaced with the university-trained doctors of philosophy. In 1904, at City College in New York started to only hire professors with the Ph.D. degree; 8 years later the same policy was applied in the hiring of instructors. In 1905, the University of Illinois in order to maintain its reputation announced that future appointments to the rank of professor would be drawn exclusively from the pool of applicants who had gone through the rigors of training for the Ph.D.

Universities spent widespread efforts to hire an increasing number of professors who wore the badge of scholarship. Universities with the prestige and the funds required to pay the higher-salaried doctorate, were the first to achieve doctoral domination. The vast complex of American universities was preparing to produce all Ph.D.s that the American system of higher education could consume. In the meantime, however, some institutions such as Princeton and Dartmouth hired faculty members with honorary Ph.D. degrees. The increase in the number of faculty members with the honorary Ph.D. in the 1870s and 1880s illustrated the need everywhere for hiring Doctors. With the increase in the production of Ph.D.s came the decline in the number of honorary Ph.D.s. At its peak in 1890, 39 honorary doctorates were awarded. However, in 1910, the corresponding number of such awards was reduced to two only.

The Ph.D. degree was regarded to have strengthened the academician, to have assured effective teaching, to have become a competitive warfare among universities, and to have emphasized organization.

In the 1880s and 1890s universities were occupied with the creation of a hierarchy of professors, thereby organizing a competitive drive toward status achievement. The creation of such a hierarchy was not as much the result of the Ph.D. degree as it was the result of the following two factors. First, it was the result of the proliferation of knowledge that expanded the scope of any particular area of human understanding. Second, it was the result of the growing undergraduate and graduate enrollment. This development in the universities was similar to happenings elsewhere in American life, particularly in business, where growth led to new career patterns.

The organization of faculty members into an academic hierarchy was a conscious and necessary design to deal efficiently and effectively with problems that could not be resolved without order and organization.

Universities added the concepts of departmentalization and specialization to the faculty hierarchy. These concepts were based on the belief in the disunity of knowledge, which was never believed by the old colleges. In old colleges, a professor had the knowledge and the interests necessary to teach several subjects. But, in the newly developed universities the old unity of knowledge belonged to the past. In universities, the search for scientific truth was greatly advancing knowledge, and specialization was increasingly dividing subject areas.

Departmentalization was required by the increase in the size of the university and the increase in the size of knowledge. Departmentalization was a method of organizing a set of academic specialists into the framework of university government. That is, it provided a formal authority that was necessary to hold together the hierarchy of academic specialists, and it also provided a formal organizational channel for the expression of their interests. Departmentalization was also a development that adequately reflected the increasing division of knowledge and the rivalry for attention, for funds, for approval, that now ensued. That is, it unleashed the competitiveness for favor, public relations, and students that was similar to other organizations.

For instance, in April 1893, the Department of Biology at the University of Chicago was divided into five new departments: zoology, botany, anatomy, neurology, and physiology. It meant five new departmental chairmanships; five new little hierarchies; five new competing domains of knowledge, ambition, and interest. The splintering of departments was meant to serve scholarship and to assure the growth of knowledge. The multiplication of departments was common.

As an organization, the university was putting together its own rationale, its own mores, and its own set of characteristics. It was growing in size and becoming capable of covering its incompetencies and elevating them to the status of untouchable.

Publication became the center of interest of the new academician. The publication of each book or each article brought the faculty member closer to the promotion to a higher rank. This showed the university's embrace of the Germanic scholarship. Accordingly, academic association held annual meetings at which scholars read their research papers. This meant a shift in emphasis from teaching to research.

This secondary role of teaching was a consequence of the university idea. It was introduced to American higher education by Johns Hopkins University. The primacy given to scientific research led to the introduction of outlets for all the productivity that was the consequence of university purpose. Competition among universities forced each university to have better professors than its rivals, and a common criterion used was the annual publication page count of its professors.

The emphasis on research sent the slow performers either to the country colleges or to exploitation and strangulation within the university. Research productivity determined who was to be promoted, when, and why. The relationship between productivity and rewards was also being established in the great American business organizations. "Publish or Perish" became the slogan. By the late nineteenth century at the University of Pennsylvania professors who spent their time and energy on teaching rather than research were told to leave. In the old colleges, excellent teacher were appreciated, this was partly because effective teaching might lead students to self-discovery and self-mastery. The university fed on research, it regurgitated research, and it promoted research. With research publication the excitement of advancing the frontiers of knowledge would come. Without research, there would be no departments, no departmental chairpersons, no hierarchy, but only teachers. When research publication requirement became an established routine in the university it would not break loose from the chains of the organization.

The research emphasis created institutions such as: learned journals, learned societies, university presses, and sabbatical leaves. In 1877, Johns Hopkins founded The American Journal of Mathematics and led the way for the universities. This was soon followed by chemistry, biology, physiology, psychology, and philology at Johns Hopkins. The University of Chicago founded journals in political economy, geology, Hebrew, astrophysics, sociology, theology, and classics. In 1898, University of Chicago journals printed a total of 150,000 copies. By 1904 Columbia was producing 35 serial publications. The production of research journals soon became one of the criteria for judging the respectability of the universities.

Learned societies produced journals that provided another outlet for research publication. The older learned societies—such as the American Philosophical Society of 1743, the American Academy of Arts and Sciences of 1780, and the American Association for the Advancement of Science of 1848 that testified to the early attraction of science—in the past had served a more general purpose and then were joined by societies of faculty who were specialized in a fragmented area of knowledge and gave scholars a means of exchanging their energies and their discoveries. Among the new wave of learned societies the American Philological Association was founded first in 1869. The American Chemical Society was founded second in 1877, the Modern Language Association was founded in 1883, the American Historical Association was founded in 1884, the American Economic Association was founded in 1885, the American Mathematical Society and the Geological Society of America, both were founded in 1888.

The annual meetings of these associations were used to read and discuss research papers, to introduce measures to formalize and standardize their particular field of knowledge, to protect their interests from rival disciplines, and to institutionalize the annual meeting as a market place for university presidents and departmental chairmen who were looking to hire new Ph.D.s. The annual meetings illustrated to the shrinking of distances, and they gathered groups of specialists who spoke in their scientific language, shared their discoveries, and returned to their campuses with a renewed sense of belonging.

University presses were formally organized by the larger, more affluent universities in order to enhance the research environment. In 1878, an office at Johns Hopkins was set up for publishing purposes, and in 1888 that office was required to publish all doctoral dissertations. In this way, the publication responsibility of the university was increased. By 1891 this activity appeared under the Johns Hopkins University Press, which was the first university press in the country. Chicago started its own in 1892, and Columbia and the University of California did theirs in 1893. Early in the twentieth century, Princeton, Yale, and Harvard each had their own university press. By 1916 the University of Chicago press had published 850 titles, 850 contributions to knowledge, 850 confirmation to reputation and promotion.

Sabbatical years and paid leaves of absence were instituted in the 1890s to facilitate research and publication, and to de-emphasize the teaching function. During these months, faculty members were relieved from other university duties to happily perform research and produce a fresh batch of articles, a startling new laboratory discovery, and a book in the university's series of scholarly studies. Such became the new life of the academic man.

For the academic man, who worked in this organizational apparatus, his reputation in the profession was more important than any commitment to a particular university. The organization with such standards, processes, and attributes produced the academic man who was loyal to professional organization but indifferent to the fate of the university at which he was working and the learning of the students whom he was teaching.

The move from the old-time college organization to the new university organization resulted in the loss of qualities that the old-time college enjoyed: the sense of unity, the sense of commitment, and the sense of close relationship. Therefore, universities directed a good deal of efforts to find alternative replacements for such lost qualities. As a result there appeared on university campuses faculty clubs and academic robes, which enhanced immeasurably the morale of the academic man. These arrangements to some extent enabled professors to form their group identity in society.

At the commencement, professors appeared in academic robes that tied the new academicians to the ancient tradition of learning, and underlined their unity and their belonging. The commencement ritual that had served the multitude of purposes of the old-time American college was redirected to serve a new purpose for the American university: the exhibition of the newly formed academic professionals organized in the order of their rank and embellished with their badges of merit.

The faculty club was organized to regain the institutional cohesiveness that the expanding size of the university made almost impossible. Participation in the faculty club was required of any self-respecting organization man. In the social setting of the faculty club, the interests of the organization were to be advanced; and it was hoped that some of the casual spirit and good fun of the old-time college could be recaptured.

The rise of the idea of university, as discussed above, played an essential role in achieving intellectual maturity by the United States. Although tremendous losses were incurred in personal security and psychological certainty due to the professionalization of the college professor, magnificent gains were also made: the tremendous conquest of ignorance, the substantial increase in the number of Americans who enjoyed intellectual pursuits, and the employment of knowledge for the service of man.

The new university professors had their own orientation. Intellect—rather than the piety of the old-time college professor—was their touchstone, and ignorance was their challenge. Their dedication to learning and advancement of knowledge made them look at times oblivious to the world around them.

Academic freedom and tenure are two additional very important gains which were made as a consequence of the formation of the idea of university. These new principles were introduced when academicians noted the disjunction between their research and society. Academicians also noted that correcting this disjunction often brought them into conflict with powerful interest groups that benefitted from the status quo, which was what the academicians sought to improve. For instance, this conflict could be with the business community, whose importance to the universities was made clear every time a new building appeared on the expanding campuses. Consequently, the fundamental standards of academic freedom and tenure were developed that strongly enhanced the capacity of the university to support the life of the mind.

The old-time colleges also discussed the question of academic freedom. This was because sectarianism had at times placed the charge of heresy on the academic community. These experiences, however, did not develop into principles to guide the life of the colleges. But, the old-time colleges had the freedom not to follow the crowd because the colleges were the preservers of the ancient tradition. Accordingly, colleges were able to defend themselves from outside attacks and to stand for unpopular causes, including the classical curriculum. The university system, with the scientific point of view and with the tradition of the German university, will strongly and purposefully benefit from the idea of academic freedom in America.

The scientific point of view, symbolized by Darwinism, victoriously confronted sectarian interests and advanced a special conception of truth and an approach for tolerating error. In effect, it invested academic freedom with an ethic. It vastly promoted secularism and evolution among scientists.

Academic freedom defined a research climate in which the scientific point of view was fundamental and the professors developed a common respect for the requirements of scholarship. The scientific method created a research climate that encouraged tolerance for error, preference for experiment and search for the unknown, indifference to tradition and inherited truth, and continuous inquiry and continuous verification. Academic freedom then rested on the evolutionary judgment and changing truth that reflected the scholar in the laboratory or at work on his manuscripts. Academic freedom would be reinforced by academicians through following the principles that guided research in the German universities, which in many different ways inspired the new American universities. For the German university professor the academic freedom meant freedom for the student and freedom for the professor. Freedom for the student meant the absence of administrative coercion. That is, the student was free to move from one university to another, to take the courses he chose, to live where he wanted, and to be free from all those restrictions that were prevalent in the English and American colleges and were obstacles to dedicated study and research. Freedom for the professor meant the right to freedom of inquiry and the right to freedom of teaching. That is, the right to study and the right to report on his findings.

The principles of academic tenure were introduced in the early decades of the twentieth century. These principles set the terms of professorial office that would protect both the academic freedom and the professor at his work. In 1878, one of the trustees at Cornell demanded the right for the Cornell board to fire professors in the same way that businessmen fire factory workers. In opposition, the academicians demanded greater job security, rank and seniority and salary schedules, rules governing permanent and temporary appointments, conditions conducive to scholarly work, and collective commitment to the principles of academic freedom. In this process, the professor was becoming professionalized, as they were successfully trying to bring university presidents and board of trustees under increasing pressure to recognize their obligations to the community of free scholars.

In 1915, the American Association of University Professors was established. It was a professional society that was most concerned with the development and protection of standards of academic freedom and tenure. Its establishment revealed the birth of the academic man in America. Now the organization man, the university model, had an organization to safeguard him against the organization itself, and to sustain him in man's ideal endeavor of the pursuit of truth and the conquest of ignorance.

2 Case Methodology and Preference for College-Like Institution

Starting in the second half of the nineteenth century, the higher education has experienced the rise to dominance of the academic profession and of the university as its principal institutional expression. The university rose in the nineteenth century and succeeded in the twentieth century. It involved the professionalization of academic life that promoted the research scholar and the research university to domination in higher education. This "academic revolution" influenced all institutions, including those designed to avoid its impact.

This "academic revolution" reflected professionalism as the dominant cultural and organizational concept in higher education. However, such professionalism has its strengths and weaknesses. Since the inception of the professionalization of higher education, there have been movements, such as "general education," that sought to expose these weaknesses and to promote alternative conception of professionalism with much different implications for curricula, faculty-student relationships, and the nature of faculty work and faculty careers.

The general education movement reached its peak during the 1930–1945 period. Its insights and principles constituted the bases for many curricular reforms and founding of new colleges in the 1960s. Colleges, such as Hampshire, Ramapo, Santa Cruz, Evergreen, and New College, came to being in the attempt to resurrect these principles and give them new meaning.

Hampshire College, for instance, was created to challenge, but not abolish, the dominant definition and forms of professionalism in higher education. It was consciously created to become a distinctive liberal arts college that opposed the influence of graduate and professional schools on undergraduate liberal arts education. It intended to avoid the extremes of "hierarchy and equalitarianism" or "specialization and freedom of choice." In this way, Hampshire College becomes a useful case study of an alternative conception of professionalism and its implications for curricular issues, student-faculty interactions, and the nature of academic work.

Professionalism started during the second half of the nineteenth century and took over law, medicine, and university teaching. Professionalization changed these occupations. More specifically, it changed their nature and underlying values that governed their practice, defined their status, and regulated their accessibility to new members. In this context, "Professional" meant someone who had gone through a difficult and long process to master an esoteric, but useful body of systematic knowledge; and had been theoretically trained before entering an apprenticeship or a practice; and had received a degree or license from a recognized institution. A "practitioner professional" meant someone with technical competence, superior skill, and a high quality of performance. "Professionals" referred to people who intended to serve some higher purpose rather than their personal gain; and who had developed codes of behavior and mechanisms of enforcement in order to ensure their ethos of service.

Professionals were given authority based on their expertise in some esoteric body of knowledge. They were given autonomy over setting standards of performance. They were given power to have control over the selection, training, and quality of new members. The culture of professionalism required amateurs to trust the integrity of trained persons, whose power was to be regarded as sacred and charismatic. Only professionals were privileged to enter and control the magic circle of scientific knowledge because only they were specialized by training and indoctrination. Amateurs were obligated to appreciate the professionals in the name of nature's universality.

The professionalization of higher education changed the conception of faculty members and their role with respect to both the college and the student. It was after professionalization that faculty members represented a distinct culture and a particular expertise to be transmitted to students. Before professionalization, the president dominated the faculty members, who were expected to follow the leader's moral and character and to develop and grow a coherent philosophy of education for all the students. They were neither expected to engage in research and scholarship, nor to represent expertise in a specialized field of study. The authority of colleges and their faculty members emanated from a religious and moral consensus, i.e., shared Christian values and beliefs in proper behavior.

But, by 1869 and the presidency of Charles Eliot at Harvard College, the higher education began to be dominated by a new mode of authority. Faculty members began to identify themselves with intellectual disciplines, to organize themselves into departments, and to base the development of their curriculum on the principle of "electives." Faculty members gained recognition for their expertise, specialization, and research. They defined the standards of performance in terms of loyalty to impersonal, professional standards of scholarship rather than to any person or institution. By 1920, professionalism started in addition to mean the guarantee of autonomy and academic freedom through the system of tenure. These characteristics were crystallized in the institutional form known as research-based university, which prepared undergraduate students for graduate work in the arts and sciences or professional school.

By 1945, the academic revolution influenced even those colleges which were founded in the 1930s as an alternative to the dominance of specialization and research. In Antioch College, for instance, from 1930 to 1950 the percentage of faculty members with Ph.D. increased from 30 to 60%. Moreover, in the 1940s, the young faculty members who were more interested in and dedicated to scholarship objected to the Antioch idea of a holistic education and close faculty-student relationship. Reed College moved from its exceeding emphasis on teaching toward the combination of teaching and research that seemed justified for effective recruitment in the academic market place.

However, the general education movement only partially accepted the dominant definition of professionalism. Its conception of professionalism and institutional forms differed significantly from the research-oriented faculty and university. It did not regard specialization, research, and pre-professional training to be the defining elements of undergraduate education. It argued for a liberal arts program that would expose students to a broad learning experience and would treat them as whole persons who play a major role in their own intellectual development. It viewed faculty members primarily as teachers of students rather than as experts in a specialized field of knowledge.

In the general education movement there were two different strands, each with a different institutional expression. The more conservative strand of the movement argued for a complete return to the old New England College. Those who supported this return to the old order, such as Robert Hutchins, Stringfellow Barr, and Scott Buchanan, sought a fixed and common curriculum, which would be required of all students. They advocated the restoration of a broad educational experience that avoided specialization but cultivated the fundamental elements of a wise and inquiring intellect. Faculty members were not to be grounded in a single discipline and dedicated to research. They were, instead, to be generalists—knowledgeable in broad areas of knowledge—and dedicated to the world of ideas.

The more liberal strand of general education movement also advocated a broad learning experience and a required curriculum in the first 2 years. However, it placed less stress on a prescribed curriculum and more on an educational program which would be developed by the student to suit their individual needs and interests. It directed its educational program toward interdisciplinary study, contemporary society, and practical experience. It preferred faculty members who were less likely to be devoted to research and scholarship and more to teaching and close faculty-student relationships.

Although the general education movement was important in American higher education, by the 1950s the emphasis on the disciplines and specialization had turned college education into a preparatory stage leading to professional life. In addition, the academic landscape was formed by requirements, prerequisites, and standardized majors. But, in the 1950s and early 1960s some of the principles of general education started to constitute the basis for an attack on professionalism in higher education as a form of oppression.

The opposition to the oppressive character of professionalism was founded on the beliefs of the liberal strand of the old general education movement, which was represented by colleges such as Antioch, Goddard, and Bennington. More specifically, the basis of their opposition was formed by their belief in the freedom of choice, students taking charge of their own education, and priority of teaching over research. A new skepticism about professionalism also added greater impetus to democratizing academic life, to sharing authority within the college, and to a more collaborative, egalitarian relationship between faculty and students.

The general education movement opposed the dominant definition and forms of professionalism by departing from the ideas, values, and beliefs prevailing in the academic culture. It also gave new meaning to those aspects it had in common with the prevailing dominant culture. Its beliefs and values opposed the research-oriented, professional-minded academic culture because it was teacher and student oriented. Its evaluation system placed less emphasis on "publish or perish" and more on student evaluation and teaching performance. It regarded college education not as a preparatory stage for graduate and professional school, but as an end in itself.

The general education movement was the proponent of freedom for both faculty members and students so that they would be their own masters in choosing what they should teach or learn. Freedom was defined as non-interference from others and greater freedom of choice and self-direction that would make students responsible for their own education and correspondingly would make educational programs geared towards meeting the particular needs and purposes of each student. Students would experience broad areas in both their academic and non-academic lives without anything prescribed by the faculty or the college. Within such broad areas of freedom, the students would evaluate alternative choices, decide, and take responsibility for their own education. Faculty members and students who would be freed from the constraints of authority and independently using their own resources, would find and achieve new levels of energy, creativity, and truth.

It is instructive to consider a case study, such as the case of Hampshire College. The New College Plan, written in 1958 by faculty from Amherst, Smith, Mount Holyoke, and the University of Massachusetts formed the basis for planning Hampshire College. This plan stressed the freedom of the faculty members and students from unnecessary structures and requirements in order to unleash the talent and creativity of the faculty members and students that come as a result of the freedom of choice.

The New College Plan was a liberal attack on professionalism. It criticized the idea that treats the course as the central unit defining the curriculum. The plan interpreted the course as the "arena of teacher power" and prescribed that both the faculty members and the students should free themselves from its tyrannical hold. In this way the faculty member would be liberated from the demands of specialization and the students would be liberated from the need to shape their learning to the demands of the faculty. Students would take charge of their own learning and faculty members would share authority with the student regarding the planning and execution of the student's academic program. The New College Plan emphasized teaching and student-centered education. It promoted fundamental values such as individualism, freedom of choice, and self-determination within a competitive market. However, it gave primacy to means, rather than ends. Therefore, it accepted some aspects of the dominant conception of professionalism, such as disciplines, research and scholarship, and pre-professional education. Students would work with faculty members in an apprentice relationship, i.e., learning the disciplines by closely working with the faculty member in practice.

The Making of a College, which was published in 1966, presented the ideas, values, and beliefs that would shape Hampshire College. It continued the basic commitment to freedom of choice and independence that formed the basis of the New College Plan. In addition, students and faculty members would be having a colleague relationship, such that both students and faculty members would become learners and teach each other.

Faculty members would act neither as narrow specialists nor as department-based disciplinarians. Hampshire College would consist of three interdisciplinary schools: humanities and arts, social science, and natural science and mathematics. Faculty members would enter into colleague relationships across disciplines to develop broad intellectual interests and areas of expertise. This would be supported by the interdisciplinary organization of Hampshire College and the emphasis on individual student freedom of choice.

The course was also abandoned as the main unit of the academic program. Instead, Hampshire College's examination system would evaluate students' accomplishments as they would go through the three divisions of study. Courses would be designed for students to gain ideas and skills in order to be able to develop and present material for examinations. In addition, students could gain ideas and skills through non-course experiences, such as field study and independent study. Course work and course examinations would not be required and course would not play the central defining role in a student's academic program. It would even be possible for students to receive their degrees from Hampshire College by successfully passing the examinations but without taking and passing any courses.

The examination system is based on a contract between the faculty members and the students. This is in contrast to the familiar course-based faculty-and-student mutual obligations that determine the student's academic progress. In Hampshire College, academic progress is determined through the examination system, in which a committee of faculty and a student develop a contract that specifies the extent of the student's work, the time-frame of the work, the method of examination, and the faculty members who would guide and evaluate the student's work.

Hampshire College has placed even greater emphasis on interdisciplinary work than the major planning documents. These documents based the academic structure on interdisciplinary schools rather than discipline-based departments. In Hampshire College, faculty and students do not perform their work in discrete disciplines but rather in the area where disciplines overlap and the exploration of particular issues and problems benefit from the contributions of several disciplines.

Hampshire College has made substantial changes in the meaning of professionalism, the basis of professional authority, the nature of the academic structure, and the character of faculty-student relationships.

Hampshire College's academic system defines professionalism differently. Its academic program is characterized by individualized relations and personalized advising and tutorials that significantly alter the faculty's responsibilities and work life. The faculty member works less as a corporate body than as an independent professional.

The faculty member's work life involves continuous one-to-one interactions, which means the application of general principles to particular cases. That is, the students present their concern and problem, the faculty members perform assessment; the students react, faculty members further assess; they negotiate and agree on what to do, how to follow-up, and how to evaluate. This emphasizes the authority of the faculty member both as expert and judge and as a representative of the institution who evaluates whether a student has fulfilled all the requirements for graduation.

The independent professional role is played more as a general practitioner than a specialist. Faculty members consult students daily on various intellectual topics and subject areas. The broad range of student interests requires a broad range of faculty expertise and competence, i.e., faculty member's interdisciplinary teaching, program development, and research. In addition, each faculty member academically advises many students at different levels of academic progress, ability, and need, which means that the faculty member plays different roles with different students. It also means that at different times with the same student the faculty member must act as adviser, friend, registrar, advocate, counselor, task-master, or evaluator. Faculty member must both have a broad repertoire, and know which role to play with which students.

3 Conclusion

This chapter discussed how, within the framework of the four paradigms, foundational philosophies underlie educational philosophies, and each educational philosophy favors a certain educational methodology, which in turn implies a certain way or method of education. More specifically, this chapter discussed how each foundational philosophy implies the specification of the type of institutional mission and administration.

References

Alpert, Richard M. 1980. Professionalism and Educational Reform: The Case of Hampshire College. *Journal of Higher Education* 51 (5): 497–518.

Aveni, Anthony. 2014. *Class Not Dismissed: Reflections on Undergraduate Education and Teaching the Liberal Arts*. Boulder, CO: University Press of Colorado.

Baltmale, Louis F. 1975. Career Education and Elitism. Paper presented at the Annual Meeting of the American Association of Community and Junior Colleges, Seattle, WA, April 13–16, 1975.

Barnett, Steve. 1988. Reframing and the Liberal Arts: Creative Decision-Making in the Global Marketplace. Working Paper 3, Corporate Council on the Liberal Arts, New York, NY.

Belford, Fontaine Maury. 1987. Liberal Arts and Leadership. *Liberal Education* 73 (2): 16–19.

Bell, T. H. 1975. The Importance of Vocational Education in the Total Education Picture. Speech prepared for the National Convention of the Future Farmers of America, November 13, 1975.

Bergen, Timothy J., Jr. 1994. The Greeks and the Education of Humanity. *Journal of General Education* 43 (1): 32–43.

Berube, Michael. 2006. *What's Liberal about the Liberal Arts?: Classroom Politics and "Bias" in Higher Education*. New York, NY: W.W. Norton & Company.

Bess, James L. 1975. Is Vocational Education the Wave of the Future? *Change* 7 (9): 46–48.

Bilsky, Manuel. 1954. Liberal Education as 'Philosophy'. *Journal of Higher Education* 25 (4): 191–196, 226–227.

Breneman, David W. 1994. *Liberal Arts Colleges: Thriving, Surviving, or Endangered?* Washington, DC: Brookings Institute.

Bryant, Paul. 1983. Reasserting the Value of the Humanities. *CEA Forum* 13 (3–4): 5–9.

Calkins, Hugh. 1969. What the Public Expects of Vocational-Technical Education. Remarks at dedication of the Center for Vocational and Technical Education, Ohio State University, September 4, 1969.

Carr, David L. 1990. Responsibility in Professional Life. U.S. Department of Education, Educational Resources Information Center (ERIC).

Chopp, Rebecca, Susan Frost, and Daniel H. Weiss, eds. 2013. *Remaking College: Innovation and the Liberal Arts*. Baltimore, MD: Johns Hopkins University Press.

Cohen, Arthur M., and Florence B. Brawer. 1982. *The American Community College*. Los Angeles, CA: ERIC Clearinghouse for Junior Colleges.

Conn, Robert H. 1989. Rear Guard on the Escalator: The Struggle to Protect the Liberal Arts Core in Higher Education. Occasional Papers, No. 80, United Methodist Board of Higher Education and Ministry, Nashville, TN.

Conrad, C., and J. Wyer. 1982. *Seven Trends in Liberal Learning*. Washington, DC: Association of Governing Boards of Universities and Colleges.

Cross, Christopher T., and Kathy Applebaum. 1998. Stretching Students' Minds Is Basic Education. *Educational Leadership* 55 (6): 74–76.

Curren, Randall R., ed. 2007. *Philosophy of Education: An Anthology*. Malden, MA: Blackwell.

Deresiewicz, William. 2015. *Excellent Sheep: The Miseducation of the American Elite and the Way to a Meaningful Life*. New York, NY: Free Press.

Draper, Chris. 2015. *Rediscovering Our Future: The Modern Liberal Arts Education Manifesto 2015*. Des Moines, IA: Press.

Farnham, Nicholas, and Adam Yarmolinsky. 1997. *Rethinking Liberal Education*. New York, NY: Oxford University Press.

Feldman, Marvin. 1979. What Is Job Creation? Why Is It Important to Vocational Education? Paper presented at the Jobs Creation Conference, Somerset, NJ, November 1, 1979.

Ferrall, Victor E. 2011. *Liberal Arts at the Brink*. Cambridge, MA: Harvard University Press.

Flynn, Thomas F., ed. 2004. *Report of a Symposium on the Liberal Arts and Business*. Washington, DC: Council of Independent Colleges.

Freeman, James O. 1996. *Idealism and Liberal Education*. Ann Arbor, MI: University of Michigan Press.

Fry, Ronald, and David Kolb. 1979. Experiential Learning Theory and Learning Experiences in Liberal Arts Education. *New Directions for Experiential Learning* 6: 79–92.

Glyer, Diana, and David L. Weeks, eds. 1998. *The Liberal Arts in Higher Education: Challenging Assumptions, Exploring Possibilities*. Lanham, MD: University Press of America.

Gray, Hanna Holborn. 1981. The Liberal Arts Revisited: Eighth David D. Henry Lecture. President's Office, University of Illinois, Urbana, IL.

Hancock, Ralph C., ed. 1999. *America, the West, and Liberal Education*. Lanham, MD: Rowman & Littlefield.

Harbert, Donald L. 1983. Vocational Education as Liberal Arts Education. *Journal of Studies in Technical Careers* 5 (2): 143–150.

Hayes, William. 2015. *The Fate of Liberal Arts in Today's Schools and Colleges*. Lanham, MD: Brown and Littlefield.

Hersh, Richard H. 1997. Intentions and Perceptions: A National Survey of Public Attitudes towards Liberal Arts Education. *Change* 29 (2): 16–23.

Hitchcock, James. 1972. The University and the Future. *Journal of General Education* 24 (1): 25–35.

Hoyt, Kenneth B. 1979. *Refining the Career Education Concept, Part IV: Monographs on Career Education*. Washington, DC: Office of Career Education.

Hutton, Todd S. 2006. The Conflation of Liberal and Professional Education: Pipedream, Aspiration, or Nascent Reality? *Liberal Education* 92 (4): 54–59.

Keller, Jo Young. 1986. Tensions between Training Career Professionals and Educating Persons for Lifelong Learning. Paper presented at the Annual Meeting of the Central States Speech Association, Cincinnati, OH, April 17–19, 1986.

Kenny, Shirley Strumm. 1993. Using Business Leaders for Academic Planning. *Planning for Higher Education* 21 (3): 21–26.

Keohane, Nannerl O. 1988. Creativity, the Classics, and the Corporation. *Liberal Education* 74 (1): 31–35.

Kimball, Roger. 1990. *Tenured Radicals: How Politics Has Corrupted Our Higher Education*. New York, NY: Harper & Row.

Koblik, Steven, and Stephen R. Graubard, eds. 2000. *Distinctively American: The Residential Liberal Arts College*. New Brunswick, NJ: Transaction Publishers.

Kuss, Hans J. 1989. Humanizing Occupational Education: Outcomes. Paper presented at the Midwest Conference of Academic Affairs Administrators, St. Louis, MI, November 30–December 2, 1989.

Lawrason, Robin E. 1984. Promoting the Liberal Arts and Instructional Development. In *Instructional Development: The State of the Art, Volume II*.

Lee, Richard E., and Immanuel Wallerstein, eds. 2015. *Overcoming the Two Cultures: Science versus the Humanities in the Modern World-System*. Boulder, CO: Paradigm Publishers.

Litz, Charles E., and Betty Bloomquist. 1980. Adult Education: Resolution of the Liberal-Vocational Debate? *Lifelong Learning: The Adult Years* 3 (8): 12–15.

McPherson, Michael S. 1998. The Economic Value of a Liberal Arts Education. *About Campus* 3 (4): 13–17.

Miles, Sue L. 1986. *The Vocational-Liberal Arts Controversy: Looking Backwards*. Sugar Grove, IL: Waubonsee Community College.

Morgan, Richard Lyon. 1977. A New Dimension in Community College Education: John Dewey Revisited. *Community College Social Science Journal* 1 (2): 74–77.

Murchland, Bernard. 1976. The Eclipse of the Liberal Arts. *Change* 8 (10): 22–62.

Noll, Donald L., and Harold E. Ball. 1979. Decision-Making in the Eighties. *College Store Journal* 47 (1): 37–49.

Nussbaum, Martha C. 1997. *Cultivating Humanity: A Classical Defense of Reform in Liberal Education*. Cambridge, MA: Harvard University Press.

Nuttall, Edmund C. 1980. Philosophy of Liberal Arts Education and Its Relationship to Life. *Journal of Thought* 15 (2): 39–46.

Olson, Paul A. 1975. *The Liberal Arts and Career Education: A Look at the Past and the Future*, Monograph on Career Education Series. Washington, DC: Office of Career Education.

O'Neill, Joseph P. 1985. The Future of the Liberal Arts. Paper presented at the Annual Meeting of the College Entrance Examination Board, New York, NY, October 30, 1985.

Pascarella, Ernest T., Gregory C. Wolniak, Tricia A. Seifert, Ty M. Cruce, and Charles F. Blaich. 2005. *Liberal Arts Colleges and Liberal Arts Education: New Evidence on Impact, ASHE Higher Education Report: Volume 31, Number 3*. Hoboken, NJ: Wiley.

Patterson, W. Brown. 1984. Defining the Educated Person: From Harvard to Harvard. *Soundings* 66 (2): 192–217.

Plaza, Oscar. 1999. Technology Education versus Liberal Arts Education? Paper presented at the Annual Conference of the International Technology Education Association, Indianapolis, IN, March 28–30, 1999.

Ridley, Dennis R., and Douglas C. Gallaer. 1993. Confirming Career Relevance in the Liberal Arts. *Journal of Career Planning and Employment* 54 (1): 40–43, 66–68.

Rivera, Miguela. 1988. Rounding Out Technical Training with Liberal Arts. *Winds of Change* 3 (1): 9–11.

Roche, Mark William. 2010. *Why Choose the Liberal Arts?* Notre Dame, IN: University of Notre Dame Press.

Roth, Michael S. 2015. *Beyond the University: Why Liberal Education Matters*. New Haven, CT: Yale University Press.

Rudolph, Frederick. 1962. *The American College and University: A History*. New York, NY: Alfred A Knopf.

Ryan, Mark B. 1980. Doldrums in the Ivies: A Proposal Restoring Self Knowledge to a Liberal Education. *Change* 12 (8): 32–38.

Sagen, H. Bradley. 1979. Careers, Competencies, and Liberal Education. *Liberal Education* 65 (2): 150–166.

Schaefer, William D. 1990. *Education without Compromise: From Chaos to Coherence in Higher Education*. San Francisco, CA: Jossey-Bass Publishers.

Schneider, Carol Geary. 2004. *Practicing Liberal Education: Formative Themes in the Re-Invention of Liberal Learning*. Washington, DC: Association of American Colleges and Universities.

Selleck, Laura. 1980. *The University Graduate and the Marketplace*. Toronto, ON, Canada: Council of Ontario Universities.

Simmons, Adele, Susan J. Kupper, Naomi S. Baron, Marcia Conner, and David Graham Burnett. 1979. Is a Core Curriculum the Best Way to Educate Students to Deal with the Future? *Change* 11 (2): 26–28.

Simpson, Michael. 1980. The Case for the Liberal Arts. *Liberal Education* 66 (3): 315–320.

Snow, Charles Percy, and Stefan Collini. 1998. *Two Cultures*. Cambridge, England: Cambridge University Press.

Stark, Joan S., and Malcolm A. Lowther. 1988. *Strengthening the Ties that Bind: Integrating Undergraduate Liberal and Professional Study*. Ann Arbor, MI: Regents of the University of Michigan.

Stark, Joan S., Malcolm A. Lowther, and Bonnie M. K. Hagerty. 1986. *Responsive Professional Education: Balancing Outcomes and Opportunities*. ASHE-ERIC Higher Education Report No. 3, Association for the Study of Higher Education (ASHE), Washington, DC.

Tichenor, Stuart. 2001. Technical Training and General Education: Can We Really Provide Both? U.S. Department of Education, Educational Resources Information Center (ERIC), December 14, 2001.

Truxal, John G. 1986. Learning to Think Like an Engineer: Why, What, and How? *Change* 18 (2): 10–19.

Turner, Frank M., ed. 1996. *The Idea of a University: John Henry Newman*. New Haven, CT: Yale University Press.

Viti, Ethel L. 1984. Liberal Arts Learning for Life. *PTA Today* 9 (4): 14–15.

Wicks, Katherine E. 1980. In Defense of the Relevance of a University Education. *School Guidance Worker* 35 (3): 5–10.

Winter, David G., David C. McClelland, and Abigail J. Stewart. 1981. *A New Case for the Liberal Arts*. San Francisco, CA: Jossey-Bass Publishers.

Woodward, Barbara L., et al. 1976. A Case for the Liberal Arts College. *Journal of National Association of College Admissions Counselors* 20 (4): 16–22.

Wyman, Thomas H. 1985. Liberal Learning and the Corporation. Speech presented by the recipient of Dickinson College's Benjamin Rush Award for Humanistic Values in Corporate Life, Carlisle, PA, November 14, 1985.

Zakaria, Fareed. 2015. *In Defense of a Liberal Education*. New York, NY: W.W. Norton and Company.

Educational Methods

This chapter builds on the discussions made in the first three chapters, distinguishes between educational methodology and educational method, shows that different educational methodologies use a given educational method differently, and argues against any attempt at ranking the lecture method in comparison with the case method.[1]

More specifically, Chap. 1 discussed how any foundational philosophy can be positioned on a continuum formed by four paradigms: functionalist, interpretive, radical humanist, and radical structuralist, as shown in Exhibit 1.1. Chapter 2 discussed the major extant educational philosophies, namely: realism; idealism and pragmatism; reconstructionism; and Marxism; and noted that they respectively correspond to the four paradigms, namely: functionalist; interpretive; radical humanist; and radical structuralist, as shown in Exhibits 2.1 and 2.2. Chapter 2 also noted that each educational philosophy underlies a certain instructional methodology, as shown in the bottom half of Exhibit 2.3. It was also noted that there is a difference between "educational method" and "educational methodology." The former refers to a tool, whereas the latter signifies an approach, an orientation, and a way of thinking about how to generate and apply educational methods. That is, educational methodologies determine the way such educational methodologies are applied to determine various aspects of the way education is performed. Chapter 2,

[1]For this literature see Ardalan (2003a, 2003b, 2006, 2008, 2013, 2015), Aveni (2014), Barnes et al. (1994), Barrow and White (1993), Barrow and Woods (1989), Blake et al. (2002), Brosio (1998), Burrell and Morgan (1979), Cahn (1996 2009), Carr (2003), Chambliss (1996), Christensen and Garvin (1991), Cromer (1997), Curren (2003, 2007), Dooley and Skinner (1977), Ellis et al. (1991), Erskine et al. (2003), Freedman (1996), Gragg (1954), Gutek (2000a, 2000b, 2003), Hancock (1999), Hare and Portelli (2001), Hickman and Alexander (1998), Kimball and Orrill (1995), Larochelle et al. (1998), Marples (1999), Mauffette-Leenders et al. (2007), McLaren (1998), Morgan (1983, 1985), Noddings (2016), Orrill (1999), Ozmon (2011), Philosophy of Education Society (2003), Popkewitz and Fendler (1999), Power (1995), Reynolds (1978), Rocha (2014), Rorty (1998), Sadovnik et al. (2000), Schrag (1995), Siegel (2012), Talisse and Hester (2002), and Winch and Gingell (1999). This chapter is based on Ardalan (2006), Erskine et al. (2003), and Mauffette-Leenders et al. (2007). This chapter is based on Ardalan (2003b).

K. Ardalan, *Case Method and Pluralist Economics*,
https://doi.org/10.1007/978-3-319-72071-5_10

furthermore, introduced the idea that when any instructional method is utilized, it is used within the bounds of that instructional methodology, educational philosophy, and foundational philosophy, as shown in the top half of Exhibit 2.3. That is, different educational methodologies use a given educational method differently.

This chapter elaborates on the way any educational methodology uses instructional methods within the bounds of its educational philosophy and foundational philosophy. This is shown by the example of the use of the case method.

This chapter also emphasizes that any attempt at ranking the lecture method in comparison with the case method translates into the ranking their underlying educational methodologies, educational philosophies, and foundational philosophies. It, however, argues that such attempt should not be made. This is because, the ranking of philosophies is self-defeating due to the fact that each philosophy is coherent and consistent based on its own underlying set of assumptions, and that there does not exist an independent point of reference to be used for evaluation and ranking. That is, this chapter argues that the existing lecture-versus-case controversy lacks context, depth, and foundation. This chapter, in conclusion, proposes paradigm diversity.

In order to understand a new paradigm, a theorist should be fully aware of the assumptions upon which his or her own paradigm is based. Moreover, to understand a new paradigm one has to explore it from within, since the concepts in one paradigm cannot easily be interpreted in terms of those of another. No attempt should be made to criticize or evaluate a paradigm from the outside. This is self-defeating since it is based on a separate paradigm. All four paradigms can be easily criticized and ruined in this way.

This chapter is organized as follows. Section 1 shows that different educational methodologies use a given educational method differently. Section 2 argues against any attempt at ranking the lecture method in comparison with the case method. Section 3 is the conclusion.

1 Educational Method

The educational philosophy specifies how an educational issue should be dealt with and, in turn, the practice of education leads to the refinement of philosophical ideas. The philosophy of education becomes important when educators recognize the need for thinking clearly about what they are doing and to see what they are doing in the larger context of society. Educational philosophy is not only a basis for generating educational ideas, but also a basis for how to provide the desired instruction, i.e., instructional methodology. In other words, each educational philosophy favors a certain educational methodology.

Chapter 1 discussed the four paradigms and emphasized that the four paradigms are very broad and basic in the sense that they fill in the whole spectrum in Exhibit 1.1. It, moreover, noted that the formation of the objective-subjective continuum in Exhibit 1.1 is based on the nature of the reality that the foundational philosophies address. In other words, in Exhibit 1.1, as one moves from the objective to the subjective end of the spectrum, the nature of reality addressed by respective worldviews changes from being objective to being subjective, i.e., from being fixed and concrete to being socially-constructed and ever-changing.

The way that an instructional method is used depends on the user's instructional methodology, which, in turn, is based on the corresponding educational philosophy and foundational philosophy. This, in the final analysis, depends on the nature of reality that it addresses.

More specifically, this section considers the case method, when it is viewed as an instructional method. It shows that different instructional methodologies use the case method differently and use different type of cases.[2] In this connection, this section looks at Dooley and Skinner (1977) and Reynolds (1978). The former categorizes alternative roles of teachers and students in the use of the case method. The latter categorizes alternative types of cases used in the case method.

Dooley and Skinner (1977) identify,[3] among other things, two extreme case teaching approaches which correspond to the two extreme positions on the objective-subjective continuum in Exhibit 1.1. More specifically, their "One Extreme" corresponds to the subjective extreme in Exhibit 1.1, and their "The Other Extreme" corresponds to the objective extreme in Exhibit 1.1:

One Extreme

The range of pedagogic philosophies employed in the case method is bounded, on the one hand, by the belief that learning is a self-acquired process. This is the philosophy that contends, in the words of Charles Gragg: "Wisdom can't be told." The student learns what he or she wants to learn and is ready to learn; the student must take full responsibility for his or her own learning. Any external elements—such as books, instructors, texts, principles, the articulated wisdom of others—can help or hurt the learning process, depending largely on whether the student is receptive to them, and perceives them as useful. But each individual can learn only at his or her own pace, in his or her own way, and according to his or her own needs.

The professor who subscribes to these assumptions believes that in a case discussion the instructor, at best, can help as a classroom traffic officer, keeping everyone from talking at once, reporting/recording the flow of analysis and conclusions. At worst, the instructor can be a foreign, intrusive, divisive element. The instructor can interfere in the learning process—can fall into the trap of assuming an understanding of what the student wants to learn and is ready to learn. But since all students are "on different tracks," the instructor inevitably gets in the way of many of them. When the professor says, "I'm going to help," he or she begins to deny the student some part of the responsibility for learning, creating student dependency instead of self-development.

According to this philosophy an instructor can offer modest assistance to students as they undergo an intensely personalized experience; the instructor who attempts to play an active role inevitably will impede, perhaps even destroy, the learning process for at least some percentage of the class. Responsibility cannot be shared. Either the student accepts the responsibility for his or her own learning, or goes to the other extreme of saying: "Here I am, instructor. Educate me."

---

[2] Ardalan (2003c), in the context of scholarly activities, similarly shows that clinical method, as a research method, is used differently by the scholars located within the functionalist paradigm than the scholars located within the interpretive paradigm.

[3] Dooley and Skinner's (1977) Table 2 is replicated in this chapter (Exhibit 10.1) for the reader's convenience.

The Other Extreme

At the other extreme is the pedagogic philosophy that the instructor is the decisive element in the learning process, that the instructor's knowledge and wisdom place him or her on "center stage," that the ultimate responsibility for making sure that the class is "effective," that "students learn something," is the instructor's. People of this persuasion believe that for the professor to play other than a dominant role, to take refuge in questions when there are answers, to act as if his or her experience, judgement and insights are not superior to those of the students, is to prevent the teaching process and the basic tenets of professorial responsibility. Wisdom can be told, and the professor should do the telling. "That's what professors are paid to do."

Time is viewed as precious. The instructor's job is to make sure maximum imparting of knowledge is achieved in the time available. When leading case discussions, the professor must maintain control, identify, and then lead students through the important aspects of a case, without letting time be wasted in fruitless arguments between uninformed and inexperienced students who have not yet learned to approach problems systematically, rigorously and efficiently. Letting students "muddle around" and master concepts themselves perhaps may be appropriate for occasional, brief intervals, but a little of this is sufficient. The instructor then must impart knowledge efficiently by showing students how to approach and handle the topic correctly. The professor constantly must make clear where he or she stands, and impart continuous feedback as to whether each student who speaks is right or wrong, and why. The instructor instructs. The student absorbs. (pp. 283–284)

Dooley and Skinner's (1977) "A Middle-Ground Viewpoint" corresponds to a mid-point on the objective-subjective continuum in Exhibit 1.1 of Chap. 1:

A Middle-Ground Viewpoint

... the instructor ... should help substantially in the learning process, and can do so without removing the student's ultimate sense of responsibility for learning. The instructor can build bridges and linkages from other courses, from case to case, and from class to class; he or she can help make the classes interesting and challenging and meaningful; can add perspective; can interject color and fun, spark and focus. (p. 284)

The other case teaching approaches which Dooley and Skinner (1977) list, in their Table 2, correspond in the same order to the intermediate points on the objective-subjective continuum in Exhibit 1.1 of Chap. 1. More specifically, in Table 2 of Dooley and Skinner (1977), as we move from top of the table to the bottom of the table, we are at the same time moving, in Exhibit 1.1 of Chap. 1, from the right (objective) end to the left (subjective) end of the horizontal axis. Dooley and Skinner (1977) identified a variety of case teaching approaches: "We contend that these ... approaches ... are only ... examples of the almost infinite array of alternative approaches utilized in 'the case method.'"[4] This infinite array of alternatives, in fact, corresponds to the infinite number of positions on the objective-subjective continuum in Exhibit 1.1 of Chap. 1.

Dooley and Skinner (1977) continue their presentation and provide four forms of instructorships. These correspond to four possibilities on the objective-subjective continuum in Exhibit 1.1 of Chap. 1. In fact, the order in which they appear in Dooley and Skinner (1977) corresponds to the order on the horizontal axis in Exhibit 1.1 of Chap. 1, i.e., the order from the subjective extreme of the continuum to the objective extreme:

[4] Dooley and Skinner (1977), p. 282.

Exhibit 10.1 Dooley and Skinner's (1977) Table 2

Table 2. A profile of pedagogy in the teaching of business administration

Cate gory	Educational objective	Case description (example)	Application of a case	Teacher's role	Student's role	Class percent age teacher talks	Teacher's preparation	Teacher's skills and knowledge required	Problems and hazards frequently encountered	Require ments for success	Judging success of class
I	Acquire knowledge	Exposition of business practice	Very poor	Narrate Expose Enlighten Provide expertise	Listen	95%	Organize facts so as to be interesting, relevant and clear	Public speaking, Clarity of thinking and lucidity Organization of material	Student impatience, boredom	Student is concerned, feels problem exists and desires knowledge	Student interest, knowledge retention, ability to playback
II	Develop concepts	Exposition of problem or in business	Poor	Explain taxonomies and inter-relation ships	Listen and question	85%	Organize facts to develop useful and meaningful inter-relationships	Cometence in theory and ability to explain it simply	Student unawareness, unconcern with problems to which concept is addressed	Student hungers for concept after much wrestling with problem without conceptual scheme	Grasp of ability to playback and verbalize

(continued)

Exhibit 10.1 (continued)

Table 2. A profile of pedagogy in the teaching of business administration

Cate gory	Educational objective	Case description (example)	Application of a case	Teacher's role	Student's role	Class percent age teacher talks	Teacher's preparation	Teacher's skills and knowledge required	Problems and hazards frequently encountered	Require ments for success	Judging success of class
III	Understand techniques	Problemette	Fair	Explain technique and its derivation and application	Work problem, examples Derive technique	70%	Understand theory and derivation and implications of technique	Ability to explain/ derive and demonstrate	Student failure to see usefulness, practically, relevance of techniques confusion	Student sees need for technique before he/ she gets it. Student derives technique himself/ herself	Ability to work problems correctly
IV	Acquire skill in use of technique	Short realistic business situation structured	Good	Question and probe to develop realism	Work out effective use of technique in business situation	33%	Understand applications and limitations and problems in use of technique	Realistic recognition of problems in use of technique	"It seems too easy; it seems too hard; it seems too universal; it seems too limited"	Realistically demanding case. Teacher can restrain self from resolving problems	Practicality of student recommend ations
V	Acquire skill in analysis of business problems	Complex unstructured slice of life	Excellent	Probe clarify inter-relate	Analyze Determine cause/effect relationships by analysis of facts and inferences	10%	Case analysis Develop many alternatives and predict possible student approaches	Questions to open up areas for discussion Careful listening Sense of realism	Teacher domination Teacher "telling" Teacher impatience, Teacher solving	Student willing to work, de-sires to analyze problem and feels competent	Thorough-ness, variety, complete-ness of analysis in breath and depth

(continued)

Exhibit 10.1 (continued)

Table 2. A profile of pedagogy in the teaching of business administration

Category	Educational objective	Case description (example)	Application of a case	Teacher's role	Student's role	Class percentage teacher talks	Teacher's preparation	Teacher's skills and knowledge required	Problems and hazards frequently encountered	Requirements for success	Judging success of class
VI	Acquire skill in synthesis of action plans	Problem with clear emphasis on action	Excellent	Challenge Question Extrapolate Role-play	Establish priorities, plan of action: Develop possible outcomes and implications	10%	Develop understanding of situation and possible approaches	Interpretation of student plan without domination	Teacher temptation to settle it with own ingenious analysis	Student feels he/she has necessary facts and is challenged to develop solution which he/she feels does exist	Creativity and realism of action plans
VII	Develop useful attitudes	V, VI, VII with emphasis on key executives	Excellent	Lift up the problem of executive attitudes	Discuss/ debate outcomes Personalize	10%	Consider variety of attitudes, present and possible	Seeing problem from its many sides	Teacher imposition of own attitudes/ values	Teacher trusts that attitudes emerges as a long-term by-product of a demanding education	Changes in attitudes, increased confidence, humility, responsibility

(continued)

Exhibit 10.1 (continued)

Table 2. A profile of pedagogy in the teaching of business administration

Cate gory	Educational objective	Case description (example)	Application of a case	Teacher's role	Student's role	Class percent age teacher talks	Teacher's preparation	Teacher's skills and knowledge required	Problems and hazards frequently encountered	Require ments for success	Judging success of class
VIII	Develop mature judgement/ wisdom	Complex, realistic, unstructured problem	Excellent	Give feedback restate listen	Discuss/ debate develop alternatives and their implications	5%	Case analysis in all possible dimensions	Self-restraint Perception of student state of progress	Teacher impatience, teacher inability to tolerate student frustration	Teacher can tolerate student frustrations	Waiting and trusting

Varying Roles of Students and Instructor

Growing out of such differences in objectives and pedagogic philosophy, understandably divergent views arise regarding instructor and student roles.

The array of alternative pedagogic roles is great. For purposes of illustration, we will "label" and describe four of the many different instructional approaches practiced under the case method.

The "Facilitator" Instructor

... the instructor's classroom role is largely non-directive, leaving responsibility primarily with the students. The instructor may write on the blackboard various data, issues, questions, principles, ideas, generalizations, concepts, and analyses that are offered by the students. But in doing so he or she plays merely the role of a recording secretary.

At the end of the class the instructor may or may not ask some student to summarize the flow of thoughts, analyses, and conclusions. Different students are likely to carry away quite different "lessons" from the class experience.

The "Coach" Instructor

... the instructor ... takes on the tasks of: (a) motivating and developing interest and generating a sense of the importance of the case and its issues; (b) linking the particular case to other facets of the course; and (c) taking active responsibility for the progress of the case analysis.

What the "Coach" instructor does not assume responsibility for is the quality of the students' analysis, for the correctness or incorrectness of student conclusions. These are student responsibilities.

The "Quarterback" Instructor

... the professor makes the subtle but important transition from the role of a coach (who attempts to help students "play their own game") to a "Quarterback" who "calls the signals," makes the crucial decisions about what is to be done, by whom and when; an plays a key role in "making things happen." There is no question about who is "in charge."

The "Demonstrator" Instructor

The instructor is the "doer." Usually employing something close to a traditional lecture, the instructor demonstrates; clarifies; performs the analysis; "walks" the student through the case facts, exhibits and figure work. ... identifies the critical problems; establishes the priorities; takes the "case apart;" presents the "correct" solution. Under this approach the student's role is largely passive. (pp. 284–288)

The objective-subjective continuum in Exhibit 1.1 of Chap. 1 is composed of an infinite number of positions, some of which would correspond to the following forms of instructorship presented by Dooley and Skinner (1977):

Still Other Forms of Instructorship

These four varieties of case instructorship represent only an illustrative sample of the pedagogic arsenal available to the teacher. Depending on preferences, convictions, talents, and ego-needs, instructors also may act as Prod, Referee, Dance Master, Choreographer, Prosecutor, Evangelist, Judge, Conductor, Soothsayer. (p. 288)

Other aspects of Dooley and Skinner's (1977) paper, especially their tables, fit very well within the philosophical context provided in Exhibit 1.1 of Chap. 1. Most prominently, the categories specified in their Table 2, and going from top to bottom, correspond to the objective-subjective continuum in Exhibit 1.1 of Chap. 1, and going from right to left.

In a similar fashion, it can be seen that Reynolds' (1978) categorization of types of cases[5] corresponds to alternative positions on the objective-subjective continuum in Exhibit 1.1 of Chap. 1. To see this, one needs to recall that the objective-subjective continuum in Exhibit 1.1 is the representation of alternative foundational philosophies and their corresponding educational philosophies, which in turn are reflected in their corresponding instructional methodologies, which require corresponding teaching materials. For instance, positions on the far right-hand side on the objective-subjective continuum in Exhibit 1.1 require "fact-based, problem-oriented, directed cases." Whereas positions on the far left-hand side on the objective-subjective continuum in Exhibit 1.1 require "qualitative, discussion-oriented, non-directed, open-ended cases." Reynolds (1978) states:

> The teacher who plans to leave two-thirds of the class time to the students should choose a case which allows for enough student analysis and interpretation to use that time effectively. The instructor who plans to use a case as the basis for a lecture should choose one which does not start too many trains of thought in diverse directions; the student whose analysis has suggested issues of social responsibility is not likely to sit still for a lecture on cost minimization. (pp. 130–131)

The other case types which Reynolds (1978) lists, in his Table 1, correspond in the same order to the intermediate points on the objective-subjective continuum in Exhibit 1.1. More specifically, in Table 1 of Reynolds (1978), as we move from top of the table to the bottom of the table, we are at the same time moving, in Exhibit 1.1 of Chap. 1, from the right (objective) end to the left (subjective) end of the horizontal axis.

This section considered the case method, when it is viewed as an instructional method. It showed that different instructional methodologies use the case method differently and use different type of cases.

2 Ranking of Lecture Method in Comparison with Case Method

The foregoing discussion noted that foundational philosophies underlie educational philosophies, and each educational philosophy underlies a certain instructional methodology, and when any instructional method is utilized, it is used within the bounds of that educational philosophy and foundational philosophy. This chapter provided an ordering of the philosophical foundations of the alternative approaches that used the case method, specified the instructor's role, the students' role, and the type of cases used. That is, this chapter showed how different educational philosophies imply alternative approaches to the utilization of the case method,

---

[5] Reynolds' (1978) Table 1 is reproduced in this chapter (Exhibit 10.2) for the reader's convenience.

Exhibit 10.2 Reynolds' (1978) Table 1

Table 1. Case characteristics and educational objectives

<table>
<tr><th>Category</th><th>Educational objective</th><th>Case description</th><th>Data dimensions</th><th>Analytical methods</th><th>Value dimensions</th></tr>
<tr><td>II</td><td>Develop concepts</td><td>Exposition of problem in Business</td><td rowspan="2">Facts clustered to highlight cause and effect relationships</td><td rowspan="2">"Worked-out example"</td><td rowspan="2">Objective function made explicit</td></tr>
<tr><td>III</td><td>Understand techniques</td><td>Problemette</td></tr>
<tr><td>IV</td><td>Acquire skill in use of techniques</td><td>Short realistic business problem, structured</td><td>Facts "selected" for relevance, but not clustered to attach meaning</td><td>Method signalled, but not worked out</td><td rowspan="3">Value system clear (usually profit-oriented), but objective function open for choice by student</td></tr>
<tr><td>V</td><td>Acquire skill in analysis of business problems</td><td>Complex, unstructured slice of life</td><td rowspan="2">More facts added, mainly within one value system, but amenable to more than one analytical method</td><td rowspan="3">No clear signals regarding methods; analytical techniques open to students' choice, including mixed and sequential analysis</td></tr>
<tr><td>VI</td><td>Acquire skill in synthesis of action plans</td><td>Problem with clear emphasis on action</td></tr>
<tr><td>VII</td><td>Develop useful attitudes</td><td>V, VI, VII with emphasis on key executives</td><td rowspan="2">Still more facts, (often including seemingly irrelevant facts), related to more than one value system; heavy use of opinions of case characters</td><td rowspan="2">Choice of value system left open to student</td></tr>
<tr><td>VIII</td><td>Develop mature judgement, wisdom</td><td>Complex, realistic, unstructured problem</td><td>No known satisfactory technique</td></tr>
</table>

specification of the instructor's role, specification of students' role, and the type of cases used.

It should be now clear that the mere ranking of the lecture method in comparison with the case method in the abstract is non-productive, since, as was noted above in the example of the case method, the case method, as any other method, can be used within the bounds of totally different educational philosophies and foundational philosophies. Consequently, the comparison of the lecture method with the case method, if it needs to be attempted at all, should be made within the appropriate context, rather than in the abstract. Based on the discussion above, an appropriate context for the comparison of the lecture method with the case method is their respective educational philosophies and foundational philosophies. In such a context, one compares instructional methodologies, rather than instructional methods. An instructional methodology is almost uniquely determined by its underlying educational philosophy and foundational philosophy.

For instance, educational realism is located on the right-hand side of the continuum in Exhibit 1.1, which implies a certain educational philosophy, which in turn implies a certain educational methodology, which strongly adheres to the lecture method as the main mode of instruction in class.

On the other hand, educational idealism and educational pragmatism are located on the left-hand side of the continuum in Exhibit 1.1, which imply certain educational philosophies, which in turn imply certain instructional methodologies, which adhere to the discussion method, including the case method, as the main mode of instruction in class.

In this way, the ranking of the lecture and the case instructional methodologies translates into the ranking of their underlying philosophies. However, the ranking of foundational philosophies is self-defeating since each foundational philosophy or paradigm is formed by a coherent set of thoughts based on a set of assumptions. Therefore, each foundational philosophy or paradigm can only be explored from within, since the concepts in one paradigm cannot easily be interpreted in terms of those of another. No attempt should be made to criticize or evaluate a paradigm from the outside. This is self-defeating since it is based on a separate paradigm. All four paradigms can be easily criticized and ruined in this way.

Moreover, there does not exist an independent point of reference to be used for such evaluation and ranking. Any attempt to evaluate or judge the significance of different philosophies may be framed by assumptions or presuppositions that have no *a priori* claim to supremacy over those of other evaluative stances.

The foregoing implies that the existing lecture-versus-case controversy lacks context, depth, and foundation. It lacks context because the comparison is done in the abstract without reference to any specific paradigmatic context. It lacks depth because it looks at the surface and sees the signs rather than looking deep down and seeing the foundational philosophies. It lacks foundation because there does not exist a neutral frame of reference for such a comparison.

This chapter proposes paradigm diversity and emphasizes its principles, implications, and requirements. Its view is that each paradigm can benefit from contributions by the other paradigms. This would entail fundamental changes in current perspectives held by the two sides involved in the lecture-versus-case debate.

To implement paradigm diversity, some fundamental changes need to be directed to the way the lecture-versus-case debate is presently viewed. The most fundamental change is to understand the multifaceted nature of education as a phenomenon. An understanding of paradigms provides a valuable means for exploring the nature of the phenomenon being investigated. Furthermore, an understanding of other paradigms provides an invaluable basis for recognizing what one is doing.

3 Conclusion

This chapter showed that different educational methodologies use a given educational method differently, and argued against any attempt at ranking the lecture method in comparison with the case method.

References

Ardalan, Kavous. 2003a. The Lecture-versus-Case Controversy: Its Philosophical Foundation. *Southwestern Economic Review* 30 (1): 99–118.

———. 2003b. Alternative Approaches Utilized in the Case Method: Their Philosophical Foundations. *Academy of Educational Leadership Journal* 30 (3): 103–120.

———. 2003c. On Clinical Research in Finance. *International Journal of Social Economics* 30 (10): 1038–1048.

———. 2006. The Philosophical Foundation of the Lecture-versus-Case Controversy: Its Implications for Faculty Teaching, Research, and Service. *International Journal of Social Economics* 33 (3): 261–281.

———. 2008. The Philosophical Foundation of the Lecture-versus-Case Controversy: Its Implications for Course Goals, Objectives, and Contents. *International Journal of Social Economics* 35 (1/2): 15–34.

———. 2013. The Philosophical Foundation of the Lecture Method of Instruction and the Case Method of Instruction: Implications for Examinations. *Contemporary Issues in Education Research* 6 (1): 1–7.

———. 2015. Chapter 3: Using Entertaining Metaphors in the Introduction of the Case Method in a Case-Based Course. In *Exploring Learning and Teaching In Higher Education*, ed. Mang Li and Yong Zhao, 69–96. New York, NY: Springer.

Aveni, Anthony. 2014. *Class Not Dismissed: Reflections on Undergraduate Education and Teaching the Liberal Arts*. Boulder, CO: University Press of Colorado.

Barnes, Louis B., Abby J. Hansen, and C. Roland Christensen. 1994. *Teaching and the Case Method: Text, Cases, and Readings*. Boston, MA: Harvard Business School.

Barrow, Robin, and Patricia White, eds. 1993. *Beyond Liberal Education: Essays in Honor of Paul H Hirst*. New York, NY: Routledge.

Barrow, Robin, and Ronald Woods. 1989. *An Introduction to Philosophy of Education*. New York, NY: Routledge.

Blake, Nigel, Paul Smeyers, Richard Smith, and Paul Standish, eds. 2002. *The Blackwell Guide to the Philosophy of Education*. New York, NY: Blackwell.

Brosio, Richard A. 1998. The Continuing Correspondence between Political Economy and Schooling: Telling the News. *Journal of Thought* 33 (3): 85–105.

Burrell, Gibson, and Gareth Morgan. 1979. *Sociological Paradigms and Organizational Analysis*. Hants, England: Gower Publishing.

Cahn, Steven M., ed. 1996. *Classic and Contemporary Readings in the Philosophy of Education*. New York, NY: McGraw-Hill College Division.

———., ed. 2009. *Philosophy of Education: The Essential Texts*. New York, NY: Routledge.

Carr, David. 2003. *Making Sense of Education: An Introduction to the Philosophy and Theory of Education*. New York, NY: Routledge.

Chambliss, J.J., ed. 1996. *Philosophy of Education: An Encyclopedia*. New York, NY: Garland Publishers.

Christensen, C. Roland, and David A. Garvin, eds. 1991. *Education for Judgment*. Cambridge, MA: Harvard Business School Press.

Cromer, Alan H. 1997. *Connected Knowledge: Science, Philosophy, and Education*. Oxford, England: Oxford University Press.

Curren, Randall R., ed. 2003. *Companion to the Philosophy of Education*. New York, NY: Blackwell.

———., ed. 2007. *Philosophy of Education: An Anthology*. Malden, MA: Blackwell.

Dooley, Arch R., and Wickham Skinner. 1977. Casing Casemethod Methods. *Academy of Management Review* 2 (2): 277–289.

Ellis, Arthur K., John J. Cogan, and Kenneth R. Howey. 1991. *Introduction to the Foundations of Education*. Upper Saddle River, NJ: Prentice Hall.

Erskine, James A., Michiel R. Leenders, and Louise A. Mauffette-Leenders. 2003. *Teaching with Cases*. 3rd ed. London, ON, Canada: Ivey Business School, University of Western Ontario, Erskine Associate Inc., and Leenders and Associates Inc..

Freedman, James O. 1996. *Idealism and Liberal Education*. Ann Harbor, MI: University of Michigan Press.

Gragg, Charles I. 1954. Because Wisdom Can't Be Told. In *The Case Method at the Harvard Business School*, ed. Malcolm P. McNair. New York, NY: McGraw-Hill.

Gutek, Gerald Lee. 2000a. *Philosophical and Ideological Perspectives on Education*. 3rd ed. New York, NY: Allyn & Bacon.

———. 2000b. *Historical and Philosophical Foundations of Education: Selected Readings*. Upper Saddle River, NJ: Prentice Hall, College Division.

———. 2003. *Philosophical and Ideological Voices in Education*. 1st ed. New York, NY: Allyn & Bacon.

Hancock, Ralph C., ed. 1999. *America, the West, and Liberal Education*. New York, NY: Rowman & Littlefield.

Hare, William, and John P. Portelli, eds. 2001. *Philosophy of Education: Introductory Readings*. 3rd ed. New York, NY: Detseling Enterprises.

Hickman, Larry, and Thomas M. Alexander, eds. 1998. *The Essential Dewey: Pragmatism, Education, Democracy*. Bloomington, IN: Indiana University Press.

Kimball, Bruce A., and Robert Orrill, eds. 1995. *The Condition of American Liberal Education: Pragmatism and a Changing Tradition*. New York, NY: College Entrance Examination Board.

Larochelle, Marie, Nadine Bednarz, and Jim Garrison, eds. 1998. *Constructivism and Education*. Cambridge, England: Cambridge University Press.

Marples, Roger, ed. 1999. *The Aims of Education*. New York, NY: Routledge.

Mauffette-Leenders, Louise A., James A. Erskine, and Michiel R. Leenders. 2007. *Learning with Cases*. 4th ed. London, ON, Canada: Ivey Publishing, Ivey Business School, University of Western Ontario.

McLaren, Peter. 1998. Revolutionary Pedagogy in Post-Revolutionary Times: Rethinking the Political Economy of Critical Education. *Educational Theory* 48 (4): 431–462.

Morgan, Gareth. 1983. *Beyond Method: Strategies for Social Research*. Beverley Hills, CA: Sage.

———. 1985. Qualitative and Action Based Research. In *Actes du Colloque, Perspective de Recherche Pour lo Praticien*, ed. Y. Allaire, M. Landry, H. Mintzberg, and G. Morgan, 81–187. Rouyn-Noranda, QC, Canada: University of Quebec at Abitibi-Temiscaminque.

Noddings, Nel. 2016. *Philosophy of Education*. Boulder, CO: Westview Press.

Orrill, Robert, ed. 1999. *Education and Democracy: Re-Imaging Liberal Learning in America*. New York, NY: College Entrance Examination Board.

Ozmon, Howard A. 2011. *Philosophical Foundations of Education*. 7th ed. New York, NY: Pearson.

Philosophy of Education Society. 2003. *Philosophy of Education 2002*. New York, NY: Philosophy of Education Society Press.

Popkewitz, Thomas S., and Lynn Fendler, eds. 1999. *Critical Theories in Education: Changing Terrains of Knowledge and Politics*. New York, NY: Routledge.

Power, Edward J. 1995. *Educational Philosophy: A History from the Ancient World to Modern America*. New York, NY: Garland Publishers.

Reynolds, John I. 1978. There's Method in Cases. *Academy of Management Review* 3 (1): 129–133.

Rocha, Samuel D. 2014. *A Primer for Philosophy and Education*. Eugene, OR: Cascade Books.

Rorty, Amelie Oksenberg, ed. 1998. *Philosophers on Education: Historical Perspectives*. New York, NY: Routledge.

Sadovnik, Alan R., Susan Semel, and Peter Cookson. 2000. *Exploring Education: An Introduction to the Foundations of Education*. 2nd ed. New York, NY: Allyn & Bacon.

Schrag, Francis. 1995. *Back to Basics: Fundamental Educational Questions Reexamined*. San Francisco, CA: Jossey-Bass Education Series.

Siegel, Harvey. 2012. *The Oxford Handbook of Philosophy of Education*. Oxford, England: Oxford University Press.

Talisse, Robert B., and D. Micah Hester. 2002. *On the Philosophy of Education*. New York, NY: Wadsworth Publishing.

Winch, Christopher, and John Gingell. 1999. *Key Concepts in the Philosophy of Education*. New York, NY: Routledge.

In-Class Introduction of the Case Methodology in Comparison to the Lecture Methodology

The purpose of this chapter is to show how professors can use entertaining metaphors when introducing the case method to their students. Students are often educated by the lecture method and, therefore, the use of the case method is new and frustrating to them. They require an introduction to the case method which is both foundational and friendly. The foundation of the case method is best introduced in simple terms and should be compared with the lecture method, with which students are most familiar. The friendly environment is best created with an approach which is most comforting to them, i.e., entertainment. This chapter shows how such a foundational and friendly introduction can be made by utilizing entertaining metaphors.

This chapter shows how entertaining metaphors can be used to increase attraction to, and learning in, the introductory session of a case-based course when the case method is introduced. Its major emphasis is on the idea that academicians should incorporate entertainment in the teaching and learning environment. The crucial role of education in the advancement of society cannot be overstated. Students are often easily attracted to the rapidly progressing world of amusement and entertainment; and away from the frequently rigid and dry world of education. For the long-term benefit of society, teachers should make the world of education more attractive. Academicians can accomplish this by incorporating entertaining material in their courses. Entertaining material, as well, plays an important role in education; as the emotion evoking qualities of such stimuli have a profound impact on learning.

This chapter shows one way to include entertaining metaphors in the introduction of the case method. It utilizes an audio-visual approach, to affect those senses in students, in order to enhance attraction and communication of the materials discussed. The audio component is performed by the professor. The visual component is covered by transparencies[1] (or a slide show) shown on an overhead screen. The transparencies

[1] These transparencies can be scanned and turned into a slide show.

K. Ardalan, *Case Method and Pluralist Economics*,
https://doi.org/10.1007/978-3-319-72071-5_11

consist of drawings and cartoons[2] which are used as metaphors. This approach enhances visualization,[3] motivation, and association in student learning.[4]

The chapter is organized as follows. Section 1 discusses the role of humor and metaphors in learning. Section 2 demonstrates how entertaining metaphors can be used in the introduction of the case method. Section 3 is the conclusion.

1 The Role of Humor and Metaphors in Learning

It is worthwhile to briefly review the literature that addresses the effect of entertainment and metaphor in education; express my own experience; then move on to an application of a combination of both in the introduction to the case method.

The Role of Humor

There are benefits to the use of entertainment and humor in teaching (Banas et al. 2011; Berk 1998; Garner 2005; Glenn 2002; Hill 1988; McCloskey 1990; Pollio and Humphreys 1996; Powell and Andersen 1985; Ziv 1988). It has been shown to have both psychological and physiological effects on learners. Psychologically, humor and laughter reduce anxiety, decrease stress, enhance self-esteem, and increase self-motivation (Banas et al. 2011; Berk 1998; Martin 2007; Mottet et al. 2006). Humor can help an individual engage the learning process by creating a positive emotional and social environment in which defences are lowered and students are better able to focus and attend to the information being presented. Additionally, humor can serve as a bridge between educators and students by creating a shared understanding and a common psychological bond (Glenn 2002).

Physiologically, humor and laughter can aid learning through improved respiration and circulation, lower pulse and blood pressure, exercise of the chest muscles, greater oxygenation of blood, and the release of endorphins into the bloodstream (Berk 1998; McGhee 1983).[5] The healing effects of laughter and humor can reduce anxiety, help relieve stress, and increase mental sharpness, which are all desirable in

[2] These drawings and cartoons were collected long time ago, and therefore, at the present time, the author of this chapter cannot find the origin of the drawings and cartoons. The authors of these drawings and cartoons are welcomed to contact the author of this chapter to claim copyright when they see their drawings and cartoons.

[3] Remember, a picture is worth a thousand words.

[4] This chapter follows Ardalan (1998) and expands on it. See also Ardalan (2008a, 2008b, 2009). This chapter is based on Ardalan (2015).

[5] See also Bohannon (1988), Brown and Kulik (1977), Christianson (1989), Christianson et al. (1991), Craik and Blankstein (1975), Ellis et al. (1971), Heuer and Reisberg (1990), Maltzman et al. (1966), Pillemer (1984), and Walker and Tarte (1963). For a broad review, see McGhee and Goldstein (1983).

pedagogical settings (Cousins 1991; Evans-Palmer 2010; Neumann et al. 2009). Students pay more attention to humorous than non-humorous material.[6] Students rehearse humorous material more than non-humorous material and the increased rehearsal, in turn, results in higher retention rates (Atkinson and Shiffrin 1968; McCartney-Matthews 2011; Schmidt 2009). There are also the elements of surprise and retrieval strategies. Students may not expect to encounter humorous materials in their experiments. In their retrieval, students may be biased with respect to retrieving humorous material or retrieving humorous material before non-humorous material.

The factors described above do not necessarily operate in isolation. Thus, physiological arousal may result in increased attention to some material. Increased attention may, in turn, result in increased rehearsal.

There is a growing body of research relating the use of humor and its positive effects on teaching and learning (Civikly 1986; Garner 2006; Skinner 2010). Students indicate that humor can increase their interest in learning, and students who have teachers with a strong orientation to humor tend to learn more. Humor as a pedagogical tool can initiate and sustain student interest and provide a means to engage in divergent thinking (Dodge and Rossett 1982). A humorous atmosphere in the classroom positively impacts student scores on divergent thinking exercises (Ziv 1983, 1988). College students report that learning is enhanced by the inclusion of instructionally-appropriate humor (Korobkin 1989; Wanzer et al. 2010). Students often have better recall of a message if it is presented with humor (Garner 2006; Hill 1988).

Students appreciate and enjoy the use of humor in the classroom (Berk 1996; Brown and Tomlin 1996; Bryant et al. 1980, 1997; Garner 2006; Pollio and Humphreys 1996). College students in describing the positive attributes of good teachers frequently mention "sense of humor" (Brown and Tomlin 1996; Buckman 2010; Kelly and Kelly 1982).

Humor establishes a connection between the instructor and the student which is the key to effective teaching (Pollio and Humphreys 1996). Effective college teachers are most often described as "enthusiastic;" and a strong sense of humor plays a major role in developing a positive learning environment (Lowman 1994; Lukehart 2009). The appropriate use of humor which fosters mutual respect enhances teaching effectiveness, and humor increases student receptivity to material by reducing anxiety in dealing with difficult material and has a positive effect on test performance (Bryant et al. 1980; Kher et al. 1999; Mantooth 2010). The positive environment of a humor-enriched lecture increases the attendance in class (Buchultz et al. 2011; Devadoss and Foltz 1996; Romer 1993; White 1992).

Humor should be used cautiously, however, as it can be an effective medium for communication or a social impediment in pedagogical settings (Garner 2003; Torok et al. 2004; Zhang 2005). The use of humor can be complicated because it may be highly personal, subjective, and contextual and it cannot always be predicted the way it will be received. Everyone has a unique perception of what is humorous and

[6] See Deckers and Devine (1981), Deckers and Hricik (1984), Isen (1985), Kaplan and Pascoe (1977), Kintsch and Bates (1977), Ohman (1979), Schmidt (1991, 1994), Suls (1972), Wanzer et al. 2010, and Zillmann et al. (1980).

defines the "sense of humor" differently (Garner 2003; Wanzer et al. 2010). Furthermore, the effective use of humor is not akin to mere joke telling, e.g., some instructors with only average student evaluations used twice as much humor as those faculty members who were more highly rated (Rhem 1998). For humor to be most effective, it must be specific, targeted, and appropriate to the subject matter. In practice, a humor may be identified as either one of the four appropriate humor categories or one of the four inappropriate humor categories (Bekelja-Wanzer et al. 2006).

Student responses confirm that teachers who use humor in their classes aid the learning process. Humor has been said to: (1) Improve attitudes toward the subject, decrease anxiety, tension, stress, and boredom; (2) Increase comprehension, cognitive retention, interest, and task performance; (3) Increase motivation to learn and satisfaction with learning, and (4) Promote creativity and divergent thinking (Willard 2006).

The Role of Metaphors

Metaphor and analogy are fundamental cognitive tools, which are used by scientists in their expert investigations (Diehl and Reese 2010; Dunbar 1993, 1995; Hesse 1966; Ng 2009), by young children (Goswami 1992; Pramling 2010), and students in their efforts to understand complex phenomena (Braasch and Goldman 2010; Mason 1996; Orgill and Thomas 2007; Paatz et al. 2004; Wormeli 2009).[7] In an analogy, the similarities between two situations, phenomena, or events are identified and the relevant information is mapped from a more familiar domain to a less familiar one.[8] In other words, analogy is essentially the transfer of a relational structure from a known domain, the source, to a lesser or unknown domain, the target (Garner 2005; Richland et al. 2004).

Analogy helps in connecting information and elaborating more comprehensive and integrated knowledge structures. That is, analogy leads to learning something more general, which is the abstraction of similarities shared by the source and target (Halpern et al. 1990; Harrison and Coll 2007; Prawat 1989; Rumelhart and Norman 1978; Vosniadou and Ortony 1989). Analogical reasoning has been investigated for some time in four-term analogy problems, which are used in IQ tests (Sternberg 1977).

When dealing with a much more complex phenomenon, a much more sophisticated process should be followed for analogical reasoning and learning (Brown and Salter 2010; Gentner 1983, 1989; Gick and Holyoak 1980, 1983). One way would be the structure-mapping approach, which refers to a structural alignment between domains. Only relational similarities shared by the source and target are preserved in the mapping of systems of predicates linked by higher-order relations, that is, relations between relations. For instance, in the analogy between the atom and the

[7] See also Gibbs (2008), Holland et al. (1986), and Holyoak and Koh (1987).

[8] See Gentner and Gentner (1983), Halpern (1987), Rigney and Lutz (1976), Royer and Cable (1976), Rumelhart and Norman (1981), Schustack and Anderson (1979), and Zheng and Song (2010).

solar system, predicates such as "bigger than" or "hot" are not mapped from the source to the target, but predicates such as "cause" are. That is, systematically, a preference for interconnected systems of relations governed by higher-order relations characterizes the structural alignment (Gentner 1983, 1989; Steinhart 2001).

Another way would be multi-constraint approach, which deals with how individuals are driven by three different types of constraint in the use of analogy: similarity, structure, and purpose. At any level of abstraction, correspondences of similarities between the concepts are implied in an analogy. Moreover, structural parallels between the source and target domains underlie analogical mapping. Finally, the analogy is used towards researcher's goal (Holyoak and Thagard 1989, 1995, 1997; Ruiz and Luciano 2011). All different approaches in analogical reasoning emphasize the mapping process through which source features are transferred to the target and a more abstract structure connecting the two domains is elaborated.

Analogy, as a cognitive tool in learning processes, mainly facilitates the coding and organization of knowledge,[9] access to and retrieval of knowledge from memory,[10] and overcoming misconceptions. Different models for teaching scientific analogies have been proposed (Brown and Salter 2010; Dagher 1997), such as bridging analogies (Brown and Clement 1989; Brice and MacMillan 2005), multiple analogies (Chiu and Lin 2005; Spiro et al. 1989), elaborate analogies (Paris and Glynn 2004), student-generated analogy (Spier-Dance et al. 2005; Wong 1993), or structural alignment (Mason 2004) models. In general, analogies are powerful tools in teaching and learning at all school levels in certain conditions (Dagher 1997; James and Scharmann 2007; Oliva et al. 2007). First, a source domain from which to draw relevant information should be accessible to students. For instance, in order to use water pump to help students understand electric circuits, students must have some knowledge about water pumps and how they work. Second, students should be able to identify the structural similarities between two domains to produce an appropriate transfer. Third, students should know for what purpose they are using the analogy. If these conditions are not met, analogies may mislead students' thought processes (Dagher 1995; Duit et al. 2001; Glynn et al. 1995; Mason 1994; Ruiz and Luciano 2011; Treagust et al. 1996).[11]

Personal Experience

My own experience in using entertaining metaphors has been positive. In the winter of 1993, I started to gradually use them in my classes. Since then, I have gathered more and more ideas, cartoons and illustrations. On a casual basis, I have found

[9] See Hutchison and Padgett (2007), Mayer and Gallini (1990), and Paivio (1971, 1986).

[10] See Halpern (1987), Hayes and Tierney (1982), Mayer and Bromage (1980), Pena and Andrade-Filho (2010), and Schustack and Anderson (1979).

[11] See also Gibbs (2008), Glynn et al. (1989), Halpern (1987), Rogers (1960), Spiro et al. (1989), and Vosniadou and Schommer (1988).

Exhibit 11.1 At the beginning of a case course, students naturally have many questions regarding different aspects of the case method: What is involved in a case and what is required of them

them, over and above what has been discussed previously, to be beneficial to the class by adding new dimensions, and creating a friendlier, relaxed environment. These characteristics encourage the students to be more attentive and interested in classes, and the course as a whole. Some indications, supporting this position are, for example, that a part-time M.B.A. (Master of Business Administration) student, who had passed the course, came back and sat through it again. Another part-time M.B.A. student asked me for a copy of the cartoons and illustrations, because he was going to use them in his presentations at work. Other students have indicated that they like the cartoons and illustrations that were displayed in this course. These indications prompted me to write this chapter in order to share my experience with colleagues.

2 Introduction of the Case Method

The lecture method is an efficient method when the transfer of knowledge is the primary objective. However, when the objective is critical thinking or problem-solving the case method offers substantial advantages. To prepare for the case method, both teachers and students must modify their traditional roles and responsibilities.[12]

Students are often brought up in an educational system which is based on the lecture method, with much structure, certainty, and control. To them, the use of the case method is new and frustrating. In the case method, students are faced with uncertainty, difficulty, complexity, which they must organize and manage it.

[12] The author has heavily benefited from the insights of Erskine et al. (2003) and Mauffette-Leenders et al. (2007). See also Christensen (1991) and Christensen and Hansen (1987).

Exhibit 11.2 There are two fundamentally different views on how to approach a problem. The view which underlies the lecture method encourages a microscopic look at the details of the issue at hand. On the other hand, the view which underlies the case method encourages not only a deep look at the details, but also a global look

And God said,

$$\frac{1}{r^2}\frac{\partial}{\partial r}(r^2 D_r) + \frac{1}{r\sin\theta}\frac{\partial}{\partial\theta}(D_\theta \sin\theta) + \frac{1}{r\sin\theta}\frac{\partial D_\phi}{\partial\phi} = 4\pi\rho,$$

$$\frac{1}{r^2}\frac{\partial}{\partial r}(r^2 B_r) + \frac{1}{r\sin\theta}\frac{\partial}{\partial\theta}(B_\theta \sin\theta) + \frac{1}{r\sin\theta}\frac{\partial B_\phi}{\partial\phi} = 0;$$

$$\frac{1}{r\sin\theta}\left[\frac{\partial}{\partial\theta}(E_\phi \sin\theta) - \frac{\partial E_\theta}{\partial\phi}\right] = -\frac{1}{c}\frac{\partial B_r}{\partial t},$$

$$\frac{1}{r}\left[\frac{1}{\sin\theta}\frac{\partial E_r}{\partial\phi} - \frac{\partial}{\partial r}(rE_\phi)\right] = -\frac{1}{c}\frac{\partial B_\theta}{\partial t},$$

$$\frac{1}{r}\left[\frac{\partial}{\partial r}(rE_\theta) - \frac{\partial E_r}{\partial\theta}\right] = -\frac{1}{c}\frac{\partial B_\phi}{\partial t};$$

$$\frac{1}{r\sin\theta}\left[\frac{\partial}{\partial\theta}(H_\phi \sin\theta) - \frac{\partial H_\theta}{\partial\phi}\right] = 4\pi j_r + \frac{1}{c}\frac{\partial D_r}{\partial t},$$

$$\frac{1}{r}\left[\frac{1}{\sin\theta}\frac{\partial H_r}{\partial\phi} - \frac{\partial}{\partial r}(rH_\phi)\right] = 4\pi j_\theta + \frac{1}{c}\frac{\partial D_\theta}{\partial t},$$

$$\frac{1}{r}\left[\frac{\partial}{\partial r}(rH_\theta) - \frac{\partial H_r}{\partial\theta}\right] = 4\pi j_\phi + \frac{1}{c}\frac{\partial D_\phi}{\partial t};$$

and there was light.

Exhibit 11.3 The view which underlies the lecture method, with its emphasis on objectivity and the observation of the object by as an observer, encourages the finding of exact relationships among the elements of a given phenomenon or issue. We see this approach in the current standard business courses and textbooks, e.g. in finance (see Brealey et al. (2011), Brealey et al. (2012), Brigham and Ehrhardt (2011), Brigham and Houston (2009), Keown et al. (2008), and Ross et al. (2008a, 2008b)), where detailed relationships is mostly expressed in exact mathematical terms. Note that, although the level of mathematics at the introductory level is not in any way high, in advanced graduate courses sophisticated mathematics is used

Exhibit 11.4 In the lecture method, therefore, the professor spends most of the class time at the board deriving or applying those exact relationships

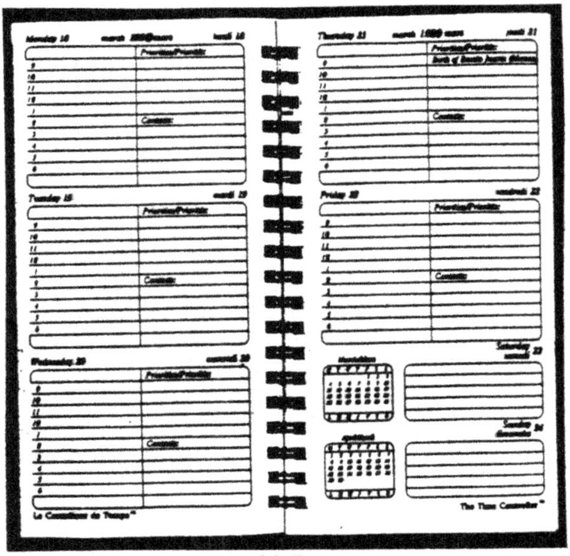

11.5

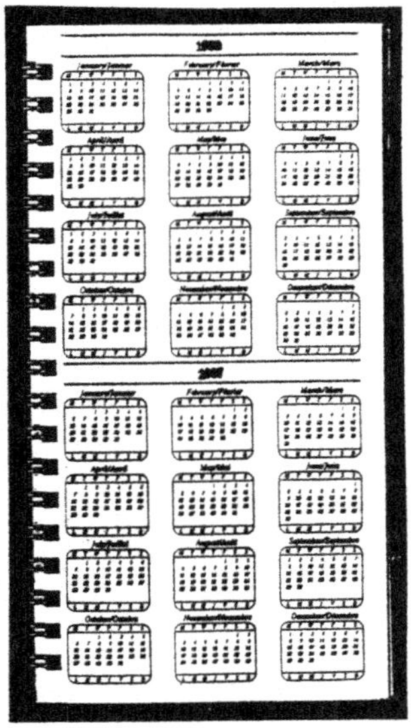

11.6

Exhibits 11.5 and 11.6 The view which underlies the case method encourages the interpretation of the details as well as the big picture. Let us look at Exhibits 11.5 and 11.6 to see that this is, in fact, what we do in our daily lives

The foundation of the case method[13] should be introduced to them in a friendly manner. The foundation is best introduced in simple terms and should be compared with the lecture method, with which they are most familiar. This is because there is a good deal of un-teaching and un-learning involved.

The lecture method has great advantages: it is efficient, and it is economical of the time, energy, and the patience of instructor and student. Students seem to possess a sureness, a precision, a firm understanding which is remarkable for the relatively short time which they have spent on acquiring their knowledge.

Compared to the lecture method, the case method has a different purpose and brings about a corresponding different result. Businesspeople must be able to solve practical problems which arise in new situations. Accordingly, education should consist of acquiring the ability to act in new situations. That is, the focus of education is not gaining knowledge but gaining skills to act.

The introduction can be made friendly by utilizing entertaining metaphors. This chapter shows how these can be accomplished generally in any business course, with some specific reference to finance, in which the use of the lecture method is often more prevalent than it is in other areas in business education.

[13] For a foundational comparison of the lecture and the case method in a philosophical context see Ardalan (2003a, 2003b). See also Ardalan (2006, 2008a, 2008b, 2013).

11.7

11.8

11.9

11.10

Exhibits 11.7, 11.8, 11.9, and 11.10 The case method places great emphasis on the role of the context. Each case needs to be seen in context, not only in terms of topic or theoretical coverage, but also in its other dimensions. This plays a crucial role in what we see, in our interpretation of the case, and the issues under consideration. In Exhibits 11.7 and 11.8, whether we see the same object as "a man washing his face" or "an embrace" reflects the important role of the context in which we interpret information. As another example, in Exhibits 11.9 and 11.10, whether we see "three penguins" or "three Asian gentlemen" reflects the critical role of the context in what we see

The entertaining metaphors approach is an audio-visual one. The audio component is performed by the professor. The visual component is covered by slides shown on an overhead screen. The slides consist of exhibits, which are used as metaphors. This approach enhances visualization, motivation, and association in student learning.

This chapter focuses on the use of entertaining metaphors in the introduction of some of the most fundamental aspects of the case method. The discussion of the other aspects of the case method can be added as well.

Exhibit 11.11 By big picture and context, we mean, what goes on in the industry, and in the national and international economies. For instance, the national budget deficit, which is a major macro-economic variable, affects all aspects of the economy and the businesses operating within it

The entertaining metaphors are so because they are cartoons and metaphorical. They are in the form of transparencies which are shown on the overhead screen while the professor introduces the course and the field. The professor discusses the topic without any reference, for the most part, to what is being shown. It is the students' role to relate what the professor is discussing to what is displayed on the overhead screen. In fact, for the student, finding the relationship between what the professor is discussing, and what is being exhibited, makes the metaphors even more entertaining. The entertaining metaphors are placed at the end of this chapter.

In the following presentation, the exhibit or slide number appears first. Next, there is a short description of the relevant material discussed in class.

The educational goal of the case method is for the students to gain practical knowledge and to be able to apply logical and correct reasoning in every subject. The case method has proven itself a most effective educational vehicle in situations where decisions are required and issues must be solved. The case method is participatory, student oriented, and involves active learning environment.

A case is a description of an actual situation, which commonly involves a challenging problem or issue which requires a decision by a person (or persons) in an organization.

Exhibit 11.12 In the lecture method, knowledge is expressed in the form of a speech. The student is not only almost always disallowed to see anything different from the lecturer, but is also required to replicate and repeat what the lecturer has presented. There is almost no allowance for the student to see the case, or the phenomenon, for himself or herself, share his or her views, and obtain insights from the views expressed by others. The lecture method of teaching and learning reminds one of ancient drawings, in which artists were limited in dimensions, and in which there was almost no opportunity for them to express themselves to any great extent

A case is a partial, historical, clinical study of a real-life situation which is faced by an administrator or managerial group. It provides substantive and process-related data which are essential to an analysis of the situation. It requires the listing of alternatives, a decision for action, and its implementation, which recognize the complexity and ambiguity of the practical world. A case is usually presented in narrative form and encourages student involvement.

A case is a record of an actual business issue which includes the surrounding facts, opinions, and prejudices upon which executive decisions would depend. These real and specific cases require students to analyze, discuss, and finally decide on the necessary action which should be taken.

In the case method, students should place themselves in the shoes of the decision maker in the business situation in order to decide what is to be done about the issue at hand. The case is basically a complex puzzle and students are required to make a decision with respect to the issues involved. Students bring their own values, age, gender, background, theoretical and practical understanding, training, skills, expertise, biases, and culture into the position and the situation in place. The decision,

Exhibit 11.13 Comparing the previous exhibit with this one is like comparing the lecture method to the case method. In this exhibit, the third dimension is brought in, and we clearly see the role and place of the artist in the drawing, as well as the drawing itself. Moreover, the artist sees the room in a special way, which is different from how most of us are accustomed to seeing a room, i.e., rectangular. The artist is seeing the room in a unique way and is sharing it with us

Exhibit 11.14 We have much in common. We have some similar interests, values, and behaviors

"I can't decide whether to go into astronautics, study business administration, or just let the government take care of me."

Exhibit 11.15 Most importantly, we all like, and are interested in, business administration

issue, or opportunity becomes theirs. Taking this responsibility is one of the major challenges in the use of cases. It is much easier to stay as an outside observer, as required by the lecture method.

In a case, there is usually an immediate issue which refers to a specific decision, problem, challenge, or opportunity faced by a decision maker. In real life, a case is not normally repeated, therefore, the purpose of being concerned with the immediate issue of a case is to develop an understanding of the basic issues underlying it. This is because basic issues tend to be commonly present. Dealing with the details of a case helps in developing an approach which is generalizable to other situations (Exhibits 11.2, 11.3, and 11.4).

In the lecture method, teaching is telling, knowledge is facts, and learning is recall. Teachers deliver factual information, and students receive it. Learning is satisfactorily completed when the student successfully transfers factual material back to the teacher at a specific time. Students go through an educational process which is devoted to finding answers, by applying rigorously defined methods to questions or problems carefully posed by others. When these students first encounter the case method of instructions they become uncomfortable, confused, and ineffectual. In the case method, the students' role, expectations, and responsibilities are much different than in the lecture method. The student is responsible for doing a thorough analysis of the case at hand.

Consider the calendar which we use every day. Exhibit 11.5 shows where we note our appointments and plans for each hour on any specific date, Wednesday, March 20, 2012. We certainly make those plans with a view to the rest of the week, for which we have other plans. The whole week is shown on both pages of the calendar. Then again, our weekly plans are made within our monthly ones. For example, our plans for March and April, which are shown on the lower half of the right-hand page of the calendar contain the week of March 20th. Our monthly plans are, in turn, made within our longer-range plans for the years 2013 and 2014. This is placed at the beginning of the same calendar, which appears in Exhibit 11.6. In

"Smoking or nonsmoking, cholesterol or non-cholesterol, caffeinated or decaffeinated?"

Exhibit 11.16 However, there are differences among us. We come to the class from different backgrounds and with different intentions

the same way we approach business cases. We look at details within a company, but never lose sight of the big picture (Exhibits 11.7, 11.8, 11.9, and 11.10).

A case mostly provides information about the background of the organization as well as the industry. That is, such information provides the context for the issue, which emphasizes one of the prime reasons for using cases. In a case, there are several decision options and the preferred one depends on the circumstances, i.e., the context. In other words, cases are useful because there do not exist standard universal solutions (Exhibits 11.11, 11.12, 11.13, 11.14, 11.15, 11.16, 11.17, and 11.18).

The case method regards truth as relative, reality as probabilistic, and structural relationships as contingent. Therefore, teaching and learning are most effectively accomplished through discussion rather than exploration. The case method regards real-world phenomena as being complex, and simple theoretical relationships as having limited use. Therefore, direct communication from the teacher to the student is of little value. The emphasis of the learning process should be on the development of understanding, judgement, and intuition (Exhibits 11.19, 11.20, and 11.21).

In order to enhance expression and exchange of ideas, participants should be well-prepared for small group discussion. Each participant uses his or her own understanding and experience to analyze the case.

Exhibit 11.17 Some of us may be interested in going into detail, while others may not be that patient. Or, some of us may be interested in and familiar with some aspects of an issue, while others may be interested in and familiar with other aspects of it. Or, some of us may see the case in a certain way, whereas others may see it in a different way

Exhibit 11.18 In the case method, we *discuss* cases. This is because each one of us interprets the case differently and looks at different aspects of it. To see this, let us look at Exhibit 11.18. What do we see? Do we see "a cowboy hat?" Or, do we see "a man?" Or, do we see "a man at the barber?" Or, do we see "a man wearing a turban?"

Exhibit 11.19 Each of us likely sees a case differently. This constitutes a spectrum for analysis and discussion. A group of us will have a similar interpretation that differs from the rest. But even that group, within itself, contains a spectrum of finer interpretations. This is very much the same as the spectrum of colors from a prism. In the same way that combining all the colors together creates a clear white light, combining our different viewpoints creates a clear view of the case

In the case method, the analysis involves the problem solving model which consists of the following steps:

(a) What are the objectives of the organization?
(b) What is the decision or the problem?
(c) What are the key relevant facts?
(d) What are the alternatives?
(e) What are the decision criteria?
(f) What is your analysis of the alternatives in view of the decision criteria?
(g) Which alternative do you recommend?
(h) What is your plan of action for implementation and what results do you expect?

Decision making is complex when students are faced with several issues with multiple objectives and decision criteria. Typically, there are several sensible course of action to a case. What is important is the students' analysis based on the available information and the student's justification for deciding on a certain alternative. Indeed, each student creates a path to an answer.

In the case method we learn by doing and by teaching others. What we learn becomes second nature and stays with us. By identifying, analyzing, and solving issues in a variety of cases we become prepared for our professional work. The case method of learning is based on the philosophy that students learn better by being actively involved in their own learning (Exhibits 11.22 and 11.23).

Exhibit 11.20 The case method states that each one of us sees the case from a different angle, and it is by sharing, and putting these together, that each one of us obtains a better perspective. The case method of learning focuses on the discussion of the cases, where the joint stakeholders are teachers and students

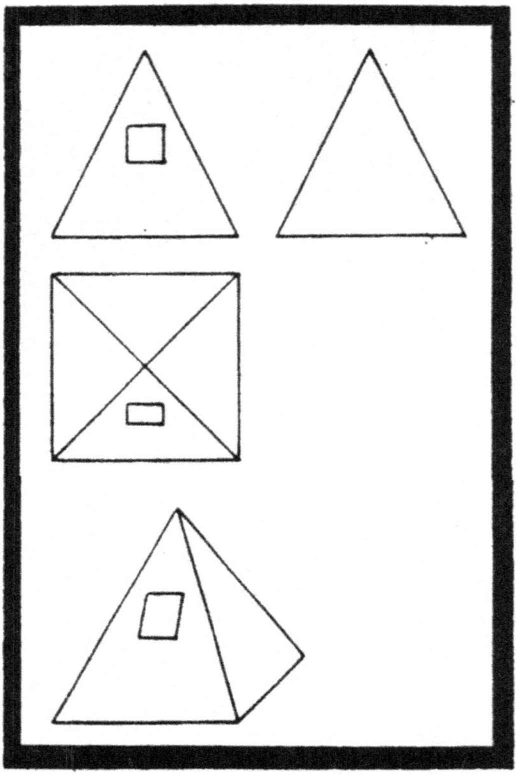

Exhibit 11.21 As we have noted, each one of us noticed a different aspect of the object; and, by sharing our observation with the rest, we came to a better understanding of the object we saw. We approach cases in the same way. That is, each of us first analyzes the case individually, then within a small group. Afterwards, we collectively discuss what each one saw, and how each one analyzed it and made a decision. Next, we exchange our ideas to get a better understanding of the case and make our own decision

Exhibit 11.22 Class participants should do their homework first by themselves, then with their group members. They should not ask for easy outside help. In this way, they learn the material better, and their problem-solving skills improve much faster. Normally, cases do not have right or wrong answers. The quality of students' solution depends largely on their decision making skills. Students should look at the case solving tasks as a process and manage it as a process

Usually, each group has a variety of skills, cultures, experiences, and expertise. Group discussion is enriched by the variety of perspectives from members with diverse backgrounds. A balance of quantitatively- and qualitatively-oriented members improves the overall learning from the group discussions. Group members share their ideas and insights. They collaborate, rather than compete. Each student reaches his or her own decisions based on individual preparation and small group discussion (Exhibits 11.24 and 11.25).

The advantage of the case method is that different analyses usually produce different correct answers. In other words, there is no one correct answer to a case. Keep in mind that, due to their nature, case classes often appear disorderly since they cannot be programmed as in the lecture method.

Effective students display the following characteristics:

1. They prepare, both through reading and analysis of the case under consideration.
2. They offer their viewpoints where these differ from the class in the expectation of:

   (a) Improving their thinking and skills at analysis.
   (b) Improving the class development of the case.

Exhibit 11.23 In discussions, participants are free to express their views, values, and attitudes with respect to any aspects of the case. They should feel free to let others know what their views are. Other participants will balance their views and preferences and change the way they saw the case accordingly. But, if some participants do not make changes in their views as per suggestions made by others, it is not that they have neglected those contributions. But, rather, that there are other views and values involved which are more persuasive to them

3. They develop their theoretical and conceptual model(s) of the field under study, as well as their skill at problem-solving.
4. They make inferences or generalizations from each case vehicle undertaken (Exhibit 11.26).

Although every case is different, the process of learning how to learn is generalizable. The case method provides students with the opportunity to develop a diverse set of skills:

1. Analytical skills
2. Critical thinking skills
3. Decision making skills
4. Application skills
5. Oral communication skills

Exhibit 11.24 Everyone should be open to suggestions. The case method strives on "the give and take" involved in case discussions. Small group discussion provides students with opportunities to check their insights, assumptions, and preparations against those of others; clarify their understanding; listen attentively and critically to others; and argue for their positions based on their individual preparation. Small group discussion uses the group synergy to push beyond the analysis reached by each individual member

6. Time management skills
7. Interpersonal or social skills
8. Creative skills
9. Written communication skills.

The fundamental principles underlying the case method and its ability to involve the student in a highly personal learning experience may be summarized as follows:

1. The primacy of situational analysis,
2. The imperative of relating analysis and action,
3. The necessity of student involvement,
4. A nontraditional instructor role, and
5. A balance of substantive and process teaching objectives.

Exhibit 11.25 After the participants do the cases by themselves and discuss them in small groups with their group members, they come to class better prepared, then the cases will be discussed in the class. It is important that everyone should feel free to express his or her ideas. The professor will express his or her analysis as well. Do not forget that his or her views are as good as that of any other participant. The professor also facilitates the discussion and the decision-making process and his or her emphasis will be to make sure that the learning process is on proper route

3 Conclusion

This chapter showed how entertaining metaphors can be used to introduce in simple terms and in a friendly manner some of the most fundamental views and principles which underlie the case method to students who have not been exposed to the case method at all and, therefore, find it new and frustrating.

This chapter showed how entertaining metaphors can be used to introduce the case method. In order to make the world of education more attractive to students, academicians can incorporate entertainment in their courses. Given the importance of the introduction to the case method, this chapter made an attempt in that direction. This approach has the capability of being applied to other fields and sub-fields of study. The author, as well, has successfully used this approach in the capital structure session and capital markets session of an introductory finance course.[14]

[14] See Ardalan (2008a, 2008b, 2009).

Exhibit 11.26 In the end, participants can make their own informed decision with respect to the issues in the case because they will have a much better view of the whole case than the limited view with which they initially started. The case method process is inductive, unlike the lecture method which is deductive

References

Ardalan, K. 1998. On the Use of Entertaining Metaphors in the Introductory Finance Course. *Financial Practice and Education* 8 (1): 108–119.

———. 2003a. The Lecture-versus-Case Controversy: Its Philosophical Foundation. *Southwestern Economic Review* 30 (1): 99–118.

———. 2003b. Alternative Approaches Utilized in the Case Method: Their Philosophical Foundations. *Academy of Educational Leadership Journal* 30 (3): 103–120.

———. 2006. The Philosophical Foundation of the Lecture-versus-Case Controversy: Its Implications for Faculty Teaching, Research, and Service. *International Journal of Social Economics* 33 (3): 261–281.

———. 2008a. The Philosophical Foundation of the Lecture-versus-Case Controversy: Its Implications for Course Goals, Objectives, and Contents. *International Journal of Social Economics* 35 (1/2): 15–34.

———. 2008b. The Capital Markets Session of the Introductory Finance Course: Incorporating Humor. *International Journal of Business Disciplines* 19 (1): 51–64.

———. 2009. The Capital Structure Session of the Introductory Finance Course: Entertaining Metaphors. *National Accounting Journal* 11 (1): 16–33.

———. 2013. The Philosophical Foundation of the Lecture Method of Instruction and the Case Method of Instruction: Implications for Examinations. *Contemporary Issues in Education Research* 6 (1): 1–7.

———. 2015. Chapter 3: Using Entertaining Metaphors in the Introduction of the Case Method in a Case-Based Course. In *Exploring Learning and Teaching In Higher Education*, ed. Mang Li and Yong Zhao, 69–96. New York, NY: Springer.

Atkinson, R.C., and R.M. Shiffrin. 1968. Human Memory: A Proposed System and Its Control Processes. In *The Psychology of Learning and Motivation: Advances in Research and Theory*, ed. K.W. Spence and J.T. Spence, vol. 2, 89–195. New York, NY: Academic Press.

Banas, J.A., N. Dunbar, D. Rodriguez, and S.J. Liu. 2011. A Review of Humor in Educational Settings: Four Decades of Research. *Communication Education* 60 (1): 115–144.

Bekelja-Wanzer, M., A. Bainbridge Frymier, A. Wojtaszczyk, and T. Smith. 2006. Appropriate and Inappropriate Uses of Humor by Teachers. *Communication Education* 55 (2): 178–196.

Berk, R. 1996. Student Ratings of Ten Strategies for Using Humor in College Teaching. *Journal of Excellence in College Teaching* 7 (3): 71–92.

———. 1998. *Professors Are from Mars, Students Are from Snickers*. Madison, WI: Mendota.

Bohannon, J.N. 1988. Flashbulb Memories of the Space Shuttle Disaster: A Tale of Two Theories. *Cognition* 29: 179–196.

Braasch, J.L.G., and S.R. Goldman. 2010. The Role of Prior Knowledge in Learning from Analogies in Science Texts. *Discourse Processes: A Multi-Disciplinary Journal* 47 (6): 447–479.

Brealey, R.A., S.C. Myers, and F. Allen. 2011. *Principles of Corporate Finance*. 10th ed. New York, NY: McGraw-Hill.

Brealey, R.A., S.C. Myers, and A.J. Marcus. 2012. *Fundamental of Corporate Finance*. 7th ed. New York, NY: McGraw-Hill.

Brice, T., and K. MacMillan. 2005. Encouraging Conceptual Change: The Use of Bridging Analogies in the Teaching of Action-Reaction Forces and the "At Rest" Condition in Physics Research Report. *International Journal of Science Education* 27 (6): 737–763.

Brigham, E.F., and M.C. Ehrhardt. 2011. *Financial Management: Theory and Practice*. 13th ed. Mason, OH: Thomson South-Western.

Brigham, E.F., and J.F. Houston. 2009. *Fundamentals of Financial Management*. 12th ed. Mason, OH: Thomson South-Western.

Brown, D.E., and J. Clement. 1989. Overcoming Misconceptions via Analogical Reasoning: Abstract Transfer versus Explanatory Model Construction. *Instructional Science* 18: 237–261.

Brown, R., and J. Kulik. 1977. Flashbulb Memories. *Cognition* 5: 73–99.

Brown, S., and S. Salter. 2010. Analogies in Science and Science Teaching. *Advances in Physiology Education* 34 (4): 167–169.

Brown, W., and J. Tomlin. 1996. Best and Worst University Teachers: The Opinion of Undergraduate Students. *College Student Journal* 30 (1): 431–434.

Bryant, J., P. Comisky, and D. Zillman. 1997. Teachers' Humor in College Classroom. *Communication Education* 28 (2): 110–118.

Bryant, J., P. Comisky, J. Crane, and D. Zillman. 1980. Relationship between College Teachers' Use of Humor in the Classroom and Students' Evaluations of Their Teachers. *Journal of Educational Psychology* 72 (4): 511–519.

Buchultz, M., E. Skapoulli, and B. Barnwell. 2011. Entextualized Humor in the Formation of Scientist Identities among U.S. Undergraduates. *Anthropology and Education Quarterly* 42 (3): 177–192.

Buckman, K.H. 2010. *Why Did the Professor Cross the Road?: How and Why College Professors Intentionally Use Humor in Their Teaching*. Ph.D. dissertation, Texas A&M University.

Chiu, M.H., and J.W. Lin. 2005. Promoting Fourth Graders' Conceptual Change of Their Understanding of Electric Current via Multiple Analogies. *Journal of Research in Science Teaching* 42 (4): 429–464.

Christensen, C. Roland. 1991. Premises and Practices of Discussion Teaching. In *Education for Judgement*, ed. C. Roland Christensen, David A. Garvin, and Ann Sweet. Boston, MA: Harvard Business School.

Christensen, C. Roland, and Abby J. Hansen. 1987. *Teaching and the Case Method: Text, Cases, and Readings*. Boston, MA: Harvard Business School.

Christianson, S.A. 1989. Flashbulb Memories: Special, but not so Special. *Memory and Cognition* 17: 435–443.

Christianson, S.A., E.F. Loftus, H. Hoffman, and G.R. Loftus. 1991. Eye Fixation and Memory for Emotional Events. *Journal of Experimental Psychology: Learning, Memory, and Cognition* 17: 693–701.

Civikly, J. 1986. Humor and Enjoyment of College Teaching. In *Communicating in College Classrooms: New Directions for Teaching and Learning*, ed. J.M. Civikly, vol. 26, 61–70. San Francisco, CA: Jossey-Bass.

Cousins, N. 1991. *Anatomy of an Illness as Perceived by the Patient*. New York, NY: Bantam.

Craik, F.I.M., and K.R. Blankstein. 1975. Psychophysiology and Human Memory. In *Research in Psychophysiology*, ed. P.H. Venables and M.J. Christie, 388–417. London, England: Wiley.

Dagher, Z. 1995. Review of Studies on the Effectiveness of Instructional Analogies in Science Education. *Science Education* 79: 295–312.

———. 1997. The Case for Analogies in Teaching Science for Understanding. In *Teaching Science for Understanding: A Human Constructivist Perspective*, ed. J.J. Mintzes, J.H. Wandersee, and J.D. Novak, 195–211. San Diego, CA: Academic.

Deckers, L., and J. Devine. 1981. Humor by Violating an Existing Expectancy. *Journal of Psychology* 108: 107–110.

Deckers, L., and D. Hricik. 1984. Orienting and Humor Response: A Synthesis. *Motivation and Emotion* 8 (3): 183–204.

Devadoss, S., and J. Foltz. 1996. Evaluation of Factors Influencing Class Attendance and Performance. *American Journal of Agricultural Economics* 78: 499–507.

Diehl, V., and D.D. Reese. 2010. Elaborated Metaphors Support Viable Inferences about Difficult Science Concepts. *Educational Psychology* 30 (7): 771–791.

Dodge, B., and A. Rossett. 1982. Heuristic for Humor in Instruction. *NSPI Journal* 5: 11–14.

Duit, R., W.M. Roth, M. Komorek, and J. Wilbers. 2001. Fostering Conceptual Change by Analogies—Between Scylla and Charybdis. *Learning and Instruction* 11: 283–303.

Dunbar, K. 1993. Concept Discovery in a Scientific Domain. *Cognitive Science* 17: 391–434.

———. 1995. How Scientists Really Reason: Scientific Reasoning in Real-World Laboratories. In *The Nature of Insight*, ed. R.J. Sternberg and J.E. Davidson, 365–395. Cambridge, MA: MIT Press.

Ellis, N.R., D.K. Detterman, D. Runcie, R.B. McCarver, and E. Craig. 1971. Amnesic Effects in Short-Term Memory. *Journal of Experimental Psychology* 89: 357–361.

Erskine, James A., Michiel R. Leenders, and Louise A. Mauffette-Leenders. 2003. *Teaching with Cases*. 3rd ed. London, ON, Canada: Ivey Business School, University of Western Ontario, Erskine Associate Inc., and Leenders and Associates Inc..

Evans-Palmer, T. 2010. The Potency of Humor and Instructional Self-Efficacy on Art Teacher Stress. *Studies in Art Education: A Journal of Issues and Research in Art Education* 51 (1): 69–83.

Garner, R. 2003. Which Came First, the Chicken or the Egg? A Foul Metaphor for Teaching. *Radical Pedagogy* 5 (2): 205–212.

———. 2005. Humor, Analogy, and Metaphor: H.A.M. It Up in Teaching. *Radical Pedagogy* 6 (2): 166–171.

———. 2006. Humor in Pedagogy: How Ha-Ha Can Lead to Aha! *College Teaching* 54 (1): 177–180.

Gentner, D. 1983. Structure-Mapping: A Theoretical Framework for Analogy. *Cognitive Science* 7 (2): 155–170.

———. 1989. The Mechanisms of Analogical Learning. In *Similarity and Analogical Reasoning*, ed. S. Vosniadou and A. Ortony, 199–241. Cambridge, MA: Cambridge University Press.

Gentner, D., and D.R. Gentner. 1983. Flowing Waters or Teeming Crowds: Mental Models of Electricity. In *Mental Models*, ed. D. Gentner and A.L. Stevens, 99–129. Hillsdale, NJ: Erlbaum.

Gibbs, R.W., Jr., ed. 2008. *The Cambridge Handbook of Metaphor and Thought*. Cambridge, England: Cambridge University Press.

Gick, M.L., and K.J. Holyoak. 1980. Analogical Problem Solving. *Cognitive Psychology* 12: 306–355.

———. 1983. Schema Induction and Analogical Transfer. *Cognitive Psychology* 15: 1–38.

Glenn, R. 2002. Brain Research: Practical Applications for the Classroom. *Teaching for Excellence* 21 (6): 1–2.

Glynn, S.M., B.K. Britton, M. Semrud-Clikeman, and K.D. Muth. 1989. Analogical Reasoning and Problem-Solving in Science Textbooks. In *Handbook of Creativity: Assessment, Research and Theory*, ed. J.A. Glover, R.R. Ronning, and C.R. Reynolds, 383–398. New York, NY: Plenum Press.

Glynn, S.M., R. Duit, and R.B. Thiele. 1995. Teaching Science with Analogies: A Strategy for Constructing Knowledge. In *Learning Science in the Schools: Research Reforming Practice*, ed. S.M. Glynn and R. Duit, 247–273. Mahwah, NJ: Lawrence Erlbaum Associates.

Goswami, U. 1992. *Analogical Reasoning in Children*. Hove, England: Lawrence Erlbaum Associates.

Halpern, D. 1987. Analogies as a Critical Thinking Skill. In *Applications of Cognitive Psychology*, ed. D.E. Berger, K. Pezdek, and W.P. Banks, 75–86. Hillsdale, NJ: Erlbaum.

Halpern, D.F., C. Hansen, and D. Riefer. 1990. Analogies as an Aid to Understanding and Memory. *Journal of Educational Psychology* 82: 298–305.

Harrison, A.G., and R.K. Coll, eds. 2007. *Using Analogies in Middle and Secondary Science Classrooms: The FAR Guide—An Interesting Way to Teach with Analogies*. Thousand Oaks, CA: Corwin Press.

Hayes, D.A., and R.J. Tierney. 1982. Developing Readers' Knowledge through Analogy. *Reading Research Quarterly* 17: 256–280.

Hesse, M.B. 1966. *Models and Analogies in Science*. Notre Dame, IN: University of Notre Dame Press.

Heuer, F., and D. Reisberg. 1990. Vivid Memories of Emotional Events: The Accuracy of Remembered Minutiae. *Memory and Cognition* 18: 496–506.

Hill, D. 1988. *Humor in the Classroom: A Handbook for Teachers*. Springfield, IL: Charles C. Thomas.

Holland, J.H., K.J. Holyoak, R.E. Nisbett, and P.R. Thagard. 1986. *Induction: Processes of Inferences, Learning, and Discovery*. Cambridge, MA: MIT Press.

Holyoak, K.J., and K. Koh. 1987. Surface and Structural Similarity in Analogical Transfer. *Memory and Cognition* 15: 332–340.

Holyoak, K.J., and P. Thagard. 1989. Analogical Mapping by Constraint Satisfaction. *Cognitive Science* 13: 295–355.

———. 1995. *Mental Leap: Analogy in Creative Thought*. Cambridge, MA: MIT Press.

———. 1997. The Analogical Mind. *American Psychologist* 52: 35–44.

Hutchison, C.B., and B.L. Padgett II. 2007. How to Create and Use Analogies Effectively in the Teaching of Science Concepts. *Science Activities: Classroom Projects and Curriculum Ideas* 44 (2): 69–72.

Isen, A.M. 1985. Asymmetry of Happiness and Sadness in Effects on Memory in Normal College Students: Comment on Hasher, Rods, Zacks, Sanft, and Doren. *Journal of Experimental Psychology: General* 114: 388–391.

James, M.C., and L.C. Scharmann. 2007. Using Analogies to Improve the Teaching Performance of Pre-service Teachers. *Journal of Research in Science Teaching* 44 (4): 565–585.

Kaplan, R.M., and G.C. Pascoe. 1977. Humorous Lectures and Humorous examples: Some Effects upon Comprehension and Retention. *Journal of Educational Psychology* 69: 61–65.

Kelly, N., andB. Kelly. 1982. Backgrounds, Education and Teaching Styles of Teaching Award Winning Professors. ERIC, ED 230080.

Keown, A.J., J.D. Martin, J.W. Petty, and D.F. Scott Jr. 2008. *Foundations of Finance: The Logic and Practice of Financial Management*. 6th ed. Upper Saddle River, NJ: Prentice Hall.

Kher, N., S. Molstad, and R. Donahue. 1999. Using Humor in the College Classroom to Enhance Teaching Effectiveness in 'Dread Courses'. *College Student Journal* 33 (3): 400–406.

Kintsch, W., and E. Bates. 1977. Recognition Memory for Statements from a Classroom lecture. *Journal of Psychology: Human Learning and Memory* 3: 150–159.

Korobkin, D. 1989. Humor in the Classroom: Considerations and Strategies. *College Teaching* 36 (4): 154–158.

Lowman, J. 1994. Professors as Performers and Motivators. *College Teaching* 42 (4): 137–141.

Lukehart, D.E. 2009. *The Use of Humor as a Teaching Strategy in Nursing Education*. Ph.D. dissertation, Capella University.

Maltzman, I., W. Kantor, and B. Langdon. 1966. Immediate and Delayed Retention, Arousal, and Orienting and Defensive Reflexes. *Psychonomic Science* 6: 445–446.

Mantooth, J.D. 2010. *The Effects of Professor Humor on College Students' Attention and Retention*. Ph.D. dissertation, Auburn University.

Martin, R.A. 2007. *The Psychology of Humor: An Integrative Approach*. Oxford, England: Elsevier Academic Press.

Mason, L. 1994. Cognitive and Meta-cognitive Aspects in Conceptual Change by Analogy. *Instructional Science* 22: 157–187.

———. 1996. Collaborative Reasoning on Self-Generated Analogies: Conceptual Growth in Understanding Scientific Phenomena. *Educational Research and Evaluation* 2: 309–350.

———. 2004. Fostering Understanding by Structural Alignment as a Route to Analogical Learning. *Instructional Science: An International Journal of Learning and Cognition* 32 (4): 293–318.

Mauffette-Leenders, Louise A., James A. Erskine, and Michiel R. Leenders. 2007. *Learning with Cases*. 4th ed. London, ON, Canada: Ivey Publishing, Ivey Business School, University of Western Ontario.

Mayer, R.E., and B.K. Bromage. 1980. Different Recall Protocols for Technical Texts Due to Advance Organizers. *Journal of Educational Psychology* 72: 209–255.

Mayer, R.E., and J.K. Gallini. 1990. When Is an Illustration Worth Ten Thousand Words? *Journal of Educational Psychology* 82: 715–726.

McCartney-Matthews, M.L. 2011. *A Funny Thing Happened on the Way to the Hippocampus: The Effects of Humor on Student Achievement and Memory Retention*. Ed.D. dissertation, Arizona State University.

McCloskey, D.N. 1990. *If You're So Smart*. Chicago, IL: The University of Chicago Press.

McGhee, P.E. 1983. The Role of Arousal and Hemispheric Lateralization in Humor. In *Handbook of Humor Research*, Basic Issues, ed. P.E. McGhee and J.H. Golstein, vol. I. New York, NY: Springer.

McGhee, P.E., and J.H. Goldstein. 1983. *Handbook of Humor Research*, Basic Issues. Vol. I. New York, NY: Springer.

Mottet, T.P., A.B. Frymier, and S.A. Bebee. 2006. Theorizing about Instructional Communication. In *Handbook of Instructional Communication*, ed. T.P. Mottet, V.P. Richmond, and J.C. McCroskey, 255–282. Boston, MA: Allyn and Bacon.

Neumann, D.L., M. Hood, and M.M. Neumann. 2009. Statistics? You Must Be Joking: The Application and Evaluation of Humor When Teaching Statistics. *Journal of Statistics Education* 17: 2.

Ng, P.T. 2009. Examining the Use of New Science Metaphors in the Learning Organization. *Learning Organization* 16 (2): 168–180.

Ohman, A. 1979. The Orienting Response, Attention, and Learning: An Information-Processing Perspective. In *The Orienting Reflex in Humans*, ed. H.D. Kimmell, E.H. van Olst, and J.E. Orlebeke, 443–471. Hillsdale, NJ: Erlbaum.

Oliva, J.M., P. Azcarate, and A. Navarrete. 2007. Teaching Models in the Use of Analogies as a Resource in the Science Classroom. *International Journal of Science Education* 29 (1): 45–66.
Orgill, M.K., and M. Thomas. 2007. Analogies and the 5E Model. *Science Teacher* 7 (1): 40–45.
Paatz, R., J. Ryder, H. Schwedes, and P. Scott. 2004. A Case Study Analyzing the Process of Analogy-Based Learning in a Teaching Unit about Simple Electric Circuits. *International Journal of Science Education* 26 (9): 1065–1081.
Paivio, A. 1971. *Imagery and Verbal Processes*. New York, NY: Holt, Rinehart and Winston.
———. 1986. *Mental Representations: A Dual Coding Approach*. New York, NY: Oxford University Press.
Paris, N.A., and S.M. Glynn. 2004. Elaborate Analogies in Science Text: Tools for Enhancing Pre-Service Teachers' Knowledge and Attitudes. *Contemporary Educational Psychology* 29 (3): 230–247.
Pena, G.P., and J.S. Andrade-Filho. 2010. Analogies in Medicine: Valuable for Learning, Reasoning, Remembering and Naming. *Advances in Health Sciences Education* 15 (4): 609–619.
Pillemer, D. 1984. Flashbulb Memories of the Assassination Attempt on President Reagan. *Cognition* 16: 63–80.
Pollio, H., and W. Humphreys. 1996. What Award-Wining Lecturers Say about Their Teaching: It's All about Connection. *College Teaching* 44 (3): 101–106.
Powell, J.P., and L.W. Andersen. 1985. Humor and Teaching in Higher Education. *Studies in Higher Education* 10: 79–90.
Pramling, N. 2010. Unearthing Metaphors: Figurativeness in Teacher-Child Talk about Soil and Related Matters. *Early Childhood Education Journal* 38 (1): 57–64.
Prawat, R.S. 1989. Promoting Access to Knowledge, Strategy, and Disposition in Students: A Research Synthesis. *Review of Educational Research* 59: 1–41.
Rhem, J. 1998. Humor in the Classroom. *National Teaching and Learning Forum* 7 (6): 10–12.
Richland, L., K. Holyoak, and J. Stigler. 2004. Analogy Use in Eighth-Grade Mathematics Classrooms. *Cognition and Instruction* 22 (1): 37–60.
Rigney, J.W., and K.A. Lutz. 1976. Effect of Graphic Analogies of Concepts in Chemistry on Learning and Attitude. *Journal of Educational Psychology* 68: 305–311.
Rogers, E.M. 1960. *Physics for the Inquiring Mind*. Princeton, NJ: Princeton University Press.
Romer, D. 1993. Do Students Go to Class? Should They? *Journal of Economic Perspectives* 7 (3): 167–174.
Ross, S.A., R.W. Westerfield, and J.F. Jaffe. 2008a. *Corporate Finance*. 8th ed. New York, NY: McGraw-Hill.
Ross, S.A., R.W. Westerfield, and B.D. Jordan. 2008b. *Fundamentals of Corporate Finance: Standard Edition*. 9th ed. New York, NY: McGraw-Hill.
Royer, M.R., and G.W. Cable. 1976. Illustrations, Analogies and Facilitative Transfer in Prose Learning. *Journal of Educational Psychology* 68: 205–209.
Ruiz, F.J., and C. Luciano. 2011. Cross-Domain Analogies as Relating Derived Relations among Two Separate Relational Networks. *Journal of Experiential Analysis of Behavior* 95 (3): 369–385.
Rumelhart, D.E., and D.A. Norman. 1978. Accretion, Tuning, and Restructuring: Three Modes of Learning. In *Semantic Factors in Cognition*, ed. J.W. Cotton and R. Klatzky. Hillsdale, NJ: Lawrence Erlbaum Associates.
———. 1981. Analogical Processes in Learning. In *Cognitive Skills and Their Aquisition*, ed. J.R. Anderson, 335–360. Hillsdale, NJ: Erlbaum.
Schmidt, S.R. 1991. Can We Have a Distinctive Theory of Memory? *Memory and Cognition* 19: 523–542.
———. 1994. Effects of Humor on Sentence Memory. *Journal of Experimental Psychology: Learning, Memory, and Cognition* 20 (4): 953–967.
———. 2009. The Humor Effect: Differential Processing and Privileged Retrieval. *Memory* 10: 127–138.

Schustack, M.W., and J.R. Anderson. 1979. Effects of Analogy to Prior Knowledge on Memory for New Information. *Journal of Verbal Behavior and Verbal Learning* 18: 565–583.
Skinner, M.E. 2010. All Joking Aside: Five Reasons to Use Humor in the Classroom. *Education Digest: Essential Readings Condensed for Quick Review* 76 (2): 19–21.
Spier-Dance, L., J. Mayer-Smith, N. Dance, and S. Khan. 2005. The Role of Student-Generated Analogies in Promoting Conceptual Understanding for Undergraduate Chemistry Students. *Research in Science and Technological Education* 23 (2): 163–178.
Spiro, R.J., P.J. Feltovich, R.L. Coulson, and D.K. Anderson. 1989. Multiple Analogies for Complex Concepts: Antidotes for Analogy-Induced Misconception in Advanced Knowledge Acquisition. In *Similarity and Analogical Reasoning*, ed. S. Vosniadou and A. Ortony, 498–531. Cambridge, England: Cambridge University Press.
Steinhart, E.C. 2001. *The Logic of Metaphor: Analogous Parts of Possible Worlds*. Dordrecht, The Netherlands: Kluwer Academic.
Sternberg, R.J. 1977. *Intelligence, Information Processing and Analogical Reasoning*. Hillsdale, NJ: Lawrence Erlbaum Associates.
Suls, J.M. 1972. A Two-Stage Model of the Appreciation of Jokes and Cartoons: An Information-Processing Analysis. In *The Psychology of Humor*, ed. J.H. Goldstein and P.E. McGhee, 81–100. New York, NY: Academic.
Torok, S.E., R.F. McMorris, and W. Lin. 2004. Is Humor an Appreciated Teaching Tool? Perceptions of Professors' Teaching Styles and Use of Humor. *College Teaching* 52: 14–20.
Treagust, D., A. Harrison, G. Venville, and Z. Dagher. 1996. Using an Analogical Teaching Approach to Engender Conceptual Change. *International Journal of Science Education* 18: 213–229.
Vosniadou, S., and A. Ortony, eds. 1989. *Similarity and Analogical Reasoning*. Cambridge, MA: Cambridge University Press.
Vosniadou, S., and M. Schommer. 1988. Explanatory Analogies Can Help Children Acquire Information from Expository Text. *Journal of Educational Psychology* 80: 524–536.
Walker, E.L., and R.D. Tarte. 1963. Memory Storage as a Function of Arousal and Time with Homogeneous and Heterogeneous Lists. *Journal of Verbal Learning and Verbal Behavior* 2: 113–119.
Wanzer, M.B., A.B. Frymier, and J. Irwin. 2010. An Explanation of the Relationship between Instruction Humor and Student Learning: Instructional Humor Processing Theory. *Communication Education* 59 (1): 1–18.
White, F. 1992. Enhancing Class Attendance. *National Association of Colleges and Teachers in Agriculture Journal* 36: 113–115.
Willard, M. 2006. Humor in the Hands of Seasoned Montessorians. *Montessori Life: A Publication of the American Montessori Society* 18 (2): 50–53.
Wong, E.D. 1993. Self-Generated Analogies as a Tool for Construction and Evaluating Explanations of Scientific Phenomena. *Journal of Research in Science Teaching* 30: 367–380.
Wormeli, R. 2009. *Metaphors and Analogies: Power Tools for Teaching any Subject*. Portland, ME: Stenhouse Publishers.
Zillmann, D., B.R. Williams, J. Bryant, K.R. Boynton, and M.A. Wolf. 1980. Acquisition of Information from Educational Television Programs as a Function of Differently Paced Humorous Inserts. *Journal of Educational Psychology* 72: 170–180.
Zhang, Q. 2005. Immediacy, Humor, Power Distance, and Classroom Communication Apprehension in Chinese College Classrooms. *Communication Quarterly* 53: 109–124.
Zheng, H.B., and W.J. Song. 2010. Metaphor Analysis in the Educational Discourse: A Critical Review. *US-China Foreign Language* 8 (9): 42–49.
Ziv, A. 1983. The Influence of Humorous Atmosphere on Divergent Thinking. *Contemporary Educational Psychology* 8: 68–75.
———. 1988. Teaching and Learning with Humor: Experiment and Replication. *Journal of Experimental Education* 6 (1): 37–44.

Pluralist Economics: A Multi-paradigmatic Look

Any explanation of an economic phenomenon is based on a worldview. The premise of this book is that any worldview can be associated with one of the four broad paradigms: functionalist, interpretive, radical humanist, and radical structuralist. This chapter takes the major extant schools of thought in economics—Neo-Classical Economics, New Institutional Economics, Behavioral Economics, Austrian Economics, Post-Keynesian Economics, Institutional Economics, Radical Economics, and Marxist Economics—and locates each of them on the map of the four paradigms, as in Exhibit 12.1. It emphasizes, as pluralist economics does, that these schools of thought in economics are equally scientific and informative; they look at economic phenomena from their certain paradigmatic viewpoint; and together they provide a more balanced understanding of the economic phenomenon under consideration. In this chapter, Sects. 1 through 8 present eight major extant schools of thought in economics, and Sect. 9 concludes the chapter.

1 Neo-Classical Economics

Neoclassical economics is an economic school of thought whose principal tenets have characterized and dominated economics since the end of the nineteenth century. During this long period, many other schools of economic thought—such as Austrians, Keynesians, Behavioralists, Institutionalists, and Marxists—have emerged in response to the changing times, or as a reaction against the dominant neoclassical paradigm. These schools of economic thought have challenged the orthodoxy of the neoclassical system. Among them, Keynesians most spectacularly challenged the orthodoxy in the post-World War II era. However, none of them has succeeded in replacing neoclassical microeconomic theory as the cornerstone of economics. The professional journals consistently publish papers which are written in the tradition of neoclassical microeconomic analysis, and macroeconomic

K. Ardalan, *Case Method and Pluralist Economics*,
https://doi.org/10.1007/978-3-319-72071-5_12

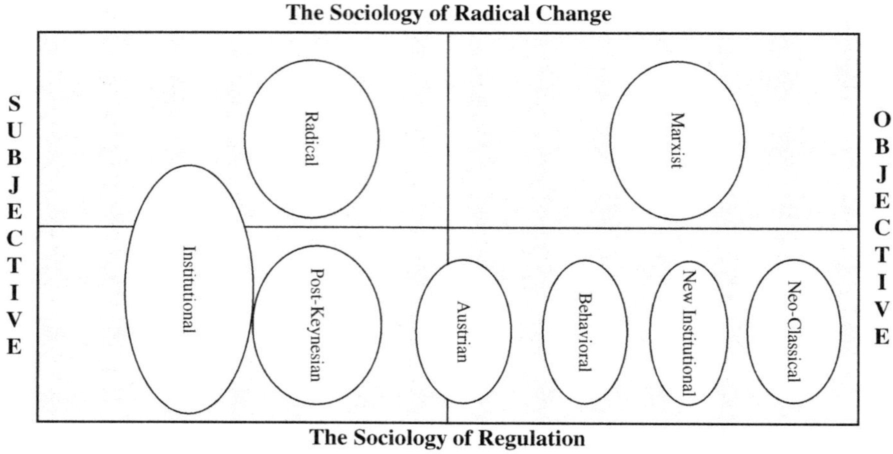

Exhibit 12.1 Major extant schools of thought in economics located within the four paradigms

analysts have increasingly paid attention to the microfoundations of their subject since the late 1960s.[1]

Neoclassical economics is founded on the simple proposition that economic agents act as constrained maximizers. People know what they want, whether they are Consumers, producers, managers, shareholders, regulators, bureaucrats, politicians, voters, husbands and wives, teachers and students, thieves, archbishops, or any other group of people. However, they cannot have all that they want. This is because they face constraints. Therefore, economic agents need to choose from among alternative possible courses of action. For instance, parents cannot spend all their time at work and be able to play with their children; consumers cannot buy all the goods and services they could possibly enjoy; philanthropists cannot contribute significant amounts to every charitable organization; and as President Lincoln has stated, politicians cannot fool all the people all of the time; neoclassical microeconomics states, it is not possible to please all the people all of the time.

Although individuals' objectives cannot be observed, and their willingness to forego some of one goal for more of some other goal depends on their subjective preference, their responses to changes in the constraints that they face can be predicted through the maximizing assumption. Such constraints are assumed to be objectively observable, e.g., a given budget and a given set of market prices; a given amount of available time; a given endowment of resources or human skills; a given

[1] For this literature see Ansperger and Varoufakis (2006), Arrow and Debreu (1954), Blaug (1980), Boland (1991), Brown (1981), Davis (1989), Davis et al. (2004), Dowling and Chin-Fang (2007), Dugger (1979), Emmet (2010), Friedman (1953), Fulton (1984), Gee (1991), Hahn (1981), Heijdra and Lowenberg (1988), Hetzel (2007), Mirowski (1987), Reder (1982), Robbins (1937), Sherman et al. (2008), Stilwell (2012), Tollison (1989), Van Horn and Mirowski (2009), Van Overtveldt (2007), Walsh and Gram (1980), Weintraub (1985a, 1985b, 2008), and Wolff and Resnick (2012). This section is based on Lavoie (1992a, 1992b) and Ricketts (1988).

technological environment; etc. When such constraints are changed, as a result prices or opportunity costs associated with various goals change, therefore a qualitative response in behavior can be predicted.

For instance, a tax levied on a commodity increases its price in terms of the alternatives foregone when a unit of it is consumed; an increase in the wage rate increases the cost of foregone leisure; a technological invention that increases the productivity of resources used in a particular activity lowers the opportunity cost of production in that particular activity. As a result of these changes people modify their behavior until the maximizing condition is reestablished, such that the use of an extra unit of the constraining resource yields the same subjective payoff no matter to which desired goal it is devoted.

The consistent and repeated applications of these principles form the distinguishing characteristics of neoclassical microeconomics, through which it has gained its strength. Such principles have been criticized by other economic school of thought. Behaviorists question neoclassicals' confidence in the purely computational capabilities of individuals. Austrians question the implication of neoclassicals' objectivity of economic constraints. Institutionalists and Marxists question the thoroughgoing individualist premises of neoclassicals. Despite these philosophical objections, the vitality of neoclassical microeconomics and its extension to areas of inquiry far beyond economics, confirm its continued influence and supremacy.

Neoclassical economics is founded on constrained maximization, and therefore it can treat the subject in a highly mathematical and formal way. The place of mathematics in microeconomics is clearly seen in the general equilibrium theory, which is one of the greatest intellectual achievements in microeconomics. General equilibrium theory gains its importance because it deals with the question of whether decisions made by various individuals are compatible with constraints which characterize the entire system. Its analysis established the necessary and sufficient conditions required for the existence and stability of a general equilibrium, which illustrates the intellectual coherence of neoclassical microeconomics.

Neoclassical economics is fairly broad and diversified as it encompasses both micro- and macro-economics as well as axiomatic general equilibrium theory and applied partial-equilibrium analysis. Nonetheless, distinct and fundamental characteristics of neoclassical economics are identifiable, consisting of either a methodological stance or a conception of what economics should be. These conceptions are the rules to which neoclassical economics adhere.

Neoclassical economics can be associated with a few presuppositions, some of which are methodological and others are technical. These presuppositions are instrumentalism, individualism, substantive rationality, and scarcity, which are applied, in the context of private property rights and market economy, to both the orthodox microeconomic and macroeconomic research programs.

1. **Instrumentalism**: Instrumentalism is the dominant epistemology in neoclassical economics. Econometrics is a typical application of instrumentalism, and is a major tool of most neoclassical economists. The empirical work done by neoclassical economists are the predictions of the more abstract neoclassical theories. Neoclassical theories are abstract, non-descriptive, and non-realistic.

Neoclassical theorists select axioms, not for their close approximation to reality, but for their ability to allow the existence and uniqueness of equilibrium. Neoclassical economists describe the world as it should be rather than as it is. Neoclassical economists rely on general equilibrium theory as the basis for their scientific inquiry, and therefore, they are forced to start from unrealistic and non-descriptive hypotheses that support their inquiry.

Meanwhile, neoclassical economists want to follow the tradition of positive science. They want to emulate natural sciences. They, therefore, must rely on empirical work, in their attempt to either verify or falsify their hypotheses. Neoclassical economists start from highly unrealistic hypotheses, and therefore, they need to test the consequences, i.e., the predictions, of their theoretical models.

Neoclassical economists have made great efforts to frame several realistic characteristics within a multitude of their neoclassical models. Such realistic characteristics have been added as auxiliary secondary hypotheses to the basic neoclassical hypotheses. In their applied work, neoclassical economists attempt to verify or falsify hypotheses, but it is the auxiliary hypotheses which are subjected to verification or falsification, not the basic hypotheses—for instance, decreasing returns and profit maximization. Neoclassical economists augment their unrealistic basic model with realistic auxiliary hypotheses, the prediction of which serves as the means to rank the validity of the auxiliary hypotheses. They believe that it is possible to arrive at a model that adequately describes the real world by adding auxiliary realistic characteristics to its unrealistic foundations.

2. Individualism: Neoclassical economists attach great importance to their microfoundations. Despite the fact that many large-scale macroeconomic models have been built without much concern for theory, neoclassical economists require sound microfoundations for such models. This is because of neoclassical economists' individualist philosophy. More specifically, individualism, based on exogenously given tastes and preferences of individuals, constitutes a central methodological characteristic of neoclassical theory.

The individual is at the core of neoclassical economics, in which the wants and the preferences of individuals are sacred. Individuals are set in the forefront of the neoclassical theory. Institutions, firms, and banks are treated as a front for the preferences of individuals. Individuals are regarded as being different in terms of their distinctive preferences, but they are all treated as equal in terms of their impact on the economy. Classes of individuals are treated an unimportant. Institutions are regarded as the veil of an aggregation of individual preferences. Otherwise, they are regarded market imperfections that threaten to disrupt the ideal individualistic world.

This philosophical view crucially influences the neoclassical theory of value. Since the preferences of individuals are at the core of neoclassical theories, they affect prices. Consequently, the neoclassical theory of value becomes subjective because no one knows the preferences of all individuals for all goods.

As a result of atomistic individualism, voluntary exchange gains its importance in neoclassical theory, and any existing social constraint takes its form as the aggregate decision of individuals. As will be noted below, the concept of voluntary exchange between atomistic individuals is quite coherent with the following two essentials of neoclassical economics.

3. Substantive rationality: This and the following presupposition of the neoclassical economics are at the level of economic technicalities, and both are based on the proper allocation of existing resources. The principle of rationality assumes that individuals make the best of any job. The principle of rationality is very powerful and is a requirement for any theory in the social sciences. The neoclassical program, similar to many other programs, is based on the principle of rationality.

However, the neoclassical program is founded on a particular kind of rationality principle. Indeed, it is intertwined with constrained maximization. Neoclassical economics is concerned, as was noted earlier and will be noted later, with the constrained optimization of scarce resources. Other research programs are perhaps concerned with different subjects of constrained maximization.

Substantive rationality is the particular type of rationality that forms the third essential of neoclassical economics. The main characteristic of substantive rationality is that it assumes individuals are capable of substantial information processing and computational performance. Substantial rationality of neoclassical economics assumes that its rational economic man is able to predict all future events, properly use probability distributions of all possible alternatives, or properly form expectations by integrating all available knowledge and information. The environmental context in which the economic agent makes decisions is always assumed to be such that the individual's substantive rationality can always be properly put into use. For instance, uncertain situations in the Knight/Keynes/Shackle sense are transformed into risky situations with known probability distributions, which assume that events are of a recurrent nature.

Substantive rationality's various versions are used in various neoclassical theories and models. The selection of a specific version of substantive rationality depends on the goal of the specific theory. For instance, rationality may be defined axiomatically, to help resolve the problems that arise in abstract neoclassical economics (e.g., existence or uniqueness of equilibrium), or to make tractable the mathematical formulations (e.g., expected utility). Sometimes, some limits may be placed on the available information in order to allow for some realism or some economic policy results.

But, in all various cases, the basic principle of substantive rationality remains in place in neoclassical economics. In all various cases, the computational abilities of the individual and the probabilistic riskiness of the environment remain in place. Neoclassical economists have modeled many realistic decision problems by elevating the computational and knowledge capabilities of the economic agents, but in doing so they have deviated from individuals' observed behavior. Substantive rationality fits very well with instrumentalism, because it allows for all possible events to be known and for their consequences to be assessed, even though this seems to be perfectly unrealistic, provided some predictions can be made.

4. Scarcity: Neoclassical economists define economics as the science of the optimal allocation of scarce resources. Consequently, the theme of scarcity prevails throughout neoclassical economics. In neoclassical economies, everything of significance is scarce, and everything has an opportunity cost. Every decision involves some form of arbitrage, i.e., sacrifice. Prices are indicators of the extent of scarcity. As early as the first course in economics, students of economics are exposed to the definition of economics as the optimal allocation of scarce resources, which in turn, exposes students to the neoclassical research program. However, this definition of economics does not necessarily apply to economics as a whole, i.e., to all schools of thought in economics.

Scarcity is clearly visible in pure exchange models, where there is no production. In pure exchange models, endowments in goods are fixed. In models with production, goods can be produced, but in such models, the endowments in productive resources are fixed. In neoclassical classical economics textbooks, the analysis starts with exchange, on which production is superimposed in the form of indirect exchange. But, in general, pure exchange models are the degenerate version of the more complete neoclassical production model. Interestingly, the structures and the main results of both models are the same. This has been accomplished through the careful addition of the supplementary hypotheses, which can be found in the various sophisticated production models, to safeguard all the main conditions and results of the pure exchange model. In neoclassical economics, production is a form of indirect exchange, which takes place between individual consumer agents who own resources, which transit through the same individual agents, whom are called producers. These producers act as arbitrageurs who attempt to benefit from existing scarcities.

Scarcity is at the foundation of neoclassical economics. It is maintained by setting a variety of conditions: full-employment, a fixed stock of money, etc. Scarcity underlies the supply and demand analysis. It gives rise to prices. It governs the economy. It explains why neoclassical economists attach so much importance to the allocation of resources and use the techniques of constrained optimization. Scarce resources imply full-employment, and therefore, all questions are about the proper use of existing resources, rather than about un-employment and the creation of new resources.

A summary of the core of the neoclassical economics is as follows:

1. Economic agents have given endowments in goods or in productive services;
2. There exists a production set;
3. Agents have ordered preferences;
4. Agents are rational, they optimize subject to constraints;
5. Agents act independently;
6. Agents have proper information;
7. There are mechanisms assuring the co-ordination of decisions.
8. There is substitution when agents make choices among goods;
9. There is substitution when techniques of production are chosen;
10. There is a law of marginal diminishing returns:
11. Each agent maximizes utility (or firms profits);
12. There exists a market for each input and output:
13. Equilibrium results from the confrontation of demand with supply;

14. Prices are the main adjustment or explanatory variable;
15. Without imperfections, or rigidities, the equilibrium would be optimal;
16. If information is imperfect, probability statements can still be made.
17. Search for the existence of an equilibrium;
18. Search for the uniqueness, stability and optimality of equilibrium;
19. Set conditions which are sufficient for the previous rules to be realized;
20. Complete the model with the required conditions;
21. Understand the real world from the completed general equilibrium model;
22. Introduce some realism, by omitting or replacing some of the conditions previously identified.

2 New Institutional Economics

New institutional economics pays close attention to the role which institutions play in the operation of economic systems. Its new and insightful literature has emerged through the consolidation of empirical and theoretical studies in such specialties as industrial organization, labor economics, economic history, comparative economic systems, and so on. It is concerned with organizational issues, and it is interest in ever extending the range of applications of the neoclassical theory that incorporates the effect of property rights and transaction costs on economic incentives and economic behavior. Its analytic approach, although different from that of neoclassical economics, is not deliberately adopted in order to set up a new and distinct type of doctrine to counter the conventional theory. Its intention, rather, is to incorporate greater institutional detail into economic models because the standard neoclassical analysis is overly abstract and incapable of dealing effectively with many problems of interest to theorists and policymakers. It is convinced that conventional microeconomics fails in current economic situations because transaction costs are greater than zero and property rights to resources are different from those of classical capitalism. It has no disagreement with the use of deductive theory, which is fundamentally rejected by the earlier historical-descriptive institutionalists. Its theorists' writings are quite diverse in style and content, but they remain committed to the tenets of orthodox marginalism, and appreciate its essential usefulness. Its emphasis is on the extension of the scope of standard micro-economic theory by taking into account some previously-neglected characteristics of the economic system.[2]

[2]For this literature see Acemoglu (2003), Alchian and Demsetz (1972), Alston et al. (1996), Brousseau and Glachant (2008), Coase (1937, 1960, 1988, 1998), Coeurderoy and Quelin (1997), Crocker and Masten (1996), Davis and North (1971), Drobak and Nye (1997), Dugger (1990), Forbes and Lederman (2009, 2010), Furubotn and Richter (1991a, 1991b, 1998, 2008), Geyskens et al. (2006), Gibbons (2010), Groenewegen et al. (2010), Hodgson (1989a, 1989b), Hutchinson (1984), Joskow (1988, 2008), Klein (1999), Libecap and Smith (1999), Macher and Richman (2008), Medema (1998), Menard and Shirley (2005), North (1986, 1990, 1991, 1994), Ostrom (2005), Pratten (2004), Richter (2005), Rutherford (1994), Rutherford (2001), Shelanski and Klein (1995), Vannoni (2002), Vromen (1995), and Williamson (1975, 1985a, 1985b, 1996, 2000, 2010). This section is based on Furubotn and Richter (1991a).

Although the traditional analysis did not completely abstract from institutional structure, its treatment of institutions was superficial. Although it recognized the existence of political, legal, monetary and other systems; either it regarded these systems as neutral in their effect on economic events and consequently it ignored them, or it took these systems as given and specified them in so perfunctory a way that meant institutional influence was not of much importance. The new institutional economics seeks to demonstrate the important economic impact of institutions. It attempts to illustrate not only that any distinct organizational structure affects incentives and behavior, but also that institutions are themselves legitimate objects of economic analysis. It uses theory to analyze institutions, to explain their operation, and to make it an integral part of the economic model. Its writers attempt to expand the applicability of neoclassical doctrine, and consequently, change the way economic activity is interpreted.

The new institutional economics systematically examines, among other things, the relationship between property rights and institutions. Property rights refer to the sanctioned behavioral relations among men with respect to the use of objects. Property rights assign specific norms of behavior with respect to things that each person, in his interactions with other persons, must observe, or bear the cost for nonobservance. This means that property rights have economic value and must be enforced in the context of society. In general, property rights are determined and enforced by a governance structure or order—i.e., a system of norms combined with the instruments that enforce this order. The enforcement of the order may be based on purely internal mechanisms, or on the expectations of specific external consequences. The new institutional economics deals with the latter. In other words, it is concerned with enforcements based on sanctions that are established either by law or by custom.

An institution is a system of norms applicable to a particular set of activities. An institution consists of informal constraints, formal rules, and the way they are enforced. Institutions play a crucial role in economic development because they regulate, at least partly, the social behavior of individual citizens. There are different theories explaining how institutions arise. At one extreme, institutions are conceived as arising "spontaneously" based on the self-interest of decision-makers, i.e., decision-makers organize themselves, which is referred to as "evolutionary rationalism." At the other extreme, institutions are thought of being organized by a central authority, which is referred to as "legal centralism" or "constructivist rationalism." The new institutional economics advocates the hypothesis of spontaneously developing institutional structure. Both hypotheses are interested in the economic analysis of institutions, and recognize that the aim of the creation of institutions is an organizational structure that will, in some sense, optimize the social behavior of people.

New institutional economics deals with both the institution of property, and the system of norms that governs the acquisition or transfer of property rights. The acquisition or transfer of rights can take place through various activities, such as inheritance or gifts, purchase agreements, order of a central authority, tortuous acts, etc. The distinction of these activities has practical importance as it specifies whether the analysis should be undertaken within the theory of the firm, public choice theory, the economic analysis of law, or some other specialty. Furthermore, it is important to differentiate between institutions in relation to law (e.g., the German civil code) and institutions in relation to rights (e.g., a concrete claim arising out of a labor contract).

New institutional economics transcends the idealized "frictionless" world of neoclassical theory by paying serious attention to the role which transaction costs play in the economy. Real resources are required in order to create, utilize, and guarantee an institution. It is costly to put the social and economic mechanism into operation. For instance, the concept of transaction costs when applied to private property rights, it suggests that resources have to be used to obtain and process information about alternatives; to negotiate, monitor, and enforce contracts; etc. Where there are transactions costs, there is a diversion of certain productive resources from the production of regular commodities to the implementation of transactions. Thus, ceteris paribus, a system that involves transaction costs has a smaller "factor endowment" than an otherwise comparable system that involves zero transaction costs.

The new institutional economics generally follows the methodology of contemporary neoclassical marginalist theory. However, for institutional analysis, it introduces several crucial changes into the orthodox theory of production and exchange, as follows.

1. Methodological individualism: An entirely new view is provided with respect to the role of individual decision-makers within an organization. That is, "society," "the state," "the people," "the firm," or "parties" are no longer conceived as collective entities that behave as if they were individual actors. The organization or collectivity per se is no longer the center of attention. Instead, the analysis of such social units is based on the positions and actions of their individual members.
2. Utility maximization: Individuals are viewed as actors who seek their own interests and maximize their utilities subject to the constraints set by the existing organizational structure. In contrast to the neoclassical practice, there is no dichotomy between the theory of consumer choice and the theory of the firm, as the utility-maximization hypothesis is extended to all individual choices. That is, an individual—whether he is the manager of a government bureau or a capitalist entrepreneur—makes his own choices and pursues his own goals within the limits set by the system in which he is operating.
3. Bounded rationality: In the analysis of the real world of institutions, it is necessary to note that individuals have only limited ability to acquire and process information. The term "bounded rationality" is used show that decision-makers are not hyper-rational. Limited rationality means that not all economic exchanges can be organized by contract and market. An individual who is "bounded rational" attempts to maximize his utility, but finds out that it is costly to do so, and that he is unable to anticipate all contingencies. This means that, with bounded

rationality (and non-zero transaction costs), it is impossible to deal with complexity in all contractually-relevant respects.

4. Opportunistic behavior: while bounded rationality leads to incomplete contracts, there can be general reliance on incomplete contracts if individuals were wholly trustworthy. However, some individuals (either principals or agents) may take dishonest actions, such as disguising preferences, distorting data, deliberately confusing issues, etc. When there is self-seeking with guile, and when it is very costly to distinguish ex ante opportunistic from non-opportunistic actors, comprehensive contracting breaks down.

The new institutional economics notes that, in the absence of bounded rationality and opportunistic behavior, all problems of economic contracting would be trivial, and the need to study economic institutions would be non-existent. However, when the actual decision making involves difficulties, and when operations are conducted in an environment of costly transactions and asymmetrical information, institutions become very important. Nonmarket forms of organization would be created in order to minimize the constraining effects of bounded rationality; and maximize transactions safeguards against the hazards of opportunism.

Property rights: In the standard model of competitive capitalism there is a legal order that provides for private property rights and freedom of contract, which are recognized as crucial. The importance of property rights becomes more evident when they are considered in connection with the concept of an "economic good." A "good" refers to anything that provides utility or satisfaction to a person. An individual must "possess" the good in order to derive satisfaction from it. However, the "owner" may not be able to derive satisfaction from his good because of the existence of many competing individuals. Such ability depends on the extent to which guarantees are provided by social norms. Factors of production are also considered as goods, i.e., they are goods which are in an "earlier stage" of consumption. A factor of production is customarily thought of as a physical entity which a firm acquires and uses (e.g., an acre of land, or a ton of fertilizer), instead of being thought as a right to perform certain physical actions. The firm owns and uses the land as a factor of production, but, in fact, what the firm possesses is the right to perform a circumscribed list of actions.

An asset or a commodity can be characterized not only by its physical properties, but also by the set of legal restrictions that govern the use and exchange of it. Two houses that are physically identical constitute two different commodities if the property rights associated with them are different; and consequently, their market values are different.

Property-rights assignments affect the allocation of resources through exchange. In an exchange of a good, an owner can only transfer to others those rights in the good than he himself possesses. The volume of exchange and the terms of trade are influenced by the prevailing property-rights structure in society, i.e., the particular rights that can be transferred legally. There are many categories of property rights, of which the right of ownership is the best known. Currently, the right of ownership in an asset consists of three components: (a) the right to use the asset (usus); (b) the right to obtain returns from the asset (usus fructus); and (c) the right to change the form, substance, and location of the asset (abusus). This last component—which means the right to experience the changes in the value of an asset—is the most fundamental component of the rights of ownership. It implies that the owner of an asset (e.g., a house) is legally free to transfer to others all rights (e.g., to sell a house), or some rights (e.g., to rent a house), in the asset at a mutually-agreed-upon price. This flexibility in the transfer of rights provides the owner with the opportunity to operate with an infinite planning horizon and, therefore, to participate in the efficient intertemporal allocation of resources.

Although the right of ownership is an exclusive right, it is limited by those restrictions that are set by the law (or custom). The imposition of restrictive measures attenuate private property rights in an asset, limits the economic options available to the asset owner, and a corresponding reduction in the value of the asset.

A particular structure of property rights in an economy affects the allocation and utilization of economic goods (resources) in a specific and predictable way. Property rights that are associated with a good affect the value of that good. Individuals tend to maximize their utility not only as consumers, but also as members of organizations (private firm, government bureau, university, etc.), as a consequence, any change in the system of property rights will have a specific and predictable effect on the allocation of resources, the composition of output, the distribution of income, etc.

The property-rights approach was developed as a reaction to the extreme simplifications of the abstract general equilibrium models that were popular among neoclassical scholars during the post-war period. It introduced a method of analysis that could be uniformly applied to various organizational structures. It formulates an optimization model that incorporates the institutional features of the system which is under consideration, which consists of: (1) a criterion function, or objective function, that specifies the decision maker's preferences with respect to the decision variables; and (2) the set of options (penalties and rewards) that is attainable by the decision maker. Then, the formal problem involves the maximization of the criterion function subject to the constraints imposed by the opportunity set.

New institutional economists have applied the model and have been able to generate valuable insights into the behavior of diverse organizations such as the modern corporation, the regulated firm, the nonprofit firm, the cooperative, the government bureau, the trade union, the codetermined firm, the socialist firm, etc. Property-rights models can deal with the role of incentives not only under circumstances of norm-abiding behavior, but also under conditions of asymmetric information that may lead to hidden actions and opportunistic behavior.

Transaction costs: The existence of positive transaction costs implies that the enforcement of rights is costly. To consider this matter and other friction-related problems, it is necessary to learn about transaction costs.

Historically, new institutional economists variously defined transaction costs as the cost of using the market; as the cost of using the price mechanism; or as the cost of exchanging ownership titles. Currently, transaction costs are broadly defined as the costs that are associated with: (1) the creation or change of an institution or organization; and (2) the use of an institution or organization.

The costs associated with institutions and the "rules of the game" increase with society's development and complexity ("civilization"). There are three basic duties/ expenditures of the sovereign: (1) defense; (2) legal system; and (3) public works and public institutions. In addition, there are costs associated with running the government. These translate into the costs incurred for guaranteeing property rights and supplying public goods. These first-type transaction costs are mostly ignored in mainstream economic theory.

The second type of transaction cost has received greater attention in the mainstream literature because these costs are more directly related to firms or markets, than to constitutional questions or governmental infrastructure. That is, there are transaction costs associated with the use of markets, as well as when entrepreneurs exercise the right to give orders within a firm.

Market transaction costs consist of the following components: (1) search and information costs; (2) bargaining and decision costs; and (3) policing and enforcement costs. Equivalently, they can be stated as follows: (1) the cost of preparing contracts; (2) the cost of concluding contracts; and (3) the cost of monitoring and enforcing the performance of a contract.

There are transactions costs associated with the manager's right to give orders within the firm. The firm concludes written or unwritten contracts with its employees, who are the owners of productive factors. The contracts indicate their tasks, their work conditions, and their division of labor within the firm, and its organizational structure. The ultimate right to give orders is normally assigned to those people who own firm-specific resources and who have the ability to take risk and analyze the firm's conditions.

Indeed, the concept of transaction costs plays a crucial role in any adequate analysis of how a capitalist market economy actually functions. The characteristics of the institutional structure (and property rights) of an economy strongly affect the level of transaction costs by affecting the rewards accrued to self-interested individuals. Given the cost of production and organizational knowledge, individuals in maximizing their utility, tend to choose an organizational structure (i.e., an institution) that minimizes transaction costs. In other words, decision-makers tend to choose that organizational form that economizes the sum of transaction cost and production cost, i.e., they economize both the transaction costs and neoclassical production costs.

3 Behavioral Economics

Behavioral economics is intended to increase the explanatory power of economics by providing it with more realistic psychological foundations. It is based on the conviction that increasing the realism of the psychological underpinnings of economic analysis results in new theoretical insights, improved predictions, and better policies. It attempts to modify the neoclassical approach to economics, which is based on utility maximization, equilibrium, and efficiency. It recognizes that the neoclassical approach to economics is useful because its theoretical framework can be applied to almost any form of economic (and even noneconomic) phenomena, and that it makes refutable predictions and suggests new theories.[3]

Behavioral economics modifies some of the assumptions made in standard economic theory in the direction of greater psychological realism. Such modifications are often not radical because they change those assumptions that are not central to the standard economic approach. For instance, the core of the neoclassical theory does not require that people disregard fairness, that they weight risky outcomes in a linear fashion, or that they discount the future exponentially at a constant rate. Other behavioral economics assumptions acknowledge human limits on computational power, willpower, and self-interest. These assumptions can be regarded as "procedurally rational" (a la Herbert Simon) because they incorporate functional heuristics for solving problems that are often so complex that even modern computer algorithms cannot exactly solve them.

Some of the neoclassical economists believe that theories should be judged based on the following three criteria: congruence with reality, generality, and tractability. Theories in behavioral economics can be judged in the same way. Behavioral economists share the modernist view that the ultimate test of a theory is how accurately it identifies the actual causes of behavior. A theory's accurate predictions provide support for the degree to which the theory has pinned down the right causes. Furthermore, more realistic assumptions are very helpful.

Theories in behavioral economics also attempt to be general. For this purpose, they add only one or two parameters to the standard model such that with specific values for the parameters the behavioral model reduces to the standard one. Then, the behavioral model can be tested against the standard model through the estimation of the values of the parameters. After such tests are successfully performed, the behavioral model can be applied as generally as the standard one.

Although adding behavioral assumptions often makes the models less tractable, many research papers have shown that it can be done. Moreover, even though behavioral models often add parameters to the standard models, they, in some cases, have been even more precise than the standard ones that assume more rationality in the context of dynamics and strategic interactions. For instance, in dynamic models,

[3]For this literature see Altman (2006), Ariely (2008), Baddeley (2013), Baker and Nofsinger (2010), Barberis and Thaler (2003), Bardsley et al. (2010), Binmore (2008), Bruni and Sugden (2007), Camerer (2003, 2006), Camerer et al. (2004), Cartwright (2011), Cassar and Friedman (2004), Conlisk (1996), Della Vigna (2009), Diamond and Vartiainen (2007), Dowling and Chin-Fang (2007), Earl (1988), Earl (1990), Forbes (2009), Frey and Benz (2004), Fudenberg (2006), Gilad and Kaish (1986), Kahneman and Tversky (1979), List (2004), Maital (2007), Mullainathan and Thaler (2000), Pesendorfer (2006), Pompian (2012), Rabin (1998), Ricciardi and Simon (2000), Roth (1995), Schmidt et al. (2008), Sent (2004), Shefrin (2002), Shiller (2003), Shiv and Fedorikhin (1999), Simon (1955, 1998), Thaler (2005, 2008a, 2008b), Tomer (2007), Tversky and Kahneman (1974, 1981), Van Raaij (1991), and Velupillai and Chen (2012). This section is based on Camerer et al. (2004).

rational expectation models often conclude with multiple paths for inflation and asset prices, while adaptive expectation models often conclude with one path. Similarly, in game theory, in those games where the mutual consistency requirement of Nash often lead to multiple equilibria, models based on cognitive algorithms often generate precise predictions.

The realism, generality, and tractability of behavioral economics can be shown through the concept of "loss-aversion." Loss-aversion refers to the idea that people have a stronger aversion to losses relative to a reference point than the desire for gains of equivalent magnitude. Many experiments have demonstrated that loss-aversion is more realistic than the standard continuous, concave, utility function over wealth. Loss-aversion has identified the instances in which predictions of standard theories have been wrong, e.g., the equity premium puzzle in finance, and asymmetry in price elasticities. Loss-aversion can also be generalized by parameterizing it as the ratio of the marginal disutility of a loss relative to the marginal utility of a gain at the reference point (i.e., the ratio of the derivatives at zero). Consequently, the standard model can be represented as its special case in which this "loss-aversion coefficient" is 1. The tractability of loss-aversion has been shown in several application, thought they have not been easy.

The methods used in behavioral economics are the same as those used in other areas of economics. Initially, behavioral economics heavily used experimental methods. More recently, however, behavioral economics has not only been using experimentation, but also has used the full range of methods employed used on other areas of economics.

Behavioral economics has heavily drawn on one of the subfields of psychology called "behavioral decision research," which typically classifies research into two categories: judgment and choice. Judgment research focuses on the processes which people use in order to estimate probabilities. Choice research focuses on the processes which people use in order to select among actions, taking into account any relevant judgments which they may have already made.

Probability judgment is central to economic life. Economics models probability judgment based on two standard principles: statistical sampling, and Bayes's rule for updating probabilities to incorporate new evidence. Bayes's rule has several features that are cognitively unrealistic. First, Bayesian updating requires a prior, which it does not specify where the prior comes from. Second, Bayesian updating involves a separation between previously-judged probabilities and the evaluations of new evidence. But this separability is violated by many cognitive mechanisms that use the previous information to interpret the new evidence. Third, subjective expected utility involves separability between probability judgments of states and utilities associated with those states. Fourth, Bayesian updating considers the order of arrival of information to be inconsequential. But, order effects are important due to the strength of recent information in working memory and of increased "rehearsal" of older memories.

Cognitive psychologists have noted that people use heuristic mechanisms that result in judgments that sometimes violate either sampling principles or Bayes's rule. For instance, people may judge the probabilities of future events based on the ease with which those events can be imagined or can be retrieved from memory. This is called "availability heuristic" and leads to several biases. One is called "hindsight bias," according to which it is easier for people to imagine events that actually did occur than the events that did not occur, and consequently people often overestimate the probability they previously attached to events that later occurred. Another bias is called the "curse of knowledge," according to which people who know a lot find it hard to imagine how little others know.

Another heuristic which people use to make probability judgments is called "representativeness." People judge conditional probabilities—e.g., P(hypothesis/data) or P(class/example)—based on the degree to which the data represents the hypothesis or the example represents the class. Representativeness, as most other heuristics, is a shortcut that provides reasonable judgments with minimal cognitive effort in many cases, but sometimes is misleading and is undisciplined by normative principles. People judge prototypical exemplars of a class to be more likely than they truly are (unless the prototype's extremity is part of the prototype). For instance, when judging whether a certain student described in a profile is a psychology major or a computer science major, people tend to focus on the extent to which the profile matches the stereotype of a psychology or computer science major. Many studies show that this practice of feature-matching leads people to underweight the "base rate"—in the example just discussed, the "base rate" refers to the overall frequency of the two majors.

Representativeness also leads to the so-called "the law of small numbers." People tend to think that small samples represent the properties of the statistical process that generated them. This is in contrast to "the law of large numbers," which guarantees that a large sample of independent draws represents the process that generated them. One of the manifestations of the law of small numbers is the so-called "gambler's fallacy," according to which people expect a tail after a coin landed heads three times in a sequence.

Choice research of behavioral economics is related to the preference theory of neoclassical economics, which incorporates several strong and testable assumptions as follows: (1) that preferences are "reference independent," i.e., preferences are not affected by the individual's transient asset position; (2) that preferences are invariant with respect to superficial variations in the descriptions of options; and (3) that elicited preferences are not influenced by the precise way in which preferences are measured as long as the method used is "incentive compatible," i.e., the method provides incentives for individuals to reveal their "true" preferences. Behavioral economists note that all of these assumptions have been significantly violated.

For instance, numerous experiments of "framing effects" illustrate that the way that choices are presented to an individual often determines the preferences that are "revealed" by the individual. The classic example of a framing effect is the "Asian disease" that threatens the lives of 600 citizens. People are asked to choose between two options. In the "positive frame," the two choices are: (A) saving 200 lives for sure, or (B) a one-third chance of saving all 600 with a two-third chance of saving no one. In the "negative frame," the two choices are: (C) 400 people dying for sure, or (D) a two-third chance of 600 dying and a one-third chance of no one dying. In terms of lives lost or at risk, A in equivalent to C; and B is equivalent to D. Nevertheless, most people choose A over B, but D over C.

The standard theory is also violated by what is called an "anchoring effect." Experimentally, this effect has been demonstrated initially in the context of judgment and then in the context of choice. In the experiment with respect to judgment, subjects were shown a number on a wheel of fortune that had a range of 0–100, and then they were asked whether the number of African nations in the United Nations was greater than or less than this number. Subsequently, they were asked about the true value. Although the number from the wheel of fortune was random, subjects' answers were strongly influenced by the number obtained from the spin of the wheel. That is, subjects seemed to "anchor" on the number obtained from the spin of the wheel, and then adjusted their answers for what they thought or knew, but adjusted insufficiently. In another experiment which was with respect to choice, subjects were shown a number which had been chosen at random and subjects were asked whether their certainty equivalent for a gamble was greater than or smaller than this number. Subsequently, the subjects were asked to specify their actual certainty equivalent for the gamble. Again, the stated values were correlated significantly with the random number.

The method of eliciting preferences can dramatically affect preferences thus revealed, even producing "preference reversals," i.e., A is preferred to B under one method of elicitation, but B is preferred to A under a different method of elicitation. The best-known experiment contrasts the choice people make between two bets versus the price people are willing to pay for the two bets when the bets are offered to them separately. More specifically, bet A offers a high probability of a small payoff, and bet B offers a small probability of a high payoff. People often choose the more conservative bet A over bet B, but are ready to pay a higher price for the riskier bet B than bet A. Another form of preference reversal occurs in marketing experiments where joint and separate evaluations of pairs of goods are elicited. People often price or evaluate item A higher than item B when the two items are evaluated independently, but people often price or evaluate item B higher than item A when the two items are evaluated concurrently.

The set of choices also affects people's preferences with respect to each choice. This is called "Context effects." Experiments have shown that people are generally attracted to options that dominate other options. Furthermore, they are drawn disproportionately to "compromise" alternatives whose attribute values lie between those of other alternatives.

All of the above findings suggest that preferences are not as defined by standard economics. Preferences are often ill-defined, highly malleable, and context-dependent. Nonetheless, people make economic decision, i.e., they choose a brand of toothpaste, a car, a job, or how to invest. Behavioral economics refers to the process by which people make choices based on such preferences as "constructing preferences."

Next, the discussion focuses on major topic areas of behavioral economics: reference-dependence/loss-aversion, and decision-making under risk/uncertainty.

Reference-dependence is in contrast to classical consumer theory's assumption that individual's preferences over various commodities are invariant with respect to the individual's current endowment or consumption. Specifically, people often prefer not to lose commodities from their consumption bundle than to gain other commodities. In an experimental study, the subjects in one group were endowed with a mug, while the subjects in another group were endowed with a pen. Both groups were allowed to exchange their good for the other. Under the assumption of preference-independence, the fractions of subjects exchanging their mug for a pen, and the fraction exchanging their pen for a mug should approximately add up to one. However, in the experiment, only 22% of the subjects made the exchange. This implies that people have a strong preference for the good in their endowment, i.e., people prefer not to lose what they own. Loss aversion has already been used to explain the following phenomena: (1) asymmetries in demand elasticities after price increases and decreases; (2) the tendency for New York City cab drivers to quit early after reaching a daily income target, producing surprising upward-sloping labor supply curves; and (3) the large gap between stock and bond returns, i.e., the "equity premium."

Decision-making under risk/uncertainty in standard economics is based on the expected-utility (EU) hypothesis that considers the utility of a risky distribution of outcomes as a probability-weighted average of the utilities of outcomes. This is a normatively-appealing hypothesis because it logically follows from seemingly reasonable axioms, e.g., the independence (or "cancellation") axiom. According to the independence axiom, when people compare two gambles, they should cancel events that have the same outcome with the same probability, i.e., their choice should be independent of all those equally-likely common outcomes. Another feature of the expected-utility hypothesis is that it simplifies matters because an individual's taste with respect to risky financial outcomes can be fully represented by the shape of the individual's utility function for money.

Many experimental studies in behavioral economics document the failures of expected utility hypothesis' predictions in simple situations where subjects can earn substantial sums of money from their choices. Such studies have also offered new theories to account for the evidence. Some of these new theories change the weighting of probabilities, but preserve a "betweenness" property that states: if A is preferred to B, then any probabilistic gamble between them is preferred to B, but dis-preferred to A, i.e., in terms of preferences, the gambles lie "between" A and B. Other new theories treat probability weights as "rank-dependent." That is, first, outcomes are ranked; then their probabilities are weighted according to the rank of outcomes within the gamble under consideration. One way to do this mathematically is to nonlinearly transform the cumulative probabilities of outcomes, and weigh the utilities of outcomes by the differences of those weighted cumulative probabilities. The best-known such theory is the cumulative prospect theory.

The above-mentioned experimental research has arrived at three clear conclusions. (1) That the two new classes of theories take more general functional forms than expected utility, and that the rank-dependent theories fit the data better than the betweenness class theories. (2) That the statistical evidence against EU is so overwhelming that it is no longer necessary to perform tests of EU against alternative theories. (3) That EU fits worst when comparing two gambles that have different sets of possible outcomes (or "support").

Prospect theory has a more accurate explanatory power than EU because it properly accounts for the psychophysics of judgment and choice. It has two main components: a probability weighting function, and a "value function," which replaces the utility function of the EU. The weighting function $w(p)$ combines two elements: (1) The level of probability weight is a way of expressing preference toward risk (if an individual does not like to gamble, he/she places low weight on any chance of winning anything); and (2) the curvature in $w(p)$ shows the degree to which people are sensitive to differences in probabilities. If people are more sensitive in the neighborhoods of possibility and certainty—i.e., changes in probability near 0 and 1—than to intermediate values, then their $w(p)$ curve will overweight low probabilities and underweight high ones. The value function is based on the insight that the utility of an outcome depends not on the absolute value of the resultant wealth, but on whether the outcome is a gain or a loss. Prospect theory also incorporates the ideas that risk-preferences are reflections at the reference point, and that preferences show "loss-aversion."

4 Austrian Economics

The Austrian school of economics was founded in 1871 when Carl Menger's *Principles of Economics* was published. Carl Menger, William Stanley Jevons, and Leon Walras brought about the marginalist revolution in economic analysis. Menger dedicated *Principles of Economics* to one of his German colleagues, William Roscher, who was one of the leading figures in the German historical school that dominated economic thought in German-speaking countries. In *Principles of Economics*, Menger argued that economic analysis is universally applicable and that the appropriate point of reference in economic analysis is man and his choices. These choices, according to Menger, are determined by the subjective preferences of the individual and the margin on which his decisions are made. The logic of choice, Menger believed, acts as the foundation for the development of a universally-valid economic theory.[4]

The historical school, in contrast, believed that economics does not lend itself to generating universal principles, and that scientific research in economics instead should focus on detailed historical examination. The German historical school

[4] For this literature see Backhaus (2005), Barry (1991), Boettke (1989, 1994, 1996), Boettke and Prychitko (1994), Dolan (1976), Gloria-Palermo (1999), Grassl and Smith (1986), Hall and Martin (2011), Kirzner (1981, 1992, 2000), Koppl (2008), Koppl et al. (2010), Lachmann (1998), Lewis (2004), Littlechild (1990), Loasby (1991), Meijer (1995), von Mises (1962, 1966), Rima (2013a, 2013b), Menger (1981), Samuels (1989), Shand (1984, 1990), and Vaughn (1994). This section is based on Boettke (2010).

thought that the English classical economists mistakenly believed in economic laws that transcend time and national boundaries. Menger's *Principles of Economics* through marginal analysis introduced new universal laws, which were aligned with the views of classical political economists. Roscher's students, especially Gustav Schmoller, in response to Menger's defense of "theory," gave the work of Menger and his followers, i.e., Eugen Bohm-Bawerk and Friedrich Wieser, the derogatory title of "Austrian school," who held faculty positions at the University of Vienna. The title has remained in effect since then.

Since the 1930s, the University of Vienna, or any other Austrian university, has produced no leading figure in the Austrian school of economics. This is because, in the 1930s and 1940s, the Austrian school moved to Britain and the United States. More specifically, the scholars associated with the Austrian approach to economic science held positions primarily at the London School of Economics (1931–1950), New York University (1944–), Auburn University (1983–), and George Mason University (1981–). Many of the ideas of the leading mid-twentieth-century Austrian economists, such as Ludwig von Mises and F.A. Hayek, are rooted in the ideas of nineteenth century classical economists, such as Adam Smith and David Hume, or early-twentieth century figures, such as Knut Wicksell, as well as Menger, Bohm-Bawerk, and Friedrich von Wieser. Contemporary Austrian school economists reflect a more diverse mix of intellectual traditions in economic science as they have been influenced by modern figures in economics, such as Armen Alchian, James Buchanan, Ronald Coase, Harold Demsetz, Axel Leijonhufvud, Douglass North, Mancur Olson, Vernon Smith, Gordon Tullock, Leland Yeager, and Oliver Williamson, as well as Israel Kirzner and Murray Rothbard. This diversity raises the possibility for someone to argue that the label "Austrian" does not possess any substantive meaning. But, one could also sensibly argue that a unique Austrian school of economics operates within the economic profession today. The following concentrates on the main propositions about economics in which Austrian economists believe. Propositions 1–3 fall under the heading of *The Science of Economics*, Propositions 4–7 fall under the heading of *Microeconomics*, and Propositions 8–10 fall under the heading of *Macroeconomics.*

Proposition 1: Only individuals choose. All economic analysis starts with man, with his purposes and plans. Only individuals make choices, and in contrast, collective entities do not make choices. Economic analysis has two main tasks. The primary task of economic analysis is to explain economic phenomena by basing it on individual purposes and plans. The secondary task of economic analysis is to follow up the unintended consequences of individual choices.

Proposition 2: The study of the market order is fundamentally about exchange behavior and the institutions within which exchanges take place. The market economy and its price system are best understood when they are regarded as a "catallaxy," and thus the studies of the market order falls in the domain of the science of "catallactics." These terms are derived from the Greek word "katallaxy," meaning exchange and bringing strangers into friendship through exchange. Catallactics requires the focus of the analysis to be placed on the exchange relationships that emerge in the market, the bargaining that characterizes the exchange process, and the institutions that constitute the context in which exchange takes place.

Proposition 3: The "facts" of the social sciences are what people believe and think. In contrast to the physical sciences, the human sciences start with the purposes and plans of individuals. Whereas the elimination of purposes and plans in the natural sciences, overcame the problem of anthropomorphism, and led to scientific advances; in the human sciences, the elimination of purposes and plans purges the science of human action of its subject matter. In the human sciences, the "facts" of the world are constituted by what the actors think and believe. The meaning that human beings place on things, practices, places, and people determines their orientation in making decisions. The goal of the sciences of human action is intelligibility, understanding, and explanation; not prediction. The human sciences can achieve this goal because human scientists are human beings who study humans, i.e., human scientists possess knowledge from within, but the natural sciences cannot pursue a goal of intelligibility because they rely on knowledge from without. Human scientists can understand purposes and plans of other human actors because human scientists themselves are human actors. The essential difference between the sciences of human action and the physical sciences can be brought to the fore through the classic thought experiment regarding a Martian observing the "data" at Grand Central Train Station in New York City. The Martian may observe that when the little hand on the clock points to eight, there is a bustle of movement as bodies exit these boxes; and that when the little hand points to five, there is a bustle of movement as bodies enter the boxes. The Martian may even develop a prediction about the direction of the little hand on the clock and the movement of bodies and boxes. But, unless the Martian has an understanding of human beings' purposes and plans (i.e., the commuting to and from work), his "scientific" understanding with respect to Grand Central Station data would be limited. The sciences of human action are qualitatively different from the natural sciences, and human sciences are impoverished when they are forced into the philosophic/scientific mold of the natural sciences.

Proposition 4: Utility and costs are subjective. All economic phenomena take effect only after they have gone through the human mind. Since the 1870s, liberal economists have come to believe that value is subjective. However, following Alfred Marshall, many liberal economists believe that costs are determined by objective conditions. Marshall used the metaphor of a pair of scissors and emphasized that in the same way that both blades of a pair of scissors cut a piece of paper, the subjective value and objective costs determine price. But, Marshall ignored the fact that costs are also subjective because they are themselves determined by the value of alternative uses of scarce resources. That is, indeed both blades of the scissors cut the paper, but the blade of supply, as well, is determined by individuals' subjective valuations. In deciding among many courses of action, an individual must choose. That is, the individual must pursue one path among many paths. The pervasiveness and importance of alternatives in choices leads to one of the defining concepts of the economic way of thinking: opportunity costs. That is, the cost of any action is the value of the highest-valued alternative forgone in taking that action. By definition, the forgone action is never taken. But, at the time of decision making, one weighs the expected benefits of an action against the expected benefits of alternative actions.

Proposition 5: The price system economizes on the information that people need to process in making their decisions. Prices summarize the prevailing terms of exchange in the market. The price system signals relevant information to market participants and helps them to realize mutual gains from exchange. For instance, when the price system informs people that the price of tin has risen, people do not need to know whether the increase in the price of tin was caused by an increase in the demand for tin or a decrease in the supply of tin. In either case, the increase in the price of tin leads them to economize on its use. In general, a change in underling conditions leads to a change in market prices, which, in turn, leads to a quick adjustment by people.

Proposition 6: Private property in the means of production is a necessary condition for rational economic calculation. Liberal economists and social thinkers have long believed that private ownership acts as a powerful incentive for the efficient allocation of scarce resources. In contrast, socialist economists and social thinkers have believed that socialism transcends these incentive problems by changing human nature. But, even if socialism changes the human nature, as assumed by socialists, socialism will fail because economic planners cannot rationally calculate the alternative uses of resources. This is because without private ownership in the means of production, there will be no market for the means of production, there will be no money prices for the means of production, there will be no money prices to reflect the relative scarcities of the means of production, and therefore, economic planners will not be able to rationally calculate the alternative uses of the means of production.

Proposition 7: The competitive market is a process of entrepreneurial Discovery. Many economists consider "competition" as a state of affairs. But, "competition" requires an activity. If competition were a state of affairs, there would be no role for entrepreneurs. But, competition is an activity, in which the entrepreneur has a huge role to play. The entrepreneur, as the agent of change, engages and pulls markets in new directions. The entrepreneur is on the look-out for unrecognized opportunities for mutual gain. By recognizing and engaging in opportunities, the entrepreneur earns a profit. The entrepreneur's discovery of opportunities, and gains from exchange, result in mutual learning and moves the market system to a more efficient allocation of resources. Entrepreneur's discovery guarantees that a free market moves closer to the most efficient use of resources. In addition, the lure of profit continually provides entrepreneurs with the incentive to seek innovations that increase productive capacity. The entrepreneur recognizes imperfections and turns them into profit opportunities. Entrepreneurship has three main characteristics: serendipity (discovery), search (conscious deliberation), and seizing the opportunity for profit. The price system and the market economy act as learning devices that provide relevant information to individuals in order to discover mutual gains and use scarce resources efficiently.

Proposition 8: Money is not neutral. Money is defined as the medium of exchange which is commonly accepted by people. In general, government policy distorts the monetary unit, and as a consequence, exchange will be distorted as well. The goal of monetary policy should be the minimization of these distortions. When an increase in money supply is not offset by a corresponding increase in money demand the result will be an increase in prices. But, all prices do not adjust instantaneously throughout the economy. Some prices adjust faster than others, which result in changes in relative prices. These changes affect the pattern of exchange and production. Thus, by its very nature, money cannot be neutral. The importance of this proposition can be seen more clearly when considering the costs of inflation. The quantity theory of money correctly stated that printing money does not increase wealth. This is because when the government doubles the money supply, money holders' ability to buy more goods is prevented because of the doubling of prices. The quantity theory of money was an important advance in economic thinking. However, a mechanical application of the quantity theory of money leads to an underestimation of the costs of inflationary monetary policy. To see this, consider the situation in which the government doubles the money supply and as a consequence prices simply double. Then, economic actors can anticipate this price adjustment by closely following money supply figures and can adjust their behavior accordingly. In this way, the cost of inflation is minimal. But, inflation has several socially-destructive characteristics. First, even if inflation is fully anticipated, it breaches the basic trust between the government and its citizens because government has used inflation to confiscate people's wealth. Second, unanticipated inflation redistributes wealth because debtors gain at the expense of creditors. Third, when the money is added somewhere in the system—e.g., through the government's purchase of bonds—and because people cannot perfectly anticipate inflation, and that some prices (e.g., the price of bonds) adjust before other prices, inflation distorts the pattern of exchange and production. Money is used for almost all transactions in a modern economy. Therefore, monetary distortions affect all those transactions. The conclusion is that the goal of monetary policy should be to minimize these monetary distortions, precisely because money is not neutral. In search of solutions to this elusive goal, Austrian economists generated some of their most innovative work that resulted in the development in the 1970s and 1980s of the literature on free banking.

Proposition 9: The capital structure consists of heterogeneous goods that have multi-specific uses that must be aligned. Car companies are designing cars which will be produced in a decade. A great challenge to them is the proper allocation of resources to meet that goal. Production is always made for meeting an uncertain future demand, and the production process requires investment in each stage of production ranging from the starting stage (mining iron ore) to the ending stage (the car dealership). In general, the values of all producer goods at every stage of production are determined by the value which consumers place on the product produced by the producer goods. The production plan involves the sequencing of various investment goods into a capital structure in order to produce the final goods in the most efficient manner. Capital goods are not homogeneous, and the same type of capital goods cannot be used to produce all the final products which the consumers desire. When a mistake is made, the capital goods cannot be reallocated quickly, and with minimal cost, toward producing the most-desired final product. Capital goods are heterogeneous and multi-specific. That is, an auto plant can make cars, but not computer chips. The proper sequencing of capital goods for the production of various consumer goods is based on price signals together with the careful economic calculations of investors. If the price system is distorted, investors will improperly sequence their capital goods. After the error is revealed, investors will adjust their investments, but, in this process, resources will be lost. Propositions 8 and 9 form the foundation of the Austrian theory of the business cycle. This explains how the government's expansionary monetary policy generates a mal-investment in the capital structure during the economic boom that must be corrected in the economic bust.

Proposition 10: Social institutions are often the result of human action, but not of human design. Many of the most important social institutions and social practices are not the result of direct human design but are the by-product of actions taken by individuals to achieve their goals. For instance, in the Midwest region of the United States, in the month of January, a student trying to get to class quickly in order to avoid the cold weather may take a short-cut across the quad rather than walk the long way around. Taking the short-cut across the quad in the snow leaves footprints. Other students, by following these footprints, turn the footprints into a path. Although the goal of each student is merely to get to class quickly in order to avoid the cold weather, as a by-product they create a path in the snow that helps other students who come later to achieve this goal more easily. This story can be used as a metaphor to illustrate that the social institutions and social practices are the product of human action, but not of human design. The market economy and its price system have come about through a similar process. People do not intentionally create a market economy with its complex array of exchanges and price signals. However, people intentionally attempt to improve their own lot in life, and their behavior results in the market system. Other social phenomena—such as money, law, language, science, and so on—owe their origins not to human design, but to people who strove to achieve their own betterment, and in the process produced an outcome that benefits the public. Not all spontaneously formed social institutions and social orders are beneficial, and, therefore, this proposition should not be regarded as an example of a Panglossian fallacy. Whether pursuing individual self-interest generates public benefits depends on the institutional context in which individuals pursue their self-interests. Individuals pursuing their self-interests can lead to the "invisible hand of market efficiency" or the "tragedy of the commons"; in one social setting, individuals generated social benefits, whereas in another social setting, individuals generated social losses. The "new institutional economics" focuses on the degree of the sensitivity of social outcomes to the institutional setting within which individuals interact. It is important to note that classical political economists and the early neoclassical economists were cognizant of this basic point of new institutional economists, and that it was only the mid-twentieth-century neoclassical fascination with formal proofs of general competitive equilibrium, on the one hand, and the Keynesian emphasis on aggregate variables, on the other, that tended to change the focus away from the institutional preconditions required for social cooperation.

These ten propositions have radical implications: (1) economic theory should be grounded in verbal logic; (2) empirical work should focus on historical narratives; and (3) public policy raises severe doubts about the ability of government officials to intervene optimally within the economic system, let alone to rationally manage the economy. The market economy develops based on individuals' natural inclination to improve their situation, which in turn leads them to discover the mutually-beneficial exchanges that will accomplish that goal. Adam Smith first systematized this message and the Austrian economists have been the proponents of this message.

5 Post-Keynesian Economics

Post-Keynesian economics constitutes a new approach to the understanding of economic phenomena. Its major characteristics can be identified and analyzed. It consists of clearly identifiable themes. Its boundaries have not been precisely defined. This is partly because, in general, boundaries are almost impossible to be precisely defined. And it is partly because the development of post-Keynesianism, as a school of economic thought, is a relatively recent phenomenon, although the ideas associated with post-Keynesianism have a long history. The post-Keynesian approach has not yet managed to be persuasive enough because: (1) it cannot be represented with a single model, although the orthodox approaches cannot be represented with a single model either; (2) it concerns itself with economic issues which are controversial; (3) it involves substantially diverse theoretical premises; (4) it is the subject of ideological objections that emanate from the orthodox character of the economics profession; and (5) it tends to define its program as a reaction to neoclassical economics.[5]

Post-Keynesian economics is comprised of different "approaches," which are reflected in different methods and different features subsumed in its models. This is as expected because in a relatively new approach there needs to exist divergences and disagreements within its ranks. Consequently, post-Keynesian methodology has been described as "horses for courses," and its mode of thought as "Babylonian," which together they mean that post-Keynesianism is a holistic and non-dualistic approach, rather than a reductionist or an atomistic approach.

The post-Keynesian school of thought has its own methodology, ideology, and content. It is unified not just by its critical attitude toward neoclassical economics,

[5]For this literature see Arestis (1990, 1996), Arestis et al. (1999), Arestis and Skouras (1985), Bohm (1989), Brown (1981), Crotty (1980), Davidson (1981), Dow (1988, 1990, 1991, 1996), Eichner (1979), Eichner and Kregel (1975), Hamouda and Harcourt (1988), Harcourt (1987, 2006), Hodgson (1989a, 1989b), Holt (2007), Holt and Pressman (2001, 2007), King (2003), Kregel (1975), Lavoie (1992a, 1992b), Lawson (1994, 1999), Lee (2002, 2009), Lee and Lavoie (2012), McKenna and Zannoni (1993), Palley (1996), Papadimitriou and Wray (2010), Pheby (1989), Rothem (1999), Sawyer (1988), Sawyer (1991), and Walters and Young (1997, 1999). This section is based on Arestis (1992).

but, more importantly, by its attempt to provide an alternative approach to that of orthodox economics. This effort might seem to face difficulty when a synthesis is aimed at in order to ascertain whether a coherent post-Keynesian model can emerge. However, because there is no uniform way of dealing with all issues in economics, there is no need to synthesize various approaches in order to conclude coherence. More specifically, within post-Keynesian economics, there are various strands of thought that deal with different issues and with different levels of abstraction at the analytical level. Notwithstanding, coherence prevails within the strands identified as post-Keynesian. The prevalence of such coherence is founded on post-Keynesianism's vision and the framework, which embrace the diversity of methods. Post-Keynesians have endeavored to provide a coherent mode of thought. For instance, they have identified a post-Keynesian research program; they have offered a synthesis of post-Keynesianism and neo-Ricardianism to produce a post-classical modus operandi; and they have offered a synthesis of a number of strands within post-Keynesian economics which is amenable to both theoretical and empirical investigation.

Post-Keynesian economics mainly aims at completing the Keynesian revolution. It attempts at a generalization of the General Theory. It inherits the principle of effective demand, as its backbone, from Keynes' General Theory. This principle had been discovered well before Keynes by Michal Kalecki. Although there are differences in the two approaches, there are common elements between Kalecki's path-breaking work and the position adopted by post-Keynesian economics, which adheres to both Kalecki and Keynes.

In what follows, the main preoccupation will be with a post-Keynesian methodological and theoretical framework that incorporates the main elements of the fundamental themes within post-Keynesianism, but does not encompass all the "approaches" that comprise the post-Keynesian school of thought. This approach stays consistent with the "horses for courses" and "Babylonian" approaches, and goes beyond them to provide a coherent framework to explain the post-Keynesian economics. Perhaps this is consistent with the expected future developments within the post-Keynesian literature, that there would be a coherent core that will form the basis for theoretical and empirical explorations.

Post-Keynesians accept the following propositions: (1) the economy is a historical process; (2) in an uncertain world, expectations have a crucial impact on economic events; (3) institutions, both economic and political, significantly shape economic events; (4) realism plays an important role; and (5) capitalism is a class-divided society.

Post-Keynesians view economics as an integral part of society that is concerned with people who are organized in groups to satisfy their material needs. Their focus of analysis is on the behavior of these groups in historical time; such that the past is immutable; and that the future is uncertain and unknowable; and that both past and future have a critical influence on the present. Consequently, it is paramount that the institutional framework within which the economic groups operate be considered clearly.

The most important institution is the large corporation or megacorp, which is organized oligopolisticly and is the dominant institution in the technically more advanced sector of the economy. Megacorps set their prices in relation to their investment, such that prices provide sufficient retained earnings to enable megacorps to finance their planned investment. In the non-oligopolistic sector of the economy, there are small firms, but, they do not behave as "perfectly competitive" firms in the neoclassical sense, instead, they behave in the way that Kalecki described as "pure imperfect competition." In any case, the production subsystem of the economy is essentially dominated by the megacorp.

On the other hand, there are the trade unions, whose members constitute a substantial proportion of workers. Trade unions enter into bargaining agreements with employers regarding conditions of employment in general and wages in particular. The interests of the trade unions and those of employers are in conflict, not harmony, such that the distribution between wages and profits is determined to a very large extent by the real wage demands of labor and the profit objectives of corporations. Actually, workers bargain over money wages, the acceptable level of which is determined by their target real wage rate, information on immediate past inflation rate, and expected future inflation rate. In this process, workers are at a disadvantage because the real wage rate that they will actually experience can be known only after the capitalists set their product prices. The resulting distribution between wages and profits is effectively determined by the capitalists' pricing decisions, and not by the wage bargaining process, unless the degree of monopoly or megacorp power is somehow reduced in the meantime. This shows a decline in the role of market as the mode of economic organization, and the necessity to find out how the resulting economic performance should be made socially acceptable to as many people as possible.

The central government's actions influence the economic activities of corporations and workers. The central government is the institution which is vested with the power to pursue Keynesian contra-cyclical policies, i.e., to reduce the amplitude of the cyclical behavior of capitalist economies. The central government, as an institution, can create money through the central bank as a lender of last resort; although most of the money in use in modern economies is credit money, which is created by the private banking system. Finally, there are international economic institutions that interact with national institutions.

The post-Keynesian paradigm partly owes its emergence to the development of the system or cybernetic framework. In this framework, the economy is considered as a group of dynamic subsystems, each of which interacts with all the other subsystems, i.e., influencing them and being influenced by them. In this way, the economic system is only one of several societal systems, each of which has its own particular dynamics. Economics in this system is not regarded as the study of how scarce resources are allocated to meet finite needs. It is, instead, regarded as the study of how actual economic systems can expand their outputs over time through the production and distribution of the resulting social surplus. The expansion path of output is generally uneven and is likely to change the nature of economic systems in unexpected ways. In other words, post-Keynesian analysis views the economy as a continually evolving system whose path cannot be predicted, and it is not only without equilibrium, but also erratic.

There are four more characteristics of the economic system that post-Keynesian analysis emphasizes. The first characteristic is the existence of uncertainty, in the sense that the future is unknown and unknowable, such that economic agents' expectations can easily prove to be wrong. Uncertainty is omnipresent in the real world, and therefore constitutes one of the central elements of the post-Keynesian analysis. Uncertainty is in the structural nature of the market economy, as market forces cannot properly account for the unknowability and unpredictability of the future, and therefore disseminate incomplete, even misleading, information. The prices of goods and services today cannot properly inform buyers or sellers about what the consequences of their collective actions will be on prices tomorrow. Knowledge about the future can only be probabilistically formed based on past events. But, the conditions under which such a probability can be ascertained are rarely met in everyday life, and therefore, such probabilities cannot be quantified. With the future being uncertain, the final stage of the uneven process of output expansion cannot be deduced; instead, the process of output expansion can be carefully and intelligently analyzed. The world is nonergodic: the observations of past events cannot produce knowledge about current and/or future events; in addition, the observations of current events provide no statistically reliable unbiased estimates about future time and/or space averages. In the presence of uncertainty, as distinct from risk, past and current events cannot be used to construct a statistical knowledge about future outcomes. The practical difference between risk and uncertainty is that in the case of risk the probability distribution of the outcomes is known (either from a priori calculations or from the observations of past experiences), but, in the case of uncertainty this is not true, because any considered situation is to a high degree unique. While the future is uncertain, decisions about the future are made all the time. Consequently, such decisions will likely turn out to be not the right ones. As a result, continued adjustments must be made over time. In this process, equilibrium is neither achieved, nor maintained. Thus, history matters.

The second characteristic of post-Keynesian economics is the existence of irreversible time, where economic agents enter into commitments well before outcomes can be predicted. During the lengthy process of production, companies pay in terms of money for their expenses—such as wages and other expenses of production—in the expectation of recouping such expenses by selling the products for money at a later date. Historical time is in sharp contrast to logical time, which is rejected in post-Keynesian economics. Logical time is closely related to rationality and logical calculus, which form two of the main characteristics of neoclassical economics. This mode of thought, consequently assumes away problems associated with historical time. It reduces uncertainty to risk, which can be quantified through the calculus of probability, as a result of which history is turned into logical time. Then, the real economy tends toward a long-period "equilibrium" position, which is stable in the sense that there is no tendency to deviate away from it; and, indeed, if for any reason the system finds itself away from this "equilibrium" position, there will be forces that will take the system back to long-period "equilibrium." Post-Keynesian economists view this type of neoclassical steady state economics as having great intellectual complexity, but also being so much out of time, and out of history, that they are practically futile and misleading. Therefore, these central concepts of neoclassical economics are completely inappropriate for an analysis that relies heavily on historical time.

The third characteristic of post-Keynesian economics is that economic agents sign contract agreements which are denominated in money. In this way, money and contracts are tightly related. This characteristic is pervasive because money comes into play along with debt contracts (which are contracts for deferred payment) and price lists (which are offers of contracts for sale or purchase). That is, money plays an important role as a link between the past and the present, as well as between the present and the future, where the past is given and unchangeable and the future is uncertain and unknowable. Indeed, it is the existence of uncertainty in the context of historical time that is both the necessary and the sufficient condition for the existence of money. There is no need for money in a stochastic, stationary, and ergodic world. The tight relationship between modern money and debt contracts underlies the proposition that money is credit-driven and demand-determined, and that the supply of and demand for money are interdependent. This is because the supply of credit essentially depends on the demand for credit. That is, in a particular period of time, the determinants of the demand for credit influence the flow of supply of credit, and thus the supply of money. Most of the demand for credit arises in relation to production. Production costs are paid before sales revenues are received. The need to bridge this gap—i.e., the working capital requirement of the industrial and commercial companies—is met by borrowing from banks in addition to the companies' internally-generated funds. The amount of borrowing from banks is dependent on the total wage bill, the raw-material and tax payments bills, and other variables, such as unexpected changes in borrowing needs. In other words, industrial and commercial companies borrow to finance their current production and distribution costs in the expectation of future sales revenues. As long as these companies can provide sound and adequate collateral at the time to their credit application, commercial banks will supply the amount of credit requested by them. Bankers accommodate businessmen's demand for funds, for invest in credit-worthy projects, at interest rates based on markup over the central bank's supply price of reserves. This means that the endogenous nature of credit money allows investment expenditures to be carried out independently of the current saving flows. Investment determines savings, rather than the reverse. In this way, money in modern capitalist economies is credit-driven and demand-determined. Central banks do not have a firm control on the amount of credit. They can only control the supply price of credit money via the discount rate, which is under their direct control.

The fourth characteristic of post-Keynesian economics is related to labor and labor markets. According to the post-Keynesian view, no labor market in the real world works in the way envisaged by neoclassical economics, where wages are determined, along with many other prices, by "market forces" in a general equilibrium framework. Instead, nominal wages are set through a bilateral administered pricing process between employers and employees. Such agreed upon nominal labor contracts prevail over some future period. The process whereby these agreements are arrived at involves "conflict" of interests between employers and employees. Wage determination is influenced not only by economic factors, but also many others, such as: political, historical, sociological, and psychological factors. After money wages are thus determined, prices adjust to money wages, not the other way round. Prices are set based on a mark-up over costs, and therefore, real wages are determined not just in labor markets but in product markets as well. It is, thus, possible to observe that higher wages are accompanied by additional demand for labor, not less. There is no functional relationship between wages and employment, because the two variables are determined independently of each other.

Methodological premises of post-Keynesian economics are as follows. (1) A free-market economic process is inherently unstable. Post-Keynesian theory attempts to present reality, be context-specific, make repeated reappraisals of current developments, and build "realistic abstractions" rather than "imaginary models." (2) An emphasis on critical realism is required. In the realist view, the economy and society is an open system; whereas in the positivist view, it is closed. Positivists believe in the occurrence of constant conjunctions of actual events. Realists believe, in contrast, that the world in general is open, and constancy, or relative endurability, lies at the level of underlying causes. For realists, explanation rather than prediction is recognized as the relevant criterion for theory assessment. This has relevance to econometric modeling. Realists use stylized facts and econometrics as the starting point for their analysis of causal mechanisms. They do not aim to generalize, or render precise, any rough empirical pattern, but to move towards an understanding of the underlying causal mechanisms that give rise to it. They regard "observations" as containing both objective and subjective elements. A certain degree of objectivity is involved when "facts" are observed, while the grouping of "facts" for purposes of theoretical analysis entails some degree of subjectivity. But, even observation is selective and hence subjective. (3) An organic, rather than atomistic, approach to economic processes is more relevant and appropriate. Post-Keynesians regard individuals as social rather than atomistic beings and therefore give considerable weight to social and economic institutions. (4) It is necessary to recognize the importance of "insufficient demand," rather than concentrating on "scarcity of resources," and to give central position to "effective demand." In exchange, individual's choice is limited, because it is determined by income, class, and the technical conditions of production, rather than by relative prices. Income and not substitution effects, along with income distribution among social classes, should be the objects of analysis. (5) Monopolies and oligopolies have socio-political as well as economic power, based on which they administer product prices. This capacity together with their power over input costs, especially wage costs, determines their gained surplus. This surplus together with their expectations and effective demand translate into investment, which is the engine for growth. (6) Individuals have limited capacity in acquiring and analyzing information. They suffer from "bounded rationality," i.e., they cannot see problems in all their complexity. They rely on group behavior and conventions. They do not optimize. Procedures and rules are set by those individuals or groups who possess power, based on their place in the social or economic hierarchy, which allows them to impose their values upon the rest.

6 Institutional Economics

The contribution of institutional economics to economic thought has distinguished institutionalism from traditional economics and melded it into a coherent body of thought. Although there is heterogeneity in institutional economics, such heterogeneity disappears as soon as institutional economics is compared with alternative economic methodological and philosophical persuasions. Despite such heterogeneity, a common thread in institutional economics is apparent that acts as an ideological nexus and binds institutionalism together to form a school.[6]

Institutional economics is distilled from the writings of major institutional economists. Its theoretical framework sets institutionalism apart from other schools of thought. More specifically, the methodologies of institutionalism and the economic orthodoxy can be contrasted. The differences in their methodologies are based on differences in their epistemologies and theories of human nature, which are in turn the foundations of differences in their ethical viewpoints.

Institutionalism places emphasis on a specific area within the broad spectrum of economic thought. Economics can be divided into the study of: (a) resource allocation; (b) levels and rates of growth of employment, income, production, and prices; (c) income distribution; and (d) the structure of power. Whereas economic orthodoxy is concerned with the first three of these categories, institutionalism emphasizes the last one.

Institutionalists do not view the standard economic theory as entirely invalid or irrelevant. They do not totally discount the efficacy of market incentives. They, rather, see the primary weakness of economic orthodoxy in its self-limiting tendencies. They criticize economic orthodoxy not for its description of the mechanics of exchange, but for its failure to account for the interaction of these processes with the economic superstructure, and for its application of the ceteris paribus assumption to the social, economic, and technological framework within which resource allocation and the level and distribution of income take place.

Institutionalists regard institutional economics as the general theory, of which economic orthodoxy is a special case. Institutionalists are concerned with the

[6] For this literature see Ayers (1951), Boettke (1989), Bowles (1998), Commons (1931, 1934, 1936), Dugger (1990), Dugger and Sherman (1994), Gruchy (1957, 1969, 1972, 1987), Hodgson (1988, 1989a, 1989b, 1998, 2000, 2002, 2003, 2004a, 2004b), Hodgson et al. (1994), Hutchinson (1984), Kapp (1968, 1976, 2011), Lawson (2005), Miller (1978), Milonakis and Fine (2008), Mirowski (1987), Myrdal (1978), Nelson and Sampat (2001), O'Hara (2007), Peterson (1987), Rima (2013a, 2013b), Rutherford (1994), Rutherford (2001), Sackrey et al. (2008), Samuels (1988, 1989), Schlicht (1998), Stanfield (1999), Stilwell (2012), Tool (1981, 1988a, 1988b), Tool and Bush (2003), Wilber and Harrison (1978), Whalen (1996), and Witte (1954). This section is based on Miller (1978).

evolving framework within which economic activities occur, such as the evolution of the power structure, the rules of the game, the process of want creation, and conflict resolution. Standard economics, in contrast, describe the special case of exchange in a world with specific assumed characteristics, which do not mostly correspond to the world.

Institutional economics is evolutionary, collective, interdisciplinary, and non-predictive. It focuses on conflict rather than harmony, on waste rather than efficiency, and on uncertainty rather than perfect knowledge. It entirely rejects the orthodoxy's view of the market as an unbiased allocational and distributional mechanism; and consistently maintains a clear distinction between private and social costs and benefits. It is mainly concerned with the existence and abuse of power and privilege, rather than the orthodoxy's machinations of the atomistic individual.

Institutionalism distinguishes between "technological" and "institutional" patterns of behavior and modes of thought, which are present in varying degrees in all cultures. "Technological," or "instrumental," thought and action is based on reasoning from cause to effect. It is non-coercive, and it can be subjected to empirical verification by checking its ability in achieving its goal. "Institutional" or "ceremonial" behavior, in contrast, is based on considering rank and status. It is enforced by social pressure and verified through appeal to authority.

Instrumental activity, i.e., the continuous advance in scientific understanding, is the driving force behind economic development. In contrast, institutions, i.e., the habits of thought shared among people, are static. Institutions are entwined with the community's status system, and are verified by such authority as custom, law, politics, religion, and morality. Thus, whereas instrumental behavior enhances development; ceremonial activity restricts or, at best, only permits change. Whereas technology involves people's creative tendencies; institutions involve people's predatory and exploitative propensities.

Technology is the state of the industrial arts, and includes the existing level of understanding and technique as well as the tools and equipment which are available and utilized by a civilization. The technology of a society is a common stock, which is collectively held and advanced by a culture. Although, the physical properties of available materials do not change over time, the people's understanding of how to use them changes. Thus, it is the people's curiosity and intelligence that act as the driving force behind technological progress. People are active forces for, rather than passive accommodators of, change. Human beings apply their creative imagination and fashion, rather than merely adapt to, their environment. Technological progress enhances new methods of provisioning, and changes in the quantity, quality, and composition of goods and services produced. Institutions, in response, adjust sluggishly and reluctantly. The existing institutions are not immutable, natural condition of economic organization.

The orthodox economic literature stresses savings (a money fund) as the cause of capital formation and industrial progress. It defends income inequality as the source of savings. Institutionalists, in contrast, emphasize that the ability of an economy to produce more emanates from science, technology, invention, and innovation; and its source is not money, but human creativity.

Institutionalists believe that all human activity takes place collectively. All transactions occur within institutions according to standards established by habits of thought. Individual tastes are shaped by emulation and social conditioning. The state of the industrial arts is a fact of group life, in the same way that mores and folkways are inherited from community. These are in contrast to the orthodoxy's concept of the hedonistic atomistic individual.

Institutionalists believe that the transactions of individuals are limited and directed by standards of law and convention. They, in contrast to the orthodoxy, do not view the discipline of economics as a mechanistic "science of choice." This is because an individual's preference and selection are governed and restrained by law and custom; by information gaps and lags; by the coercion of the less powerful resulted from the more powerful; and by manipulated market forces based on the ability of those with market power who can interfere with it.

Institutionalists conceive of private ownership not as a "natural" condition, but as having evolved through historical conditions and subject to human control. Property rights establish both power over use and power in exchange, especially as industrialization proceeds and transactions are increasingly taking place between competing collectivities. Property rights establish the right of super-ordinates to direct and control sub-ordinates.

Conflicts of interest which result from scarcity are settled by goal-seeking individuals. People use their outmost power, whether granted or exacted, to achieve their goals, which are set in conjunction with their expectations about the future. Transactions may seem to be taking place between relative equals. But, the existing working rules in society also sanction coercion, i.e., the direction of some people by others. The result of the settlement of such conflicts is an indeterminate and imprecise compromise, rather than a unique, calculable, automatic solution. The compromise is based on the use of power within "reasonable" limits, as set by laws and customs, which have been and continue to be established on a case-by-case basis, especially when existing working rules no longer function satisfactorily. The outcome of all transactions is uncertain and transitory; and it is dependent on customary methods of procedure, varying expectations about the future, and relative power. The system is always in the state of flux, and it is never in the state of equilibrium imposed by outside forces.

Institutionalists, thus, do not envision the market as a neutral mechanism for allocational efficiency and distributional equity. They, rather, view the market as biased in many important respects. The prevailing structure of power is reflected in the existing operation of the market, such that not only the market controls, but also it is itself controlled. Terms of exchange is based on the existing power relations between negotiators. Institutionalists view the market as an institution that is constrained, which is in contrast to what the orthodoxy views as "free market."

Institutionalists note that the economic system is often characterized by waste, rather than the orthodoxy's efficiency. They challenge the traditional economics' utility theory of value as well as the competitive model, which are based on the fundamental belief that all expenditures and productive effort are equally legitimate. They describe and explain the wasteful consumption practices of the monied classes.

They explain that the demand for goods is often based, not upon its utility, but upon the status that the possession confers upon the possessor. In other words, it is the show of expensiveness that is valued; it is accumulation for its own sake that is the goal; it is the medium that is the message.

Institutionalists call into question the concept of "consumer sovereignty" by reference to the manipulation of consumer wants by producers. When choices are subjected to manipulation, they are neither inherent nor informed. When demand is increased as much by manipulation as by intrinsic desires, then scarce resources are wasted in the production of goods of low social and individual serviceability, while public needs are ignored.

Institutionalists have also directed attention towards another form of waste: the underutilization of productive resources. They note the sabotage of industrial output by industrialists to create values. They identify the causal factors for business cycle and its resultant unemployment. They emphasize the waste of resources as a result of unemployment; and insist that while labor is a variable cost for business, it is a fixed cost for society. In the same way that a business suffers if it does not fully utilize its fixed plant and equipment, society suffers if it does not fully utilize its labor force.

Institutionalists portray an economic system that often involves inequity, rather than justice. They observe the orthodoxy's notion that each factor of production receives the equivalent of its marginal product is incorrect. This is because no factor of production produces in isolation, but as part of an industrial system. Whereas the orthodoxy claims that the common practice is to reward those with scarce skills, institutionalists state that the scarcity is often contrived.

Institutionalists distinguish private and social costs and benefits. They direct attention to externalities, and their concerns include and transcend the physical environment. They note that with industrialization, interdependencies multiply, and externalities proliferate. They also maintain that the existing social structure victimizes certain groups, and that this victimization constitutes a social cost.

Institutionalists describe a perpetually evolving environment which is subject to human dominance, which is made possible through humans continued development of methods of control. In the process of changing the environment, the human agent changes, which is the most profound development of all.

Institutionalists envision unceasing change, in which no pattern necessarily exists. Scientific understanding continuously expands, but its direction cannot be foretold, because it varies with the types of inquiries and the types of inquirers. Neither the growth of scientific understanding nor the development of an economy follows any law or principle.

Institutionalists view technology as the dynamic force in society. They, accordingly, regard human intelligence as the basic driving force. Their moral imperative is free inquiry, i.e., freedom of thought and experimentation. Growth of understanding not only leads to an increase in productive potential, but also it facilitates an escape from tradition and authority as well as the creation of new working rules.

Institutionalists, thus, view economics as indeterminate and experimental. They conceive of economic knowledge not as the discovery of universal principles (as the orthodox does), but as the creation of tools of control in order to achieve a more reasonable society or an increased serviceability. This is to be achieved through trial and error in a search not for perfection (as in the orthodoxy), but for an improved accommodation.

Institutionalists, then, view the function of economists as not providing prediction (as in the orthodoxy), but performing critical inquiry and problem-solving. Traditional economists examine a specific institution, i.e., the market, which has a moral beneficence or is neutral. Institutionalist economists, in contrast, search for the underlying bias of the current institutional structure and attempt to recognize how such institutions can be changed in order to disperse power and privilege with the aim of creating a more reasonable society.

Institutional and orthodox schools of economics are based on different methodologies which are, in turn, based on different epistemologies and theories of human nature, which are, in turn, the bases of different ethical outlooks. Institutional economists have historically criticized orthodox theorists for their specific method of abstraction, their reliance on a priori reasoning, and their static, marginal approach.

Institutionalists criticize the orthodox method of abstraction not because of abstraction per se, but because of that from which the orthodox theory abstracts. Institutionalists well understand that in the method of abstraction, theory is based on certain selected variables while leaving other relevant factors out of consideration. The orthodox economics focuses on "rational economic men" whose goals are profit or utility maximization. Institutionalists criticize this hedonistic psychology of traditional theory. They conceive of persons as active and sometimes irrational agents operating within an institutional framework which conditions and controls their behavior, while it is itself altered by the change in behavior.

Institutionalists call into question the explanatory and descriptive power of the orthodoxy's model which posits the institutional and technological framework as exogenous, given, and fixed. Furthermore, without the ability to explain, the model cannot have the capacity to predict. Institutionalists view the environmental milieu as both controlled and controlling, i.e., the environment is simultaneously a dependent and an independent variable. Individuals shape and are shaped by their environment. In other words, individuals create and are the creatures of their environment. The interface of individuals and their environment is one of continuous interaction and evolutionary change.

Institutionalists challenge both the models which traditional theorists construct based on disputable assumptions, and the portrayal of these models as the goals of economic conduct and organization. They direct attention to the limited scope of admitted variables in the orthodox formulation. That is, the focus on the rational economic man whose transaction take place within a competitive market economy; the identification of the market with competition; and the equivalency of the model with the ideal. They contend that the orthodox theorists unrealistically portray the competitive market as the existing economic reality and as an ideal state toward which the economy would move in the absence of undesirable collusion or intervention.

Institutionalists also criticize orthodox theorists for their a priori methods. That is, orthodox theorists apply reasoning based on general principles, but without regard to the facts of experience. Institutionalists believe that traditional economists rely on revelation, rather than observation, as the appropriate method of science. That is, orthodox theorists assume the existence of a set of natural laws and rights which are discoverable solely through the application of reason. Institutionalists also believe that conventional theorists attribute merit and truth to this set of natural laws and rights, and as a result the system becomes an apologetic for the existing institutional structure. Specific institutions, such as ownership and free contract, are regarded as "natural," rather than as the human creations. These institutions, consequently, are taken as given, and are considered beyond the scope of professional inquiry. The role of the economists reduces to the discovery and interpretation of universal principles. Theory, in orthodoxy's view, is strictly a logical construct with no need for reference to the facts.

7 Radical Economics

The idea of socialism developed historically in opposition to capitalism. Accordingly, the basic goals of socialist movement have been set in reaction to the inherent problems of capitalism. At its core, socialism has been committed to the following objectives[7]:

1. Equity: In capitalism, there are severe inequalities of income and wealth. In opposition, socialism aims at an egalitarian distribution of economic outcomes and opportunities by class race, gender, region, etc.
2. Democracy: In capitalism, liberal democracy in the political sphere has characterized the most democratic societies. In opposition, socialism aims at economic democracy, which enables people to exercise control over their own economic fate.
3. Solidarity: In capitalism, it is the individual who is celebrated. In opposition, socialism aims at solidarity among the members of all communities covering small neighborhoods to the whole society, by encouraging people to develop themselves as social beings rather than individual beings.
4. Efficiency: In capitalism, inefficiency is endemic. In opposition, socialism aims at the wise and non-wasteful use of resources so that economic and social goals can be more successfully achieved.

[7] For this literature see Albert et al. (1986), Amariglio et al. (1996), Amariglio et al. (1993), Amariglio and Ruccio (1994), Arestis and Sawyer (1994), Baiman et al. (2000), Bowles and Edwards (1990), Cullenberg (1994), Dugger and Sherman (1994), Edwards and MacEwan (1970), Hahnel (2002), Kotz et al. (1994), Lippit (1996), Milberg (1991), Nell (1981), O'Connor (1984, 1994), Palermo (2007), Panitch and Leys (1999), Prychitko (1998), Resnick and Wolff (1987), Roberts and Feiner (1992), Sawyer (1989), Scott (1991), Sherman (1987), Ward (1977), and Wolff and Resnick (2012). This section is based on Wiesskopf (1992).

In order to achieve these socialist goals, liberal-democratic socialists (radical economists) advocate market socialism, but communitarian socialists (Marxist economists) advocate participatory socialism.

Liberal-democratic socialists place emphasis on democracy, and they see liberal democracy—i.e., a political system based on constitutionally protected civil rights and liberties, democratic elections, etc.—as a vital prerequisite for a socialist society. That is, socialist economic institutions that aim at achieving socialist goals, such as equity and solidarity, must be built upon a liberal-democratic political foundation. They do not regard the construction of socialist society as the replacement of "bourgeois democratic institutions" by a totally different and superior form of democracy, but as deepening the democratic nature of such institutions and extending them from the political to the social and economic arenas. They never considered the political authoritarian character of Communist Party-directed societies as exemplars of socialism.

Liberal-democratic socialists favor democratic market socialism, which is a combination of: (1) liberal democracy; (2) an economic system mainly characterized by collective ownership of the means of production; and (3) the use of markets as the main means of resource allocation and distribution, but subject to some government planning, intervention, and regulation. Collective ownership of the means of production is intended to achieve equity and justice in both economic and political spheres; markets are expected to promote individual freedom of choice and efficient allocation of resources; and government regulation is enforced in order to ensure that general interest prevails over particular interests, and to limit the development of substantial inequities.

The idea of a market-based form of socialism was seriously promoted in the 1920s by the social-democratic wing of Marxism as a desirable alterative to the market-less form of socialism, which was associated with Marx's vision of full communism as well as advocated by the Bolshevik wing of Marxism. The first systematic theoretical exposition of the functioning of a market-based socialist economy was made in the 1930s by Oskar Lange, who has since then been known as the pioneer of market socialism. Lange's original model consisted of: (1) actual markets (in consumer goods and labor); (2) simulated markets (in producer goods); and (3) a limited but important role for central planning (e.g., in controlling the rate of investment and the distribution of income). In this system, all enterprises are owned by the government, but run by independent managers who follow profit-maximizing rules. Since the exposition of Lange's market socialism model, many economists—who have been either from or interested in the post-World War II Eastern European countries—have done a great deal of work to improve upon Lange's model, especially in view of various problems raised by critics.

Although the continuing literature on the conceptualization of market socialism has resulted in a variety of different models, they all share the same set of goals. Market socialism seeks to attain the socialist goals of equity, democracy, and solidarity through retaining one major feature of capitalist economies—the market—but replacing another major feature of capitalism—private ownership of the means of production. Market socialism also involves some form of social ownership of enterprises for at least the major sectors and/or the most important enterprises in the economy.

"Ownership," as a complex concept, encompasses various rights, which can be assigned to various people. Market socialism identifies and distinguishes two such rights: (1) the right to enterprise control; and (2) the right to enterprise income. The right to control involves the prerogatives and responsibilities of management. That is, those who control the enterprise (or their representatives) are entitled to make the decisions about: how the enterprise will be operated; who will work in it and under what conditions; if any aspects of the enterprise need to be expanded, contracted, sold, or liquidated; etc. The right to income involves the claim to the monetary surplus generated by the enterprise. That is, it is the entitlement to claim the net (or residual) income after all fixed obligations have been paid.

In capitalism, an enterprise is owned by private individuals or shareholders, who appoint management and have (ultimate) control over management according to the nature and the number of their share ownership. It is possible for a small number of individuals or shareholders to have predominant control. In market socialism, enterprise control is not private, but social. That is, the control of a market socialist enterprise is held by the people in the community. Each member of the community—in principle—can equally influence the management of the enterprise. In practice, this (ultimate) control is usually exercised through the appointment of managerial staff. Depending on the nature of the community, the vested control rights can usually be exercised through one of the following two ways:

1. Public management: In this alternative, an enterprise is run by managers, whom are appointed by and are held accountable to an agency of the government—at the national, regional, or local level. The government agency represents the relevant politically-constituted community of citizens.
2. Worker self-management: In this alternative, an enterprise is run by managers, whom are appointed by and are held accountable to those who work in the enterprise—or their elected representatives. The control rights ultimately rest with the community of enterprise workers, on a one-person one-vote basis.

In capitalism, ownership by private individuals or shareholders determines not only control rights but also income rights. The extent of these rights is determined according to the nature and the number of their share ownership. In market socialism, income rights are not held privately, but socially. The monetary surplus of the market socialist enterprise belongs to the community of people, and shared among them on a relatively egalitarian basis. Depending on the nature of the community, the income rights can usually be exercised through one of the following two ways:

1. Public surplus appropriation: In this alternative, the monetary surplus of the enterprise is distributed to an agency of government—at the national, regional or local level. The government agency represents the corresponding community of citizens.
2. Worker surplus appropriation: In this alternative, the monetary surplus of the enterprise is distributed to the enterprise workers.

In general, the two different ways of assigning control rights and the two different ways of assigning income rights can combine to generate a matrix of four different possible market socialist models. This can happen because there is no a priori reason for each set of rights to be assigned in the same way. However, most contemporary advocates of market socialism fall into one of the two schools of thought and favor one of the following two models: (1) one school favors what may be called the "public enterprise model," which is characterized by public management and public surplus appropriation; and (2) the other school favors what may be called the "worker enterprise model," which is characterized by worker self-management and worker surplus appropriation.

Although market socialism most clearly distinguishes itself from (market) capitalism by the replacement of social for private control and income rights at the enterprise level, market socialism also generally requires a greater degree of government intervention into markets than is the norm in capitalism. Such intervention is not primarily of the kind of quantitative controls, i.e., not of the kind associated with the discredited system of centrally-planned socialism. Instead, government intervention involves more government provision of public goods and services, public capital formation, regulation of enterprises, and use of taxes and subsidies to internalize external effects that would otherwise be ignored by individual consumers and producers in the market environment. The objective here is to use the market—rather than replace it—but shape the environment in which the market operates, such that market price and cost valuations will approximate the social benefits and costs. With respect to government intervention, the difference between market socialism and (market) capitalism is one of degree rather than kind. In a market socialist system, the government intervenes in economic life slightly more than the governments in the more regulated (e.g., social-democratic) capitalist systems. The essential difference between market socialism and (market) capitalism is constituted by the public control and income rights in enterprises

Market socialism has been challenged on several grounds in regard to its ability to meet socialist goals with social ownership forms in the context of markets, i.e., whether market socialism is socialist enough. The first challenge is the idea that the market system systematically undermines efforts to serve general public interests. That is, in the market environment, people are encouraged to better themselves at the expense of others—e.g., through individual rent-seeking behavior, the formation of self-aggrandizing coalitions, etc. As a result, markets appear to generate a systematic tendency for the general social interest to be undermined by the pursuit of particular private interests.

Although the idea of this challenge is theoretically plausible, it is not decisive. Rent-seeking behavior and self-aggrandizing coalitions can and will occur in any economic system that allows some people to live better than others. This is why every system requires institutions that limit antisocial behavior. That problem can be eradicated only by an economic system that controls the individual patterns of living to the extent that it can preclude any individual from enjoying the gains from self-interested behavior. This solution to the problem of such behavior, therefore, comes only at the expense of strict limits on privacy and freedom of choice. This is a high price which market socialists are unwilling to pay.

The second challenge to the market socialism model is the idea that market systems unfairly reward good luck. In market capitalist economies, owners of property are rewarded, in the form of capital income, for the productive contributions of their property. Such rewards to property ownership not only are the source of unequal distribution in society, but also they are generally not necessary to assure deployment of the property in production. In market socialist economies, owners of labor power are rewarded, in the form of labor income, for the productive contributions of their labor. Yet market socialism, like capitalism, rewards people's natural abilities, even though such rewards may not be necessary to assure the deployment of those natural abilities in production. Moreover, worker self-management forms of market socialism are likely to reward those people who work in prosperous areas or enterprises despite the fact that they do not necessarily work harder or longer than other people who work in less prosperous areas or enterprises.

Although the idea of this challenge has some merits, it ignores the degree of difference between market socialism and (market) capitalism. In a more just economic system, people would be rewarded differently based on their different personal effort and personal sacrifice, not based on the luck of the genetic or economic draw. Although the market socialist system does not achieve this ideal, it gets substantially much closer to this ideal than the capitalist system does. Furthermore, in market socialism, the extent to which unwarranted returns to some people, due to their genetic or economic luck, result in differentials a progressive system of income taxation is applied to diminish such differentials.

The third challenge to the market socialism model is the idea that any kind of market system leads to inequalities that contradict the socialist goals of equity and democracy. That is, market socialism generates a minority of elites of "coordinators"—e.g., public investment bankers, public enterprise directors, self-managed firm managers, and government planners—who, over time, gain disproportionate economic and political power, similar to what capitalists do in a market capitalist system.

Although the idea of this challenge is meritorious, it ignores the degree of difference between the results of market socialism and (market) capitalism. There is no doubt that in market socialism, there are some people who occupy high positions, and make key decisions, as well as have greater power, and earn higher income than most of the population. That is, inequalities of income and power exist in market socialism, but they are much smaller than what they are in capitalism. This is because market socialism eliminates property ownership, and therefore, it eliminates returns to property ownership, which is the predominant source of inequalities under capitalism. In market socialism, there are inequalities that correspond to differential skills, talents, and responsibilities, but there are no inequalities that correspond to the propertied capitalist class in capitalism.

The fourth challenge to the market socialism model is the idea that markets undermine solidarity and community. This is because markets breed selfishness and competitiveness on the part of producers and consumers. As a consequence, markets divide people instead of uniting them, encourage indifference to other people instead of empathy for them, and therefore, discourage the development of public-spirited community consciousness and solidarity.

Although the idea of this challenge is insightful, it overlooks the fact that the difference between the results of market socialism and (market) capitalism is a matter of degrees. There is no doubt that market transactions cause people to think in terms of their own individual (or family) welfare, and set aside consideration for others. In addition, markets encourage anonymity, autonomy, and mobility rather than community, empathy, and solidarity. There is no doubt that market socialism, as a result, does not provide direct support for a culture of community, empathy, and solidarity. However, market socialism provides an environment which is less amenable to the development of such characteristics than (market) capitalism. Indeed, market socialism by providing a greater egalitarianism and stronger democracy it attenuates the consequences of unfettered markets and unrestricted private property ownership.

The fifth challenge to the market socialism model is whether market socialism is more successful than social-democratic variants of capitalism in achieving socialist goals. The market-socialist approach is superior to the social-democratic approach in achieving socialist objectives, because it redefines and reassigns—to workers or communities—rights that form the point of departure for markets. In this way, market socialism intervenes in the market system before markets operate, which is in contrast to social democracy that intervenes in the market system after markets operate. Consequently, social democracy can be weakened or disintegrated through political challenge, because tax-and-subsidy schemes and government regulation are much easier to reverse than property rights. Moreover, social democracy maintains properly-owning capitalists who form a disproportionately powerful class with interest in challenging social-democratic government policies. Although in market socialism there is a managerial class with disproportionate power, its power is less disproportionate because enterprise control rights and personal wealth are not as highly concentrated as in social-democratic capitalism.

8 Marxist Economics

As noted in the radical humanist section, the idea of socialism developed historically in opposition to capitalism. Accordingly, the basic goals of socialist movement have been set in reaction to the inherent problems of capitalism. At its core, socialism has been committed to the following objectives[8]:

[8]For this literature see Amin (1974, 1988), Baran and Sweezy (1966), Brewer (2001), Desai (1979), Fine (1980), Foster and McChesney (2004), Howard and King (1975, 1992), King (1990), Kotz (1991), Mandel (1968), McLellan (2000), Mermelstein (1970), Panitch and Leys (1999), Scott (1991), Singer (1999), Stilwell (2012), Sweezy (1942), Sweezy and Magdoff (1972), Wallerstein (1974), and Warren (1980). This section is based on Wiesskopf (1992).

1. Equity: In capitalism, there are severe inequalities of income and wealth. In opposition, socialism aims at an egalitarian distribution of economic outcomes and opportunities by class race, gender, region, etc.
2. Democracy: In capitalism, liberal democracy in the political sphere has characterized the most democratic societies. In opposition, socialism aims at economic democracy, which enables people to exercise control over their own economic fate.
3. Solidarity: In capitalism, it is the individual who is celebrated. In opposition, socialism aims at solidarity among the members of all communities covering small neighborhoods to the whole society, by encouraging people to develop themselves as social beings rather than individual beings.
4. Efficiency: In capitalism, inefficiency is endemic. In opposition, socialism aims at the wise and non-wasteful use of resources so that economic and social goals can be more successfully achieved.

In order to achieve these socialist goals, liberal-democratic socialists (radical economists) advocate market socialism, but communitarian socialists (Marxist economists) advocate participatory socialism.

Communitarian socialists, similarly to liberal-democratic socialists, are committed to democracy, but the kind of democracy they advocate is a democracy of a less liberal and more participatory kind. In their vision, the socialist goal of solidarity receives the greatest emphasis. That is, people develop and sustain solidarity as active participating members of their communities ranging from their neighborhood and their workplace to their society as a whole. In their view, the political and economic institutions of liberal democratic capitalism need to be revolutionarily transformed into an egalitarian participatory society, in which people jointly and directly control their own fate. Communitarian socialists reject the communist-party-directed socialism because it not only retains many of the individualistic patterns and hierarchical structures of capitalist societies, but also it betrays democratic ideals.

Communitarian socialists advocate a form of democratic participatory socialism, in which not only there is collective social control of the means of production, but also there are decentralized participatory planning institutions, which replace markets as a mechanism for resource allocation and distribution. Thus, not only private property, but also markets are abolished. Consequently, expressed in Marxist terms, both exploitation and alienation are overcome. Instead of acting as independent self-interested individuals responding to market signals in the economic arena, people act as interdependent social beings, through communitarian participation, making consumption and production decisions.

Although, in recent years, market socialism has gained relative popularity on the Left; a much older socialist tradition has always rejected the idea of maintaining markets, except during a transitional phase after capitalism. Karl Marx wanted to rid humans not only of the inequalities through the abolition of private property, but also of the alienation and commodity fetishism through the abolition of the market system. This was the Marxism of the Russian Bolshevik revolutionaries, and Soviet socialism maintained it as an important part of its ideology, though not its practice, for decades after the Revolution of 1917. Indeed, none of the communist-party-directed socialist economies of the U.S.S.R., Eastern Europe, China, Cuba, etc., dispensed with markets, but they only limited the operation of markets in many ways.

Contemporary participatory socialists support the market-less Marxist ideal, but of a kind which is very different from that of the Bolshevik tradition. First of all, they insist on a democratic political framework, which is in sharp contrast to the authoritarian rule associated with the communist-party-directed socialist economies. Second, they insist on a process of decentralized planning based on the participation of all people as equals, which is in sharp contrast to the hierarchical central planning used as the main alternative to market exchange.

Similarly to market socialism, models of market-less participatory socialism have been developed in various ways. Although such models of participatory socialism differ in many respects, they all share the common goal of the replacement of market forces—which allocate resources based on individual economic agents who act in their own best interest and in response to market signals—by a system of decentralized and coordinated planning—which allocates resources based on negotiation among relevant groups of workers, consumers, community residents and citizens in general.

The participatory system is typically constituted by two basic decision-making units: workplace workers' councils and neighborhood consumers' councils, in which workplace and neighborhood communities decide with respect to production and consumption. Of course, these basic decision-making units are embedded in a related larger network of politically-constituted bodies whose concerns transcend the limited scope of individual workplaces and neighborhoods. Planning boards play a crucial role in the network of non-market decision-making institutions. The planning boards collect and disseminate information as well as coordinate the decisions of separate councils and entities such that decentralized production and consumption plans which come from all the workplaces and neighborhoods converge to a comprehensive overall plan of production and consumption. In their decision-making, they consider not only quantitative data about production and consumption processes, but also qualitative ramifications of each production and consumption activity.

Advocates of participatory socialism believe that it can attain the socialist goals of egalitarianism, democracy, and solidarity far more successfully than market socialism—because there are no markets—and it can perform at least as efficiently as a market system—even though there are no markets. Advocates of market socialism, in contrast, find the omission of market forces highly impractical and problematic; and they find the feasibility, and at times even the desirability, of a participatory socialist system questionable.

Participatory socialism has been challenged on several grounds, of which the main ones are as follows. The first challenge is the idea that in a complex economy, the allocation of resources through participatory decision-making institutions places huge demands on information processing and disproportionate demands on people's time.

Advocates of the market system follow Adam Smith's original exposition of the "invisible hand" and emphasize the role of market prices in processing the enormous amount of information necessary for coordinated economic decision-making in a complex economy, and in disseminating such information in a simple manner to individual economic actors, such that they have both the information and the incentive to act in an economically efficient manner. Some other economists believe that the only alternative method of resource allocation, in a complex economy, is through a centralized, hierarchical system of administrative commands, which has been discredited by the experience of the communist-party-directed socialist economies. Participatory socialists take up this challenge and develop a third method of resource allocation that avoids both the use of markets and the hierarchy of an administrative command system.

The participatory socialist model replaces the market without using administrative commands. This model requires a vast network of an enormous number of decision-making bodies on which individual members sit, process information, deliberate, and arrive at decisions. It requires these decision-making bodies to perform a detailed analysis of both the qualitative and the quantitative implications of alternative ways of resource allocation. This places on the system a staggering set of requirements: (a) to involve all members of society in group decision-making processes; (b) to compile an enormous amount of economic information and to make it available to individuals engaged in economic decision-making; (c) to develop a system of accounting for the measurement and comparison of the social value of different production and consumption activities so that individual decision-makers can gauge the overall social consequences of any given set of decisions; (d) to find a way for the individual members of any given decision-making body to decide in a harmonious and timely fashion; and (e) to develop a system to assure that the myriad separate micro decisions when aggregated form a consistent pattern of resource allocation for the economy as a whole.

There is doubt regarding how these requirements can possibly be functionally met. Even if computer technology can be used to process and disseminate the enormous amount of information needed to make the system work, people do not necessarily provide the needed information in an unbiased manner. And even if all the needed information can be accurately compiled, the participatory planning requires each individual to dedicate so much time, interest, and energy in decision-making meetings that most people feel overwhelmed.

The second challenge to participatory socialism is the idea that the process of democratic decision-making is so complex and problematic that it should be limited to a small range of critical decision-making areas.

Advocates of participatory socialism place great emphasis on democracy both as a desirable goal in itself and as the best means to arrive at decisions that truly reflect people's interests. However, they tend to ignore the many problems involved in establishing fair and efficient democratic decision-making processes, such as: (1) the complex and critical nature of choice among alternative voting conventions: simple majority, supermajority, and consensus; (2) the distinction between constitutionally-protected rights and democratic voting; and (3) the weighing of various people's votes according to the extent to which they are affected by a pending decision.

Advocates of participatory socialism favor political forms of economic decision-making on the grounds that people take into account the larger social context and the interdependence of their decisions. However, the politicization of all decisions leads to excessive conflict, strife, and anger as well as to the formation of political groups that reduce the diversity of individual views and preferences to the lowest common-denominator platforms and programs. Advocates of participatory socialism favor direct participatory democracy over indirect representative democracy on the grounds that people listen to and confront each other as directly as possible in arriving at decisions. However, the practice of participatory democracy is so difficult, time-consuming, and emotionally draining that it has to be limited to a relatively small range of decisions.

Advocates of participatory socialism favor decentralized and negotiated planning on the grounds that it assures egalitarianism in economic decision-making. However, in practice, it is possible for some people to exercise much greater influence over decisions than others. Although such disproportionate influence may not arise from disproportionate wealth or income, it is possible for it to arise from disproportionate interest in and aptitude for the relevant decision-making processes. Different people have different abilities in accessing and processing information; in negotiating with others; and in influencing group decision-making. As a result, political and economic inequalities can arise in market-less as well as in market societies.

The third challenge to participatory socialism is the idea that it is not efficient to allocate labor without using the market-determined incentive system that rewards individuals according to the value of their work contributions.

Advocates of participatory socialism argue that their model is more efficient (and equitable) than the market system because, in their model, people are rewarded for their work according to their effort rather than results. Their model links the individual's consumption opportunities to the individual's input into the production process, i.e., the amount of personal effort made or personal sacrifice endured. They favor their model over the market system, in which individuals' rewards for work are linked to the market-determined value of their output, which depends on variables—such as natural talent, job location, and the vagaries of market demand—over which individuals have little or no control.

Participatory socialism model leads to greater equity in the reward for labor than the market-based alternative. Advocates of participatory socialism argue that their model provides the most efficient incentive as people are rewarded according to their personal input that best motivates people to apply the one factor which is under their control. However, their claim of greater efficiency is misguided because their personal-input reward system is flawed on two counts:

First, there is immense difficulty in observing and measuring an individual's sacrifice or work effort, and determining how much of the work result is due to such personal input rather than to other aspects of the work. Even if quantitative indices of personal input are developed, they tend to encourage the substitution of quantity for quality of effort. Moreover, people tend to associate good performance with their personal input, and bad performance with bad lucks.

Second, even if there are no measurement problems, an incentive structure that rewards individuals according to their personal input is inefficient. Although it can lead to greater work effort and sacrifice on the part of individuals, it cannot assure that such effort and sacrifice are expended in a desirable way. The social good is best served by undertaking those activities whose results are highly valued relative to the cost of undertaking those activities. In order to motivate people to direct their efforts the most socially-desirable goods, it is therefore necessary to reward their activities based on the value of work output rather than based on the quantity of work input. If market valuations of output do not properly reflect the social interest, then those output valuations need to be modified.

The fourth challenge to participatory socialism is the idea that a participatory economic system requires that people's basic consciousness to have already been transformed from one that is individually-oriented to one that is socially-oriented.

Advocates of market socialism assume that individuals behave as homo economicus, who seek to maximize their individual rewards. Advocates of market socialism seek to achieve socialist goals through structuring the market environment such that self-interested individuals make decisions that have socially-desirable consequences. In contrast, advocates of participatory socialism are highly critical of market-oriented motivational schemes and seek to diminish the role of incentives which are based on individual's material self-interest. There are some possible alternative incentives. On the positive motivational side, people can derive satisfaction from: (a) the enjoyable parts of their work; (b) the social confirmation which they receive for a job well done; (c) the confirmation that they well performed their responsibilities to others in the society; and/or (d) the enjoyment by others from activities to which they contributed. On the negative motivational side, people can be discouraged from antisocial behavior by: (e) the watchfulness and peer pressure of others; and/or (f) the inability of hiding excessively high consumption or excessively low production behavior in a society which is committed to egalitarianism.

In order for such mechanisms to become a working system of motivation that can replace the incentive system of individual's material self-interest, there needs to be a wholesale conversion of human behavior patterns from "homo economicus" to what may be called "homo socialis." That is, a wholesale conversion of individual's consciousness from individually-oriented to socially-oriented. One of the fundamental premises of Marxism is that the behavior of people is strongly influenced by their socioeconomic environment, i.e., people's values and behavior change as historical and socioeconomic conditions change. Accordingly, in a participatory economic environment people might develop the solidaristic and cooperative attitudes which reinforce the workings of a participatory socialist system. However, what is not clear is the process whereby the needed institutions, values, and behavior emerge.

9 Conclusion

This chapter briefly discussed eight major extant school of thought in economics, namely: Neo-Classical Economics, New Institutional Economics, Behavioral Economics, Austrian Economics, Post-Keynesian Economics, Institutional Economics, Radical Economics, and Marxist Economics. It noted that any explanation of an economic phenomenon is based on a worldview. It reiterated the premise of this book—i.e., that any worldview can be associated with one of the four broad paradigms: functionalist, interpretive, radical humanist, and radical structuralist—and located each of the schools of thought on the map of the four paradigms, as in Exhibit 12.1. It emphasizes, as pluralist economics does, that these schools of thought in economics are equally scientific and informative; they look at economic phenomena from their certain paradigmatic viewpoint; and together they provide a more balanced understanding of the economic phenomenon under consideration.

Each paradigm is logically coherent—in terms of its underlying assumptions—and conceptualizes and studies the phenomenon in a certain way, and generates distinctive kinds of insight and understanding. Therefore, different paradigms in combination provide a broader understanding of the phenomenon under consideration. An understanding of different paradigms leads to a better understanding of the multi-faceted nature of the phenomenon.

References

Acemoglu, D. 2003. Root Causes: A Historical Approach to Assessing the Role of Institutions in Economic Development. *Finance and Development* 40 (2): 27–30.

Albert, Michael, Leslie Cagan, Noam Chomsky, Robin Hahnel, Mel King, Lydia Sargent, and Holly Sklar. 1986. *Liberating Theory*. New York, NY: South End Press.

Alchian, Armen, and H. Demsetz. 1972. Production, Information Costs, and Economic Organization. *American Economic Review* 62: 777–795.

Alston, L.J., G.D. Libecap, and R. Schneider. 1996. The Determinants and Impact of Property Rights: Land Titles on the Brazilian Frontier. *Journal of Law, Economics and Organization* 12: 25–61.

Altman, Morris. 2006. *Handbook of Contemporary Behavioral Economics: Foundations and Developments*. Armonk, NY: M.E. Sharpe.

Amariglio, Jack, Antonio Callari, Stephen Resnick, David Ruccio, and Richard D. Wolff. 1996. Chapter 8: Nondeterminist Marxism: The Birth of a Postmodern Tradition in Economics. In *Beyond Neoclassical Economics: Heterodox Approaches to Economic Theory*, ed. Fred E. Foldvary, 134–147. Cheltenham, England: Edward Elgar Publishing.

Amariglio, Jack, Stephen Resnik, and Richard D. Wolff. 1993. Division and Difference in the 'Discipline' of Economics. *Critical Inquiry* 17: 108–137. Reprinted in Messer-Davidow, E, Shumway, D.R., and Sylvan, D.J., eds. 1994. *Knowledges: Historical and Critical Studies in Disciplinarity*. Charlottsville, VA: University of Virginia Press, pp. 150–184.

Amariglio, Jack, and David F. Ruccio. 1994. Postmodernism, Marxism, and the Critique of Modern Economic Thought. *Rethinking Marxism* 7 (3): 7–35.

Amin, Samir. 1974. *Accumulation on a World Scale: A Critique of the Theory of Underdevelopment*. New York, NY: Monthly Review Press.

———. 1988. Accumulation on a World Scale: Thirty Years Later. *Rethinking Marxism* 1 (2): 54–75.

Ansperger, Christian, and Yanis Varoufakis. 2006. What is Neoclassical Economics. *Post-Autistic Review* 38 (1): 2–13.

Arestis, Philip. 1990. Post-Keynesianism: A New Approach to Economics. *Review of Social Economy* 48 (3): 222–246.

———. 1992. *The Post-Keynesian Approach to Economics: An Alternative Analysis of Economic Theory and Policy*. Aldershot, England: Edward Elgar Publishing.

———. 1996. Post-Keynesian Economics: Towards Coherence. *Cambridge Journal of Economics* 20: 111–135.

Arestis, Philip, Stephen P. Dunn, and Malcolm Sawyer. 1999. Post Keynesian Economics and Its Critics. *Journal of Post Keynesian Economics* 21 (4): 527–549.

Arestis, Philip, and Malcolm Sawyer, eds. 1994. *The Elgar Companion to Radical Political Economy*. Aldershot, Hants, England: Edward Elgar Publishing.

Arestis, Philip, and Thanos Skouras, eds. 1985. *Post Keynesian Economic Theory: A Challenge to Neo-Classical Economics*. Brighton, England: Wheatsheaf Books.

Arrow, K.J., and G. Debreu. 1954. Existence of an Equilibrium for a Competitive Economy. *Econometrica* 22 (3): 265–290.

Ariely, D. 2008. *Predictably Irrational: The Hidden Forces that Shape Our Decisions*. New York, NY: Harper Collins.

Ayers, Clarence E. 1951. The Co-Ordinates of Institutionalism. *American Economic Review* 41: 47–55.

Backhaus, Jurgen G., ed. 2005. *Modern Applications of Austrian Thought*. New York, NY: Routledge.

Baddeley, Michelle. 2013. *Behavioral Economics and Finance*. New York, NY: Routledge.

Baiman, Ron, Heather Boushey, and Dawn Saunders, eds. 2000. *Political Economy and Contemporary Capitalism: Radical Perspectives on Economic Theory and Policy*. Armonk, NY: M.E. Sharpe.

Baker, H. Kent, and John R. Nofsinger, eds. 2010. *Behavioral Finance: Investors, Corporations, and Markets*. Hoboken, NJ: Wiley.

Baran, Paul, and Paul Sweezy. 1966. *Monopoly Capital*. London, England: Penguin Books.

Barberis, Nicholas, and Richard Thaler. 2003. A Survey of Behavioral Finance. In *Handbook of the Economics of Finance*, ed. G.M. Constantinides, M. Harris, and R. Stulz. Amsterdam, The Netherlands: Elsevier Science B.V.

Bardsley, N., R. Cubitt, G. Loomes, P. Moffat, C. Starmer, and R. Sugden. 2010. *Experimental Economics: Rethinking the Rules*. Princeton, NJ: Princeton University Press.

Barry, Norman P. 1991. Chapter 5: Austrian Economics: A Dissent from Orthodoxy. In *Companion to Contemporary Economic Thought*, ed. David Greenaway, Michael Bleaney, and Ian Stewart, 68–87. London, England: Routledge.

Binmore, Ken. 2008. Review of Behavioral Economics and Its Applications. *Economic Journal* 118 (529): 248–251.

Blaug, Mark. 1980. Economic Methodology in One Easy Lesson. *British Review of Economic Issues* 2 (5): 1–16.

Boettke, Peter J. 1989. Evolution and Economics: Austrian as Institutionalists. *Research in the History of Thought and Methodology* 6: 73–91.

———., ed. 1994. *The Elgar Companion to Austrian Economics*. Cheltenham, England: Edward Elgar Publishing.

———. 1996. Chapter 2: What Is Wrong with Neoclassical Economics (and What Is Still Wrong with Austrian Economics)? In *Beyond Neoclassical Economics: Heterodox Approaches to Economic Theory*, ed. Fred E. Foldvary, 22–40. Cheltenham, England: Edward Elgar Publishing.

———. 2010. *Handbook on Contemporary Austrian Economics*. Northampton, MA: Edward Elgar Publishing.

Boettke, Peter J., and David L. Prychitko, eds. 1994. *The Market Process: Essays in Contemporary Austrian Economics*. Brookfield, Vermont: Edward Elgar Publishing.

Bohm, Stephan. 1989. Chapter 4: Subjectivism and Post-Keynesianism: Towards a Better Understanding. In *New Directions in Post-Keynesian Economics*, ed. John Pheby, 59–93. Aldershot, Hants, England: Edward Elgar Publishing.

Boland, Lawrence A. 1991. Chapter 6: Current Views on Economic Positivism. In *Companion to Contemporary Economic Thought*, ed. David Greenaway, Michael Bleaney, and Ian Stewart, 88–104. London, England: Routledge.

Bowles, Samuel. 1998. Endogenous Preferences: The Cultural Consequences of Markets and other Economic Institutions. *Journal of Economic Literature* 36 (1): 75–111.

Bowles, Samuel, and Richard Edwards, eds. 1990. *Radical Political Economy, Volumes I and II*. Aldershot, Hants, England: Edward Elgar Publishing.

Brewer, Anthony. 2001. *Marxist Theories of Imperialism: A Critical Survey*. London, England: Routledge and Kegan Paul.

Brousseau, Eric, and Jean-Michel Glachant, eds. 2008. *New Institutional Economics: A Guidebook*. Cambridge, England: Cambridge University Press.

Brown, Elba K. 1981. The Neoclassical and Post-Keynesian Research Programs: The Methodological Issues. *Review of Social Economy* 39 (2): 111–132.

Bruni, L., and R. Sugden. 2007. The Road Not Taken: How Psychology Was Removed from Economics, and How It Might Be Brought Back. *Economic Journal* 117: 146–173.

Camerer, Colin F. 2003. *Behavioral Game Theory: Experiments in Strategic Interaction*. Princeton, NJ: Princeton University Press.

———. 2006. Behavioral Economics. In *Advances in Economics and Econometrics: Theory and Applications, Ninth World Congress*, ed. Richard Blundell, Whitney K. Newey, and Rorsten Persson, vol. II. Cambridge, England: Cambridge University Press.

Camerer, Colin F., George Loewenstein, and Matthew Rabin, eds. 2004. *Advances in Behavioral Economics*. Princeton, NJ: Princeton University Press.

Cartwright, Edward. 2011. *Behavioral Economics*. New York, NY: Routledge.

Cassar, A., and D. Friedman. 2004. *Economics Lab: An Introduction to Experimental Economics*. London, England: Routledge.

Coase, Ronald H. 1937. The Nature of the Firm. *Economica* 4 (16): 386–405. Reprinted in Coase, Ronald H. 1988. *The Firm, the Market and the Law*. Chicago, IL: University of Chicago Press, pp. 55–75.

———. 1960. The Problem of Social Cost. *Journal of Law and Economics* 3 (1): 1–44.

———. 1988. *The Firm, the Market, and the Law*. Chicago, IL: University of Chicago Press.

———. 1998. The New Institutional Economics. *American Economic Review Papers and Proceedings* 88 (2): 72–74.

Coeurderoy, R., and B. Quelin. 1997. Transaction Cost Theory: A Survey of Empirical Studies on Vertical Integration. *Review of Economic Policy* 107 (2): 145–181.

Commons, John R. 1931. Institutional Economics. *American Economic Review* 21 (4): 648–657.

———. 1934. *Institutional Economics*. London, England: Mamillan.

———. 1936. Institutional Economics. *American Economic Review* 26 (1): 237–249.

Conlisk, J. 1996. Why Bounded Rationality. *Journal of Economic Literature* 34: 669–700.

Crocker, K.J., and S.E. Masten. 1996. Regulation and Administered Contracts Revisited: Lesson from Transaction-Cost Economics for Public Utility Regulation. *Journal of Regulation Economics* 9: 5–40.

Crotty, James R. 1980. Post-Keynesian Economic Theory: An Overview and Evaluation. *American Economic Review* 70 (2): 20–25.

Cullenberg, Stephen. 1994. *The Falling Rate of Profit: Recasting the Marxian Debate*. Boulder, CO: Pluto Press.

Davidson, Paul. 1981. Chapter 10: Post Keynesian Economics: Solving the Crisis in Economic Theory. In *The Crisis in Economic Theory*, ed. Daniel Bell and Irving Kristol, 151–173. New York, NY: Basic Books.

Davis, John B. 1989. Axiomatic General Equilibrium Theory and Referentiality. *Journal of Post Keynesian Economics* 11 (3): 424–438.

Davis, John B., Alain Marciano, and Jochen Runde, eds. 2004. *The Elgar Companion to Economics and Philosophy*. Cheltenham, England: Edward Elgar Publishing.

Davis, Lance E., and Douglass C. North. 1971. *Institutional Change and American Economic Growth*. New York, NY: Cambridge University Press.

Della Vigna, Stefano. 2009. Psychology and Economics: Evidence from the Field. *Journal of Economic Literature* 47 (2): 315–372.

Desai, Meghnad. 1979. *Marxian Economics*. Oxford, England: Basil Blackwell.

Diamond, Peter, and Hannu Vartiainen. 2007. *Behavioral Economics and Its Applications*. Princeton, NJ: Princeton University Press.

Dolan, Edwin G., ed. 1976. *The Foundations of Modern Austrian Economics*. Kansas City, KS: Sheed and Ward.

Dow, Sheila C. 1988. Post Keynesian Economics: Conceptual Underpinnings. *British Review of Economic Issues* 10 (23): 1–18.

———. 1990. Post Keynesianism as Political Economy: A Methodological Discussion. *Review of Political Economy* 2 (3): 345–358.

———. 1991. Chapter 7: The Post-Keynesian School. In *A Modern Guide to Economic Thought: An Introduction to Comparative Schools of Thought in Economics*, ed. Douglas Mair and Anne G. Miller, 176–206. Aldershot, Hants, England: Edward Elgar Publishing.

———. 1996. *The Methodology of Macroeconomics Thought: A Conceptual Analysis of Schools of Thought in Economics*. Cheltenham, England: Edward Elgar Publishing.

Dowling, John Malcolm, and Yap Chin-Fang. 2007. *Modern Developments in Behavioral Economics: Social Science Perspectives on Choice and Decision Making*. London, England: World Scientific.

Drobak, John N., and John V.C. Nye, eds. 1997. *The Frontiers of the New Institutional Economics*. New York, NY: Academic.

Dugger, William M. 1979. Methodological Differences Between Institutional and Neoclassical Economics. *Journal of Economic Issues* 13 (4): 899–909. Reprinted in Samuels, Warren J., ed. 1988. *Institutional Economics, Volumes I, II, and III*. Aldershot, Hants, England: Edward Elgar Publishing, Chapter 5, pp. 84–94.

———. 1990. The New Institutionalism: New But Not Institutionalist. *Journal of Economic Issues* 24 (2): 423–431.

Dugger, William M., and Howard J. Sherman. 1994. Comparisons of Marxism and Institutionalism. *Journal of Economic Issues* 28 (1): 101–127. Reprinted in Prychitko, David L., ed. 1998. *Why Economists Disagree: An Introduction to the Alternative Schools of Thought*, Albany, NY: State University of New York Press, Chapter 9, pp. 211–236.

Earl, Peter E., ed. 1988. *Behavioral Economics, volumes I and II*. Aldershot, England: Edward Elgar Publishing.

———. 1990. Economics and Psychology: A Survey. *Economic Journal* 100: 718–755.

Edwards, Richard, and Arthur MacEwan. 1970. A Radical Approach to Economics: Basis for a New Curriculum. *American Economic Review* 60 (2): 352–363.

Eichner, Alfred S., ed. 1979. *A Guide to Post-Keynesian Economics*. While Plains, NY: M.E. Sharpe.

Eichner, Alfred S., and J.A. Kregel. 1975. An Essay on Post-Keynesian Theory: A New Paradigm in Economics. *Journal of Economic Literature* 13 (4): 1293–1314. Reprinted in Prychitko, David L., ed. 1998. *Why Economists Disagree: An Introduction to the Alternative Schools of Thought*, Albany, NY: State University of New York Press, Chapter 5, pp. 83–114.

Emmet, Ross B., ed. 2010. *The Elgar Companion to the Chicago School of Economics*. Cheltenham, England: Edward Elgar Publishing.

Fine, Ben. 1980. *Economic Theory and Ideology*. London, England: Edward Arnold Publishers.

Forbes, Silke Januszewski, and Mara Lederman. 2009. Adaptation and Vertical Integration in the Airline Industry. *American Economic Review* 99 (5): 1831–1849.

———. 2010. Does Vertical Integration Affect Firm Performance? Evidence from the Airline Industry. *RAND Journal of Economics* 41 (4): 765–790.

Forbes, W. 2009. *Behavioral Finance*. Chichester, England: Wiley.

Foster, John Bellamy, and Robert W. McChesney. 2004. *Pox Americana: Exposing the American Empire*. New York, NY: Monthly Review Press.

Frey, Bruno S., and Matthias Benz. 2004. Chapter 4: From Imperialism to Inspiration: A Survey of Economics and Psychology. In *The Elgar Companion to Economics and Philosophy*, ed. John B. Davis, Alain Marciano, and Jochen Runde, 61–83. Cheltenham, England: Edward Elgar Publishing.

Friedman, Milton. 1953. *Essays in Positive Economics*. Chicago, IL: University of Chicago Press.

Fudenberg, Drew. 2006. Advancing beyond Advances in Behavioral Economics. *Journal of Economic Literature* 44 (3): 694–711.

Fulton, G. 1984. Research Programmes in Economics. *History of Political Economy* 16 (2): 187–205.

Furubotn, Eirik G., and Rudolf Richter. 1991a. The New Institutional Economics: An Assessment. In *The New Institutional Economics: A Collection of Articles from the Journal of Institutional and Theoretical Economics*, ed. Eirik G. Furubotn and Rudolf Richter, 1–32. College Station, TX: Texas A&M University Press.

———, eds. 1991b. *The New Institutional Economics: A Collection of Articles from the Journal of Institutional and Theoretical Economics*. College Station, TX: Texas A&M University Press.

———. 1998. *Institutions and Economic Theory: The Contribution of the New Institutional Economics*. 2nd ed. Ann Arbor, MI: University of Michigan Press.

———. 2008. The New Institutional Economics: A Different Approach to Economic Analysis. *Economic Affairs* 28 (3): 15–23.

Gee, J.M. Alec. 1991. Chapter 4: The Neoclassical School. In *A Modern Guide to Economic Thought: An Introduction to Comparative Schools of Thought in Economics*, ed. Douglas Mair and Anne G. Miller, 71–108. Aldershot, Hants, England: Edward Elgar Publishing.

Geyskens, Inge, Jan-Benedict E.M. Steenkamp, and Nirmalya Kumar. 2006. Make, Buy, or Ally: A Meta-Analysis of Transaction Cost Theory. *Academy of Management Journal* 49 (3): 519–543.

Gibbons, Robert S. 2010. Transaction-Cost Economics: Past, Present, and Future? *Scandinavian Journal of Economics* 112 (2): 263–288.

Gilad, Benjamin, and Stanley Kaish, eds. 1986. *Handbook of Behavioral Economics, Volumes A and B*. Greenwich, CT: JAI Press.

Gloria-Palermo, Sandye. 1999. *The Evolution of Austrian Economics: From Menger to Lachmann*. New York, NY: Routledge.

Grassl, Wolfgang, and Barry Smith, eds. 1986. *Austrian Economics: Historical and Philosophical Background*. New York, NY: New York University Press.

Groenewegen, John, Spithoven, Antoon, and Van Den Berg, Annette, (2010), Institutional Economics: An Introduction, New York, NY: Palgrave Macmillan.

Gruchy, Allan Garfield. 1957. Institutional Economics, A New Look at Institutionalism: Discussion. *American Economic Review* 47 (Suppl 2): 13–27.

———. 1969. Neoinstitutionalism and the Economics of Dissent. *Journal of Economic Issues* 3: 3–17.

———. 1972. *Contemporary Economic Thought: The Contribution of Neo-Institutional Economics*. Clifton, NJ: Augustus Kelley Publishers.

———. 1987. *The Reconstruction of Economics: An Analysis of the Fundamentals of Institutional Economics*. Westport, CT: Greenwood Press.

Hahn, Frank. 1981. Chapter 8: General Equilibrium Theory. In *The Crisis in Economic Theory*, ed. Daniel Bell and Irving Kristol, 123–138. New York, NY: Basic Books.

Hahnel, Robin. 2002. *The ABCs of Political Economy: A Modern Approach*. London, England: Pluto Press.

Hamouda, O.F., and G.C. Harcourt. 1988. Post Keynesianism: From Criticism to Coherence? *Bulletin of Economic Research* 40 (1): 1–33. Reprinted in Pheby, J., ed. 1988. *New Directions in Post-Keynesian Economics*, Aldershot, Hants, England: Edward Elgar Publishing.

Harcourt, G.C. 1987. Post-Keynesian Economics. In *The New Palgrave: A Dictionary of Economics*, ed. John Eatwell, Murray Milgate, and Peter Newman, vol. 3, 924–928. London, England: Macmillan.

———. 2006. *The Structure of Post-Keynesian Economics: The Core Contributions of the Pioneers*. Cambridge, England: Cambridge University Press.

Heijdra, Ben J., and Anthon D. Lowenberg. 1988. The Neoclassical Economic Research Program: Some Lakatosian and other Considerations. *Australian Economic Papers* 27 (1): 272–284.

Hetzel, Robert L. 2007. The Contributions of Milton Friedman to Economics. *Economic Quarterly* 93 (1): 1–30.

Hodgson, Geoffrey Martin. 1988. *Economics and Institutions: A Manifesto for a Modern Institutional Economics*. Philadelphia, PA: University of Pennsylvania Press.

———. 1989a. Institutional Economic Theory: The Old versus the New. *Review of Political Economy* 1 (3): 249–270. Reprinted in Prychitko, David L., ed. 1998. *Why Economists Disagree: An Introduction to the Alternative Schools of Thought*, Albany, NY: State University of New York Press, Chapter 7, pp. 155–178.

———. 1989b. Chapter 5: Post-Keynesianism and Institutionalism: The Missing Link. In *New Directions in Post-Keynesian Economics*, ed. John Pheby, 94–123. Aldershot, Hants, England: Edward Elgar Publishing.

———. 1998. The Approach of Institutional Economics. *Journal of Economic Literature* 36 (1): 166–192.

———. 2000. What Is the Essence of Institutional Economics. *Journal of Economic Issues* 34 (2): 317–329.

———, ed. 2002. *A Modern Reader in Institutional and Evolutionary Economics: Key Concepts*. Cheltenham, England: Edward Elgar Publishing.

———, ed. 2003. *Recent Developments in Institutional Economics*. Cheltenham, England: Edward Elgar Publishing.

———. 2004a. *The Evolution of Institutional Economics: Agency, Structure and Darwinism in American Institutionalism*. London, England: Routledge.

———. 2004b. Chapter 5: Institutional Economics: From Menger and Veblen to Coase and North. In *The Elgar Companion to Economics and Philosophy*, ed. John B. Davis, Alain Marciano, and Jochen Runde, 84–101. Cheltenham, England: Edward Elgar Publishing.

Hodgson, Geoffrey Martin, Warren J. Samuels, and Marc R. Tool, eds. 1994. *The Elgar Companion to Institutional and Evolutionary Economics*. Aldershot, England: Edward Elgar Publishing.

Holt, Richard P.F. 2007. Chapter 6: What is Post Keynesian Economics. In *Post-Keynesian Macroeconomics: Essays in Honor of Ingrid Rima*, ed. Mathew Forstater, Gary Mongiovi, and Steven Pressman, 89–107. London, England: Routledge.

Holt, Richard P.F., and Steven Pressman, eds. 2001. *A New Guide to Post Keynesian Economics*. London, England: Routledge.

———, eds. 2007. *Empirical Post Keynesian Economics: Looking at the Real World*. Armonk, NY: M.E. Sharpe.

Howard, M.C., and J.E. King. 1975. *The Political Economy of Marx*. Harlow, Essex, England: Longman Group.

———. 1992. *A History of Marxian Economics*. Princeton, NJ: Princeton University Press.

Hall, Joshua C., and Adam Martin. 2011. Austrian Economics: Methodology, Concepts, and Implications for Economic Education. *Journal of Economics and Finance Education* 10 (2).

Hutchinson, Terence W. 1984. Institutional Economics Old and New. *Journal of Institutional and Theoretical Economics* 140: 20–29. Reprinted in Furubotn, Eirik G., and Rudolf Richter., eds. 1991. *The New Institutional Economics: A Collection of Articles from the Journal of Institutional and Theoretical Economics*. College Station, TX: Texas A&M University Press, pp. 35–44.

Joskow, Paul L. 1988. Asset Specifity and the Structure of Vertical Relationships: Empirical Evidence. *Journal of Law, Economics and Organization* 4: 95–117.

———. 2008. Introduction to New Institutional Economics: A Report Card. In *New Institutional Economics: A Guidebook*, ed. Eric Brousseau and Jean-Michel Glachant, 1–19. Cambridge, England: Cambridge University Press.

Kahneman, Daniel, and Amos Tversky. 1979. Prospect Theory: An Analysis of Decision under Risk. *Econometrica* 47 (2): 263–291.

Kapp, K. William. 1968. In Defense of Institutional Economics. *Swedish Journal of Economics* 70: 1–18.

———. 1976. The Nature and Significance of Institutional Economics. *Kyklos* 29 (2): 209–232.

Kapp, Karl William. 2011. *The Foundations of Institutional Economics*. New York, NY: Routledge.

King, John E., ed. 1990. *Marxian Economics, Volumes I, II, and III*. Hants, England: Edward Elgar Publishing.

———., ed. 2003. *The Elgar Companion to Post Keynesian Economics*. Cheltenham, England: Edward Elgar Publishing.

Kirzner, Israel M. 1981. Chapter 7: The 'Austrian' Perspective. In *The Crisis in Economic Theory*, ed. Daniel Bell and Irving Kristol, 111–122. New York, NY: Basic Books.

———. 1992. *The Meaning of Market Process: Essays in the Development of Modern Austrian Economics*. New York, NY: Routledge.

———. 2000. *Driving Force of the Market: Essays in Austrian Economics*. New York, NY: Routledge.

Klein, P. 1999. New Institutional Economics. In *Encyclopedia of Law and Economics*, ed. B. Bouckaert and G. De Geest, vol. 1. Cheltenham, England: Edward Elgar Publishing.

Koppl, Roger, ed. 2008. *Explorations in Austrian Economics*. Bingley, England: JAI Press.

Koppl, Roger, Steven Horwitz, and Pierre Desrochers, eds. 2010. *Advances in Austrian Economics: What Is So Austrian about Austrian Economics?* Bingley, England: Emerald.

Kotz, David M. 1991. Accumulation, Money, and Credit in the Circuit of Capital. *Rethinking Marxism* 4 (2): 119–133.

Kotz, David M., Terrence McDonough, and Michael Reich, eds. 1994. *Social Structures of Accumulation: The Political Economy of Growth and Crisis*. Cambridge, England: Cambridge University Press.

Kregel, J.A. 1975. *The Reconstruction of Political Economy: An Introduction to Post-Keynesian Economics*. London, England: Macmillan.

Lachmann, Ludwig M. 1998. Chapter 3: From Mises to Shackle: An Essay on Austrian Economics and the Kaleidic Society. In *Why Economists Disagree: An Introduction to the Alternative Schools of Thought*, ed. David L. Prychitko, 53–66. Albany, NY: State University of New York Press.

Lavoie, Marc. 1992a. *Foundations of Post-Keynesian Economic Analysis*. Cheltenham, England: Edward Elgar Publishing.

———. 1992b. Toward a New Research Programme for Post-Keynesianism and Neo-Ricardianism. *Review of Political Economy* 4 (1): 37–78.

Lawson, Tony. 1994. The Nature of Post Keynesianism and Its Links to other Traditions: A Realist Perspective. *Journal of Post Keynesian Economics* 16 (4): 503–538. Reprinted in Prychitko, David L., ed. 1998. *Why Economists Disagree: An Introduction to the Contemporary Schools of Thought*, New York, NY: State University of New York Press, Chapter 6, pp. 115–154.

———. 1999. Connections and Distinctions: Post Keynesianism and Critical Realism. *Journal of Post Keynesian Economics* 22 (1): 3–14.

———. 2005. The Nature of Institutional Economics. *Evolutionary and Institutional Economics Review* 2 (1): 7–20.

Lee, Frederic S. 2002. Theory Foundation and Methodological Foundations of Post Keynesian Economics. *Cambridge Journal of Economics* 26 (4): 789–804. Reprinted in Downward, Paul., ed. 2003. *Applied Economics and the Critical Realist Critique*, New York, NY: Routledge.

———. 2009. Chapter 5: The History of Post Keynesian Economics in America, 1971-95. In *A History of Heterodox Economics: Challenging the Mainstream in the Twentieth Century*, ed. Frederic S. Lee, 78–96. New York, NY: Routledge.

Lee, Frederic S., and Marc Lavoie. 2012. *In Defense of Post-Keynesian and Heterodox Economics: Responses to Their Critics*. New York, NY: Routledge.

Lewis, Paul A. (2004). Structure and Agency in Economic Analysis: The Case of Austrian Economics and the Material Embeddedness of Socio-Economic Life. In Davis, John B., List, John. (2004). Neoclassical Theory versus Prospect Theory: Evidence from the Marketplace. *Econometrica*, 72 (2), 615–625.

Libecap, G.D., and J.L. Smith. 1999. The Self-Enforcing Provisions of Oil and Gas Unit Operating Agreements: Theory and Evidence. *Journal of Law, Economics and Organization* 15 (2): 526–548.

Lippit, Victor D., ed. 1996. *Radical Political Economy: Explorations in Alternative Economic Analysis*. Armonk, NY: M.E. Sharpe.

List, John. 2004. Neoclassical Theory versus Prospect Theory: Evidence from the Marketplace. *Econometrica* 72 (2): 615–625.

Littlechild, Stephen, ed. 1990. *Austrian Economics*. Vol. I, II, III. Aldershot, England: Edward Elgar Publishing.

Loasby, Brian J. 1991. Chapter 3: The Austrian School. In *A Modern Guide to Economic Thought: An Introduction to Comparative Schools of Thought in Economics*, ed. D. Mair and A.G. Miller, 40–70. Aldershot, Hants, England: Edward Elgar Publishing.

Macher, J.T., and B.D. Richman. 2008. Transaction Cost Economics: An Assessment of Empirical Research in the Social Sciences. *Business and Politics* 10 (1): 1–63.

Maital, Shlomo, ed. 2007. *Recent Developments in Behavioral Economics*. Cheltenham, England: Edward Elgar Publishing.

Mandel, Ernest. 1968. *Marxist Economic Theory*. New York, NY: Monthly Review Press.

McKenna, Edward J., and Diane C. Zannoni. 1993. Philosophical Foundations of Post Keynesian Economics. *Journal of Post Keynesian Economics* 15 (3): 395–407.

McLellan, David, ed. 2000. *Karl Marx: Selected Writings*. Oxford, England: Oxford University Press.

Medema, Steven, ed. 1998. *Coasian Economics: Law and Economics and the New Institutional Economics*. Boston, MA: Kluwer Academic Publishing.

Meijer, Gerrit, ed. 1995. *New Perspectives on Austrian Economics*. New York, NY: Routledge.

Menard, Claude, and Mary M. Shirley, eds. 2005. *Handbook of New Institutional Economics*. Dordrecht, The Netherlands: Springer.

Menger, Carl. 1981. *Principles of Economics*. New York, NY: New York University Press.

Mermelstein, David, ed. 1970. *Economics: Mainstream Readings and Radical Critiques*. New York, NY: Random House.

Milberg, William. 1991. Marxism, Poststructuralism, and the Discourse of Economics. *Rethinking Marxism* 4 (2): 92–104.

Miller, Edythes S. 1978. Institutional Economics: Philosophy, Methodology and Theory. *Social Science Journal* 15 (1): 13–25. Reprinted in Samuels, Warren J., ed. 1988. *Institutional Economics, Volume II*, Aldershot, Hants, England: Edward Elgar Publishing, Chapter 3, pp. 50–62.

Milonakis, Dimitris, and Ben Fine. 2008. *From Political Economy to Economics: Method, the Social and the Historical in the Evolution of Economic Theory*. New York, NY: Routledge.

Mirowski, Philip. 1987. The Philosophical Bases of Institutionalist Economics. *Journal of Economic Issues* 21 (3): 1001–1038.

Mullainathan, Sendhil, and Richard Thaler. 2000. Behavioral Economics. In *International Encyclopedia of the Social and Behavioral Sciences*. Cambridge, MA: MIT Press.

Myrdal, Gunnar. 1978. Institutional Economics. *Journal of Economic Issues* 12 (4): 771–783.

Nell, Edward J. 1981. Chapter 11: Value and Capital in Marxian Economics. In *The Crisis in Economic Theory*, ed. Daniel Bell and Irving Kristol, 174–200. New York, NY: Basic Books.

Nelson, Richard R., and Bhaven N. Sampat. 2001. Making Sense of Institutions as a Factor Shaping Economic Performance. *Journal of Economic Behavior and Organization* 44 (1): 31–54.

North, Douglass C. 1986. The New Institutional Economics. *Journal of Institutional and Theoretical Economics* 142: 230–237.

———. 1990. *Institutions, Institutional Change and Economic Performance*. Cambridge, England: Cambridge University Press.

———. 1991. Institutions. *Journal of Economic Perspectives* 5 (1): 97–112.

———. 1994. Economic Performance through Time. *American Economic Review* 84 (3): 359–368.

O'Connor, James. 1984. *Accumulation Crisis*. New York, NY: Basil Blackwell.

O'Connor, Martin, ed. 1994. *Is Capitalism Sustainable?: Political Economy and the Politics of Ecology*. New York, NY: Guildford Press.

O'Hara, Phillip Anthony. 2007. Principles of Institutional-Evolutionary Political Economy: Converging Themes from the Schools of Heterodoxy. *Journal of Economic Issues* 41 (1): 1–42.

Ostrom, Elinor. 2005. Chapter 30: Doing Institutional Analysis: Digging Deeper than Markets and Hierarchies. In *Handbook of New Institutional Economics*, ed. Claude Menard and Mary M. Shirley, 819–848. Dordrecht, The Netherlands: Springer.

Palermo, Giulio. 2007. The Ontology of Economic Power in Capitalism: Mainstream Economics and Marx. *Cambridge Journal of Economics* 31 (4): 539–561.

Palley, Thomas I. 1996. *Post Keynesian Economics: Debt, Distribution and the Macro Economy*. New York, NY: St. Matin's Press.

Papadimitriou, Dimitri B., and L. Randall Wray, eds. 2010. *The Elgar Companion to Hyman Minsky*. Cheltenham, England: Edward Elgar Publishing.

Panitch, Leo, and Colin Leys, eds. 1999. *Global Capitalism versus Democracy: Socialist Register 1999*. New York, NY: Monthly Review Press.

Pesendorfer, Wolfgang. 2006. Behavioral Economics Comes of Age: A Review Essay on Advances in Behavioral Economics. *Journal of Economic Literature* 44 (3): 712–721.

Peterson, Wallace C. 1987. Macroeconomic Theory and Policy in an Institutionalist Perspective. *Journal of Economic Issues* 21 (4): 1587–1622.

Pheby, John, ed. 1989. *New Directions in Post-Keynesian Economics*. Aldershot, Hants, England: Edward Elgar Publishing.

Pompian, Michael M. 2012. *Behavioral Finance and Wealth Management: How to Build Investment Strategies that Account for Investor Biases*. Hoboken, NJ: Wiley.

Pratten, Stephen. 2004. Chapter 17: The Conflict Between Formalism and Realisticness in Modern Economics: The Case of the New Institutional Economics. In *The Elgar Companion to Economics and Philosophy*, ed. John B. Davis, Alain Marciano, and Jochen Runde, 339–363. Cheltenham, England: Edward Elgar Publishing.

Prychitko, David L., ed. 1998. *Why Economists Disagree: An Introduction to the Alternative Schools of Thought*. Albany, NY: State University of New York Press.

Rabin, Matthew. 1998. Psychology and Economics. *Journal of Economic Literature* 36 (1): 11–46.

Reder, Melvin W. 1982. Chicago Economics: Permanence and Change. *Journal of Economic Literature* 20 (1): 1–38.

Resnick, Stephen A., and Richard D. Wolff. 1987. *Knowledge and Class: A Marxian Critique of Political Economy*. Chicago, IL: University of Chicago Press.

Ricciardi, Victor, and Helen K. Simon. 2000. What Is Behavioral Finance? *Business, Education and Technology Journal* 2 (2): 1–9.

Richter, R. 2005. The New Institutional Economics: Its Start, Its Meaning, Its Prospects. *European Business Organization Law Review* 6: 161–200.

Ricketts, Martin, ed. 1988. *Neoclassical Microeconomics*. Vol. I, II. Aldershot, England: Edward Elgar Publishing.

Rima, Ingrid. 2013a. Chapter 8: German-Austrian Economics. In *A Primer on Heterodox Economics*, ed. Ingrid Rima. New York, NY: Routledge.

———. 2013b. *A Primer on Heterodox Economics*. New York, NY: Routledge.

Robbins, Lionell. 1937. *An Essay on the Nature and Significance of Economic Science*. London, England: Macmillan.

Roberts, Bruce, and Susan Feiner, eds. 1992. *Radical Economics*. Boston, MA: Kluwer Academic Publishers.

Roth, A. 1995. Introduction to Experimental Economics. In *Handbook of Experimental Economics*, ed. J. Kagel and A. Roth. Princeton, NJ: Princeton University Press.

Rothem, Roy J. 1999. Post Keynesian Economics and Realist Philosophy. *Journal of Post Keynesian Economics* 22 (1): 71–103.

Rutherford, Malcolm. 1994. *Institutions in Economics: The Old and the New Institutionalism*. Cambridge, England: Cambridge University Press.

———. 2001. Institutional Economics: Then and Now. *Journal of Economic Perspectives* 15 (3): 173–194.

Sackrey, Charles, Geoffrey Schneider, and Janet Knoedler. 2008. *Introduction to Political Economy*. New York, NY: Dollars and Sense.

Samuels, Warren J., ed. 1988. *Institutional Economics*. Vol. I, II, and III. Aldershot, Hants, England: Edward Elgar Publishing.

———. 1989. Austrian and Institutional Economics: Some Common Elements. *Research in the History of Economic Thought and Methodology* 6: 53–72.

Sawyer, Malcolm C., ed. 1988. *Post-Keynesian Economics*. Aldershot, England: Edward Elgar Publishing.

———. 1989. *The Challenge of Radical Political Economy: An Introduction to the Alternatives to Neoclassical Economics*. Savage, MD: Barnes and Noble Books.

———. 1991. Chapter 11: Post-Keynesian Macroeconomics. In *Companion to Contemporary Economic Thought*, ed. David Greenaway, Michael Bleaney, and Ian Stewart, 184–206. London, England: Routledge.

Schlicht, Ekkehart. 1998. Chapter 15: The Texture of Customs. In *On Custom in the Economy*, 269–275. Oxford, England: Claredon Press.

Schmidt, U., C. Starmer, and R. Sugden. 2008. Third Generation Prospect Theory. *Journal of Risk and Uncertainty* 36: 203–223.

Scott, Andrew. 1991. Chapter 9: Marxian and Radical Economics. In *A Modern Guide to Economic Thought: An Introduction to Comparative Schools of Thought in Economics*, ed. Douglas Mair and Anne G. Miller, 233–262. Aldershot, Hants, England: Edward Elgar Publishing.

Sent, E.M. 2004. Behavioral Economics: How Psychology Made Its (Limited) Way Back into Economics. *History of Political Economy* 36: 735–760.

Shand, Alexander H. 1984. *The Capitalist Alternative: An Introduction to Neo-Austrian Economics*. New York, NY: New York University Press.

———. 1990. *Free Market Morality: The Political Economy of the Austrian School*. London, England: Routledge.

Shefrin, Hersh. 2002. *Beyond Greed and Fear: Understanding Behavioral Finance and the Psychology of Investing*. Oxford, England: Oxford University Press.

Shelanski, Howard A., and Peter G. Klein. 1995. Empirical Research in Transaction Cost Economics: A Review and Assessment. *Journal of Law, Economics, and Organization* 11 (2): 335–361.

Sherman, Howard J. 1987. *Foundations of Radical Political Economy*. Armonk, NY: M.E. Sharpe.

Sherman, Howard J., E.K. Hunt, Reynold F. Nesiba, Philip A. O'Hara, and Barbara Wiens-Tuers. 2008. *Economics: An Introduction to Traditional and Progressive Views*. Armonk, NY: M.E. Sharpe.

Shiller, R.J. 2003. From Efficient Markets Theory to Behavioral Finance. *Journal of Economic Perspectives* 17: 83–104.

Shiv, B., and A. Fedorikhin. 1999. Heart and Mind in Conflict: The Interplay of Affect and Cognition in consumer Decision Making. *Journal of Consumer Research* 26: 278–292.

Simon, Herbert A. 1955. A Behavioral Model of Rational Choice. *Quarterly Journal of Economics* 69: 99–118.

———. 1998. Behavioral Economics. In *The New Palgrave Dictionary of Economics*, ed. J. Eatwell, M. Milgate, and P. Newman, vol. 1. London, England: Macmillan.

Singer, Daniel. 1999. *Whose Millennium? Theirs or Ours?* New York, NY: Monthly Review Press.

Stanfield, James Ronald. 1999. The Scope, Method, and Significance of Original Institutional Economics. *Journal of Economic Issues* 33 (2): 231–255.

Stilwell, Frank. 2012. *Political Economy: The Contest of Economic Ideas*. Oxford, England: Oxford University Press.

Sweezy, Paul M. 1942. *The Theory of Capitalist Development: Principles of Marxian Political Economy*. New York, NY: Monthly Review Press.

Sweezy, Paul M., and Harry Magdoff. 1972. *The Dynamics of U.S. Capitalism: Corporate Structure, Inflation, Credit, Gold, and the Dollar*. New York, NY: Monthly Review Press.

Thaler, R.H., ed. 2005. *Advances in Behavioral Finance*. New York, NY: Russell Sage Foundations.

———. 2008a. Mental Accounting and Consumer Choice: Anatomy of a Failure. *Marketing Science* 27: 1–14.

———. 2008b. Mental Accounting and Consumer Choice. *Marketing Science* 27: 15–25.

Tollison, Robert D. 1989. Chicago Political Economy. *Public Choice* 63 (3): 293–298.

Tomer, John F. 2007. What Is Behavioral Economics? *Journal of Socio-Economics* 36 (3): 463–479.

Tool, Marc R. 1981. The Compulsive Shift to Institutional Analysis. *Journal of Economic Issues* 15 (3): 569–592.

———. 1988a. *Evolutionary Economics, Volume I: Foundations of Institutional Thought*. Armonk, NY: M.E. Shape.

———. 1988b. *Evolutionary Economics, Volume II: Institutional Theory and Policy*. Armonk, NY: M.E. Shape.

Tool, Marc R., and Paul Dale Bush, eds. 2003. *Institutional Analysis and Economic Policy*. Boston, MA: Kluwer Academic Publishers.

Tversky, A., and D. Kahneman. 1974. Judgment under Uncertainty: Heuristics and Biases. *Science* 185: 1124–1131.

———. 1981. The Framing of Decisions and the Psychology of Choice. *Science* 211: 453–458.

Van Horn, Robert, and Philip Mirowski. 2009. The Rise of Chicago School of Economics and the Birth of Neoliberalism. In *The Road from Mont Pelerin: The Making of the Neoliberal Thought Collective*, ed. P. Mirowski and D. Plehwe. Cambridge, MA: Harvard University Press.

Vannoni, D. 2002. Empirical Studies of Vertical Integration: The Transaction Cost Orthodoxy. *International Review of Economics and Business* 49: 113–141.

Van Overtveldt, Johan. 2007. *The Chicago School: How the University of Chicago Assembled the Thinkers Who Revolutionized Economics and Business*. Chicago, IL: Agate.

Van Raaij, W. Fred. 1991. Chapter 40: Economics and Psychology. In *Companion to Contemporary Economic Thought*, ed. David Greenaway, Michael Bleaney, and Ian Stewart, 797–811. London, England: Routledge.

Vaughn, Karen I. 1994. *Austrian Economics in America: The Migration of a Tradition*. New York, NY: Cambridge University Press.

Velupillai, Kumaraswamy, and Shu-Heng Chen, eds. 2012. *Behavioral Economics*. New York, NY: Routledge.

von Mises, Ludwig. 1962. *The Ultimate Foundation of Economic Science: An Essay on Method*. Princeton, NJ: D. Van Nostrand Company.

———. 1966. *Human Action: A Treaties on Economics*. Chicago, IL: Henry Regnery.

Vromen, Jack J. 1995. *Economic Evolution: An Inquiry into the Foundations of New Institutional Economics*. London, England: Routledge.

Wallerstein, Immanuel. 1974. *The Modern World-System*. San Diego, CA: Academic.

Walsh, Vivian, and Harvey Gram. 1980. *Classical and Neoclassical Theories of General Equilibrium: Historical Origins and Mathematical Structure*. Oxford, England: Oxford University Press.

Walters, Bernard, and David Young. 1997. On the Coherence of Post-Keynesian Economics. *Scottish Journal of Political Economy* 44 (3): 329–349.

———. 1999. Is Critical Realism the Appropriate Basis for Post Keynesianism? *Journal of Post Keynesian Economics* 22 (1): 105–123.

Ward, Dwayne. 1977. *Toward a Critical Political Economics: A Critique of Liberal and Radical Economic Thought*. Santa Monica, CA: Goodyear Publishing Company.

Warren, Bill. 1980. *Imperialism: Pioneer of Capitalism*. London, England: Verso.

Weintraub, E. Roy. 1985a. *General Equilibrium Analysis: Studies in Appraisal*. Cambridge, England: Cambridge University Press.

———. 1985b. Appraising General Equilibrium Analysis. *Economics and Philosophy* 1 (1): 23–37.

———. 2008. Mathematics and Economics. In *The New Palgrave Dictionary of Economics*, ed. Steven Durlauf and Lawrence Blume. New York, NY: Palgrave Macmillan.

Whalen, Charles J. 1996. Chapter 5: The Institutional Approach to Political Economy. In *Beyond Neoclassical Economics: Heterodox Approaches to Economic Theory*, ed. Fred E. Foldvary, 83–99. Cheltenham, England: Edward Elgar Publishing.

Wiesskopf, Thomas E. 1992. Toward a Socialism for the Future in the Wake of the Demise of the Socialism of the Past. *Review of Radical Political Economics* 24 (3/4). Reprinted in Prychitko, David L., ed. 1998. *Why Economists Disagree: An Introduction to the Alternative Schools of Thought*, Albany, NY: State University of New York Press, Chapter 11, pp. 275–306.

Wilber, Charles K., and Robert S. Harrison. 1978. The Methodological Basis of Institutional Economics: Pattern Model, Story Telling, and Holism. *Journal of Economic Issues* 12 (1): 61–89.

Williamson, Oliver E. 1975. *Markets and Hierarchies: Analysis and Antitrust Implications*. New York, NY: Free Press.

———. 1985a. *The Economic Institutions of Capitalism: Firms, Markets and Relational Contracting*. New York, NY: Free Press.

———. 1985b. Reflections on the New Institutional Economics. *Journal of Institutional and Theoretical Economics* 141: 187–195.

———. 1996. *The Mechanisms of Governance*. New York, NY: Oxford University Press.

———. 2000. The New Institutional Economics: Taking Stock, Looking Ahead. *Journal of Economic Literature* 38 (3): 595–613.

———. 2010. Transaction Cost Economics: The Natural Progression. *American Economic Review* 100 (3): 673–690.

Witte, Edwin E. 1954. Institutional Economics as Seen by an Institutional Economist. *Southern Economic Journal* 21 (2): 131–140.

Wolff, Richard D., and Stephen A. Resnick. 2012. *Contending Economic Theories: Neoclassical, Keynesian, and Marxian*. Cambridge, MA: MIT Press.

Conclusion

Social theory can usefully be conceived in terms of four key paradigms: functionalist, interpretive, radical humanist, and radical structuralist. The four paradigms are founded upon different assumptions about the nature of social science and the nature of society. Each generates theories, concepts, and analytical tools which are different from those of other paradigms.

All theories are based on a philosophy of science and a theory of society. Many theorists appear to be unaware of, or ignore, the assumptions underlying these philosophies. They emphasize only some aspects of the phenomenon and ignore others. Unless they bring out the basic philosophical assumptions of the theories, their analysis can be misleading; since by emphasizing differences between theories, they imply diversity in approach. While there appear to be different kinds of theory, they are founded on a certain philosophy, worldview, or paradigm. This becomes evident when these theories are related to the wider background of social theory.

The functionalist paradigm has provided the framework for current mainstream in academic research, and accounts for the largest proportion of theory and research in academic fields.

In order to understand a new paradigm, theorists should be fully aware of assumptions upon which their own paradigm is based. Moreover, to understand a new paradigm one has to explore it from within, since the concepts in one paradigm cannot easily be interpreted in terms of those of another. No attempt should be made to criticize or evaluate a paradigm from the outside. This is self-defeating since it is based on a separate paradigm. All four paradigms can be easily criticized and ruined in this way.

These four paradigms are of paramount importance to any scientist, because the process of learning about a favored paradigm is also the process of learning what that paradigm is not. The knowledge of paradigms makes scientists aware of the boundaries within which they approach their subject. Each of the four paradigms implies a different way of social theorizing.

Scientists often approach their subject from a frame of reference based upon assumptions that are taken-for-granted. Since these assumptions are continually

K. Ardalan, *Case Method and Pluralist Economics*,
https://doi.org/10.1007/978-3-319-72071-5_13

affirmed and reinforced, they remain not only unquestioned, but also beyond conscious awareness. In this way, most researchers tend to favor the functionalist paradigm.

The partial nature of this view only becomes apparent when the researcher exposes basic assumptions to the challenge of alternative ways of seeing, and starts to appreciate these alternatives in their own terms. To do this, one has to explore other paradigms from within, since the concepts in one paradigm cannot easily be interpreted in terms of those of another.

The diversity of research possibilities referred to in this book is vast. While each paradigm advocates a research strategy that is logically coherent, in terms of underlying assumptions, these vary from paradigm to paradigm. The phenomenon to be researched can be conceptualized and studied in many different ways, each generating distinctive kinds of insight and understanding. There are many different ways of studying the same social phenomenon, and given that the insights generated by any one approach are at best partial and incomplete, the social researcher can gain much by reflecting on the nature and merits of different approaches. It is clear that social scientists, like other generators of knowledge, deal with the realization of possible types of knowledge, which are connected with the particular paradigm adopted.

The mainstream academic research is based upon the functionalist paradigm; and, for the most part, theorists are not always entirely aware of the traditions to which they belong. This book recommends a serious conscious thinking about the social philosophy upon which social research is based and of the alternative avenues for development.

Academic research can gain much by exploiting the new perspectives coming from the other paradigms. An understanding of different paradigms leads to a better understanding of the multi-faceted nature of social phenomenon. Although a researcher may decide to conduct research from the point of view of a certain paradigm, an understanding of the nature of other paradigms leads to a better understanding of what one is doing.

Paradigm diversity is based on the idea that more than one theoretical construction can be placed upon a given collection of data. In other words, any single theory, research method, or particular empirical study is incapable of explaining the nature of reality in all of its complexities.

It is possible to establish exact solutions to problems, if one defines the boundary and domain of reality. Functionalist research, through its research approach, defines an area in which objectivity and truth can be found. Any change in the research approach, or any change in the area of applicability, would tend to result in the break down of such objectivity and truth.

The knowledge generated through functionalist research relates to certain aspects of the phenomenon under consideration. Recognition of the existence of the phenomenon beyond that dictated by the research approach, results in the recognition of the limitations of the knowledge generated within the confines of that approach.

It is almost impossible to find foundational solution to the problem of creating specific kind of knowledge. Researchers are encouraged to explore what is possible by identifying untapped possibilities. By comparing a favored research approach in relation to others, the nature, strengths, and limitations of the favored approach become evident. By understanding what others do, researchers are able to understand what they are not doing. This leads to the development and refinement of the favored research approach. The concern is not about deciding which research approach is best, or with substituting one for another. The concern is about the merits of diversity, which seeks to enrich research rather than constrain it, through a search for an optimum way of doing diverse research.

There is no unique evaluative perspective for assessing knowledge generated by different research approaches. Therefore, it becomes necessary to get beyond the idea that knowledge is foundational and can be evaluated in an absolute way.

Different research approaches provide different interpretations of a phenomenon, and understand the phenomenon in a particular way. Some may be supporting a traditional view, others saying something new. In this way, knowledge is treated as being tentative rather than absolute.

All research approaches have something to contribute. The interaction among them may lead to synthesis, compromise, consensus, transformation, polarization, or simply clarification and improved understanding of differences. Such interaction, which is based on differences of viewpoints, is not concerned with reaching consensus or an end point that establishes a foundational truth. On the contrary, it is concerned with learning from the process itself, and to encourage the interaction to continue so long as disagreement lasts. Likewise, it is not concerned with producing uniformity, but promoting improved diversity.

Paradigm diversity is based on the idea that research is a creative process and that there are many ways of doing research. This approach leads to the development of knowledge in many different, and sometimes contradictory, directions such that new ways of knowing will emerge. There can be no objective criteria for choosing between alternative perspectives. The number of ways of generating new knowledge is bounded only by the ingenuity of researchers in inventing new approaches.

The functionalist paradigm regards research as a technical activity and depersonalizes the research process. It removes responsibility from the researcher and reduces him or her to an agent engaged in what the institutionalized research demands.

Paradigm diversity reorients the role of the researchers and places responsibility for the conduct and consequences of research directly with them. Researchers examine the nature of their activity to choose an appropriate approach and develop a capacity to observe and question what they are doing, and take responsibility for making intelligent choices which are open to realize the many potential types of knowledge.

To implement paradigm diversity, some fundamental changes need to be directed to the way research is presently managed in academic fields. In other words, paradigm diversity implies and requires changes. The most fundamental change is to understand the multifaceted nature of social phenomena.

An understanding of paradigms provides a valuable means for exploring the nature of the phenomenon being investigated. Furthermore, an understanding of other paradigms provides an invaluable basis for recognizing what one is doing.

It is interesting to note that this recommendation is consistent with the four paradigms:

1. It increases efficiency in research: This is because, diversity in the research approach prevents or delays reaching the point of diminishing marginal return. Therefore, the recommendation is consistent with the functionalist paradigm, which emphasizes purposive rationality and the benefit of diversification.
2. It advocates diversity in research approach: This is consistent with the interpretive paradigm, which emphasizes shared multiple realities.
3. It leads to the realization of researchers' full potentials: This is consistent with the radical humanist paradigm, which emphasizes human beings' emancipation from the structures which limit their potential for development.
4. It enhances class awareness: This is consistent with the radical structuralist paradigm, which emphasizes class struggle.

Knowledge is ultimately a product of the researcher's paradigmatic approach to the multifaceted social phenomenon. Viewed from this angle, the pursuit of knowledge is seen as much an ethical, moral, ideological, and political activity, as a technical one. Mainstream academic research can gain much from the contributions of the other paradigms.

CPSIA information can be obtained
at www.ICGtesting.com
Printed in the USA
LVOW13*1713280118
564338LV00008B/314/P

9 783319 720708